C000148373

LES AMES

Also published by Christopher Helm:

The Christopher Helm County Cricket Histories:

Derbyshire
John Shawcross, with a personal view by
Bob Taylor

Glamorgan
Andrew Hignell, with a personal view by
Tony Lewis

Hampshire
Peter Wynne-Thomas, with a personal view by
John Arlott

Lancashire
Peter Wynne-Thomas, with a personal view by
Brian Statham

Middlesex
David Lemmon, with a personal view by
Denis Compton

Surrey
David Lemmon, with a personal view by
Peter May

Worcestershire
David Lemmon, with a personal view by
Basil D'Oliveira

Yorkshire
Anthony Woodhouse, with a personal view by
Sir Leonard Hutton

An Ashes Anthology
Peter Arnold and Peter Wynne-Thomas

The Crisis of Captaincy
David Lemmon

LES AMES

Alan Hill
Foreword by R.E.S. Wyatt

I love to walk the fields; they are to me
A legacy no evil can destroy;
They, like a spell, set every rapture free
That cheer'd me when a boy.
Play—pastime—all Time's blotting pen conceal'd,
Comes like a new-born joy,
To greet me in the field.

From the poem *Summer Images* by John Clare.
Copyright © Eric Robinson 1967.
Reproduced by permission of Curtis Brown Ltd., London.

CHRISTOPHER HELM
London

© 1990 Alan Hill and R. E. S. Wyatt

Christopher Helm (Publishers) Ltd,
Imperial House, 21–25 North Street,
Bromley, Kent BR1 1SD

ISBN 0-7470-1412-4

A CIP catalogue record for this book
is available from the British Library

All rights reserved. No reproduction, copy
or transmission of this publication may be
made without written permission.

No paragraph of this publication may be
reproduced, copied or transmitted save
with written permission or in accordance
with the provisions of the Copyright Act
1956 (as amended), or under the terms of
any licence permitting limited copying
issued by the Copyright Licensing Agency,
7 Ridgmount Street, London WC1E 7AE.

Any person who does any unauthorised act
in relation to this publication may be liable
to criminal prosecution and civil claims for
damages.

Typeset by Cotswold Typesetting Ltd, Cheltenham
Printed and bound in Great Britain by
Biddles Ltd, Guildford & King's Lynn

CONTENTS

For Jean, a dear friend, who loved Kent cricket.

ACKNOWLEDGEMENTS

Whether people adopt a 'low profile' it is usually because they are ducking to avoid or prevent a calamity overtaking them. Others, like my revered subject, Les Ames, are simply ill at ease in the celebrity spotlight. For all his achievements as a cricketer and administrator with Kent and England over 50 years, Les remains essentially a private man, without a trace of conceit. He exudes, in the words of one former colleague, 'an aura of kindness and commonsense.'

One of the reasons why he retains the affection and esteem of a wide circle of friends is his unyielding honesty. It is a precept not without its dangers; but for Les it has become a charming virtue. He has found it an invaluable guide over a long and worthy life. In all his dealings he is resolutely direct. He has never minced matters with either his cricket peers, or the young men of Kent, who came under his rule during his years as the county's secretary-manager. Only a very special man would deserve the tribute paid to Les by former Kent stalwart, Derek Ufton: 'With complete honesty, I can say that Les was my hero when I was a kid; he was my hero as a player; and he is still my hero today.'

Les Ames shared with Hedley Verity, his old England associate, a rare steel and purpose in proceeding from humble origins to achieve distinction as a cricketer. A biography of him was long overdue. It has been a privilege to chronicle his deeds as the finest wicket-keeper batsman in the history of the game. I am especially grateful to Les, and his delightful wife, Bunty, for being so hospitable during our conversations at their Canterbury home. Without Les's assistance and his marvellous recall of cricketers and events, this book would have lacked substance and value. He has also checked the manuscript and given it his unqualified seal of approval. I count this verdict as a special boon and a signal that he does not regard my intrusion as a calamity. Here in Sussex my wife, Betty, has been an uncomplaining aide amid her other preoccupations. She has been an alert scrutineer, not allowing the merest comma to elude her vigilance.

For my descriptions of Ames's boyhood at Elham and his schooldays at Folkestone I am indebted to Mrs Nell Ashby (Les's sister); Miss Mary Smith; Mr Fred Castle; Mr Herbie Palmer; Mr A. E. Cole; Mr Jack Godden; Mr Alan Philpott (Head of P.E. at Harvey Grammar School); and Mr O. Ford. Mr Chris Taylor, the Kent CCC Curator, has been a constant source of encouragement. His assistance with the loan of county year books and other material is much appreciated. I must also acknowledge the courtesy and help of Mr Stephen Green, the MCC Curator at Lord's; the British Newspaper Library staff at

Colindale, London; Mr Howard Milton, The Cricket Society Librarian; Mr Chris Harte, Australian Cricket Society, Adelaide; and Mr H. A. Osborne, Hon. Librarian, Sussex County Cricket Club. Mr Jim Wrigglesworth, of Outwood, Surrey, has carried out researches relating to Ames's association with 'Tich' Freeman and his rivalry with George Duckworth.

My allies on the Kent scene have included many of Ames's contemporaries and post-war friends and colleagues. For their invaluable recollections I am grateful to Howard Levett, Claude Lewis, Doug Wright, Jack Davies, David Clark, Colin Cowdrey, Godfrey Evans, Tony Pawson, Colin Page, Derek Ufton, Alan Shirreff, Derek Underwood and Alan Knott.

Sir George Allen's death, after a severe illness, in late 1989, marked the end of a distinguished life devoted to cricket. I was the fortunate recipient of his kindness on many occasions. Gubby and Bob Wyatt, the two senior England captains and two of Ames's lifelong friends, guided me along Les's international path. Along with other friends, Tom Pearce, Wilf Wooller, Doug Insole and the late Norman Yardley, they delved into their treasury of memories to provide many vital components for this portrait. They helped me to evoke the spirit of an adventurous and captivating cricketer. Their handsome contributions reflected their undiminished respect and admiration for Les as a gentleman of the game and a wise administrator.

Sir Leonard Hutton has recalled Ames's friendship on his first overseas tour to South Africa before the Second World War; and how Les was held in high esteem by the Yorkshire team of the 1930s. E. M. ('Lyn') Wellings, John Arlott and Jim Swanton, among the senior cricket writers, have saluted the all-round merits of Ames. Wellings, who accompanied the MCC team on the riot-strewn tour of Pakistan in 1969, was especially fervent in his praise of Les as a manager in circumstances of extreme provocation. Ken Grieves and Cyril Washbrook, in Lancashire, and Reg Simpson, in Nottinghamshire, have endorsed my own belief that Ames's post-war batting accomplishments, which yielded over 9,000 runs, should have led to further England recognition.

From Australia my postbag has included the reminiscences of former Test rivals, Sir Donald Bradman, W. J. O'Reilly, W. A. Brown, L. S. Darling, L. P. J. O'Brien and K. E. Rigg, all of whom remember the qualities which combined to make Ames the complete craftsman in both his cricket roles. The testimony of Bradman and O'Reilly is particularly revealing. In their view, Les was indisputably the finest wicket-keeper batsman of all time.

All my correspondents, without exception, describe Les Ames as the perfect gentleman, who was admired and respected by everyone. If I needed further corroboration that this book should be written, the answer came in a letter from the Australian, Leo O'Brien: 'The memories Les holds of his career are precious because he belongs to an era of quality, which I fear has gone forever.'

Alan Hill,
Lindfield, Sussex   1990

FOREWORD

by R. E. S. Wyatt

I feel honoured to be invited to write a short foreword to the biography of the greatest wicket-keeper batsman of all time. For many years I have been an admirer of the subject of this biography which I consider to be much overdue. The author, after much research, has portrayed the life of Les Ames from his earliest days until, as an octogenarian, he was honoured in Canterbury Cathedral by receiving the insignia of the Master of Arts from Kent University.

During these years owing to keenness, determination and intelligence he has given great service to the game of cricket, not only as a player but also as an administrator, at the same time providing much pleasure for thousands of followers of cricket by his artistry with the bat and his quiet efficiency as a wicket-keeper. As a batsman Ames always believed in attack and in wresting the initiative from the bowlers as soon as possible by his quickness of foot and correct stroke play.

Mr Alan Hill describes beautifully the frequent scenes on the Kent grounds during the 1930s when Ames and Woolley were in full flow and had complete command of the bowling. Woolley, known as the 'Pride of Kent', was the best left-hander I ever saw against really fast bowling which was also countered by Ames with courage and skill.

Les always appeared to be enjoying his cricket. He played the game in the best spirit and in the way cricket was originally intended to be played. He never, at any time, showed any sign of dissent when confronted with a doubtful umpiring decision. In fact he is the epitome of a gentleman both on and off the field and a great credit to his profession.

This is a book which will revive the memories of those who watched some glorious cricket between the wars and which, I hope, will heighten the appreciation of the beauty of the pre-war game among the younger readers.

1
A CHILD IN THE SMILING VALLEY

We were so thrilled with Leslie's performances.
He hit the ball as high as our church tower.

MARY SMITH, *retired teacher and*
Elham historian.

———————

'Ames is little good at anything but sport which won't get him anywhere,' was the daunting verdict in an end-of-term report from Harvey Grammar School, Folkestone. The indictment against the inattentive student carried a lash more weighty than the cane for the cricket-mad boy from Elham. Les Ames, in his 85th year, metaphorically cowered in the corner of the classroom. Across a lifetime, the criticism of his masters, justifiable and well-meaning, left him shaking his head in rueful remembrance. 'It wasn't my happiest time,' he said. Homework, hastily completed, often with the help of schoolfriends, usually took second place to cricket which held him in thrall from his earliest days.

His elder sister, Nell recalled: 'Les used to dread his school reports arriving at home.' As the term moved on to the day of reckoning, he went through untold agonies about the daily post. Each day he would ask his parents if the report had arrived, so that he could run out and hide until their anger had abated.

On the cricket field the powers of concentration and resolution, which eluded the negligent schoolboy, surfaced as proof of the aptitude he summoned in the right situation. Ames's fanaticism and zest for the game was to take him, with a swiftness which still astonishes, to the pinnacle of fame as a cricketer. But he was not allowed to forget his lack of bookishness even after he had achieved distinction as a member of Douglas Jardine's England team in Australia in 1932-3. On his return from Australia, a dinner was held to honour him at Folkestone. Ames joined in the laughter when one of his former Harvey Grammar School teachers wryly reminded him of the school report prophecy. It probably afforded the now seasoned world traveller, but still modest Les, more delight than the acclaim of his cricket peers.

Sporting and scholastic strengths infrequently coincide. Les, like the majority of his professional contemporaries, did not aspire to academic distinction. He was, in the words of one close friend, just a 'typical village boy', without any pretensions to grandeur.

A child of the Edwardian era, Les Ames was born on 3 December 1905 in the smiling valley of Elham, amid the farmlands of Kent between Canterbury and Folkestone. His parents, Harold and Edith Ames, christened him Leslie Ethelbert George, the intriguing middle name after a sixth-century king of Kent. The newly-installed Vicar of Elham, the Reverend Alard de Bourbel, anxious to perpetuate the names of local saints, was probably persuasive in this choice.

Congenial Elham, and the snugness of a warm, friendly and stable community, heaped its blessings on the young Ames. At the turn of the century the tranquillity of Elham was undisturbed by the screech of traffic; even now it still has presence and the air of a village with a prestigious past. The square in the centre of the village, with its surrounding venerable timbered buildings and the twelfth-century church of St Mary, its massive flint tower spearing the sky, evokes a time when Elham was a busy market centre for the nearby farms and hamlets.

In the uneasy days when this corner of east Kent, along with the rest of southern England, marshalled its forces to resist the might of Napoleon, the Duke of Wellington set up his headquarters in the fifteenth-century Smithies Arms (now the site of the Abbots Fireside Hotel). This picturesque building is still there and looks across the road at the Rose and Crown, in the upper room of which the local magistrates used to meet for their fortnightly Sessions. There is a legend that the man upon whom Baroness Orczy modelled the fictional Scarlet Pimpernel, dined at the Rose and Crown while he changed horses during one of his errands of mercy to revolutionary France to rescue the aristocrats from the guillotine.

The Rose and Crown, with its large yard and excellent stabling, did a bustling trade in post-horses. Francis Mackinnon, the chief of the Scottish clan Mackinnon (later to befriend the young Les Ames) remembered how, when a young boy in the 1850s, he walked from his home at nearby Acryse Place to board the coach at Elham to travel to cricket at Canterbury.

The stagecoach was ousted in the late-nineteenth-century by the Elham Valley Railway line, running between Dover and Canterbury. The neat and spruce Elham station, with its flowerbeds and climbing roses and sparkling brasswork, typified the country stations of the old South Eastern Railway. The charms of this rural ride, which lasted for 50 years, until the Second World War, linked the communities in the valley. The arrival of the railway did not, however, meet with the approval of one Elham centenarian resident. When asked if she had travelled on the new line, she expressed a preference for the stagecoach. The trains, she said, went too fast, making it impossible to look at the passing scenery.

Canterbury Cricket Week always brought a flurry of extra traffic to the line. Spectators travelled on an augmented service to Canterbury South which was conveniently close to the St Lawrence ground. Special trains ran from all parts of Kent to the city and the service from Deal was routed via Folkestone and thence up the valley to Canterbury. On arrival at Canterbury, reported one observer, 'the crowds poured forth from the long train, giving the unfortunate ticket collector a taste of something more akin to Charing Cross at rush hour.'

The ting-ting of the bells of the trains, attired in their gleaming green and crimson liveries, was the sound which greeted and harried young Les Ames in his sprints to catch the 8.10 morning train to school at Folkestone. It was not uncommon for Elham stationmaster William Cheeseman or signalman Bill Young to hold up the train as Les and his friends, waving frantically, raced down the hill to the station. On winter evenings the rows of oil lamps dotted along the platforms twinkled reassuringly for the schoolboys returning home in the gathering dusk.

Elham's older residents retained vivid memories of the athleticism of the Ames family. Herbie Palmer, a North Elham farmer, recalled an example of Les's agility on one journey home from school. It was an act of daring not calculated to please the Elham station staff. 'The train stopped just outside the station opposite a pair of white gates. Les opened the carriage door and jumped down on the track. He then hurdled the gates to take a short cut home past the vicarage.' Les's disregard for his own safety was, to say the least, indiscreet; but his boyish imprudence revealed him as a gymnast in the mould of his grandfather. Harold Ames senior, at 70, was still nimble enough to place his hand on a five-bar gate and leap over.

To the east of Elham railway station Running Hill climbed up to the Chalk Pit, a happy playground for generations of the village children. The charmingly named Duck Street led from the station approach up beside the church, with the King's Arms in one corner, and into the square. Beyond the High Street, with its assortment of cottages, shop and inns, once rose one of Elham's two windmills, a landmark visible for miles around.

Below the windmill in Elham's network of streets the sounds of cricket were only silenced at nightfall. One faded photograph, taken in the gardens of Kingpost (the home of Miss Mary Smith, the daughter of the village postmaster) gives a delightful glimpse of Les Ames as a sturdy three-year-old batsman. There he stands with a dogged expression, leaning on a makeshift bat and guarding the roughly hewn wickets.

Sturdy defence: Les, as a three-year-old, practising in an Elham Garden (L. Ames)

A letter to an uncle at Northiam a few years later amusingly demonstrated his undiminished enthusiasm for cricket. 'Thank you very much for the nice letter and fag cards. I have broken two windows at cricket this summer.' He did not mention any reprimands, appearing to observe that the wreckage was a tribute to his big hitting, which was undoubtedly the case.

That the Ames family of Elham were a cricket force to be reckoned with, in more ways than one, was revealed by the story of two disgruntled rivals from neighbouring villages. In parenthesis it should be said that Les's father, Harold, was a slow left-arm bowler of local renown. He rarely averaged more than 4 runs per wicket. In the view of his son, he was good enough to have played at county level. Grandfather Ames, a builder by trade, was the Elham umpire for 30 years. The old man's powers of execution were said by some envious opponents to err on the side of nepotism. The gravity of the situation confronting Elham's rivals was being discussed in a pub at Lyminge. One man asked: 'Are you playing Elham this year?' His friend replied: 'No, we're not going over there. Waste of time going there, with all them Ames. The lad gets all the runs, father takes the wickets, and granddad gives you out.'

Another Elham man, Fred Castle, along with Ames and H. J. Hubble, nephew of Jack Hubble, the Kent wicket-keeper in the 1920s, formed a trio of villagers who played first-class cricket. Ames and the younger Hubble joined the Kent staff together in 1925. Castle's promise was checked by an eye injury, sustained in a road accident. He played with some distinction for Somerset after the Second World War, but a full-time cricket career was jettisoned in favour of teaching.

Castle, four years junior to Ames, remembered with affection his friendship with Les and the great benefits of growing up in the Kent village. 'We were lucky to be brought up at Elham because there was such a lovely spirit about the place. Everybody worked together. It was just one big happy family.' Of his friendship with Les he said: 'He was a marvellous pal. You always knew where you stood with him. He didn't consider himself superior to the rest of us, which he wasn't—apart from his wonderful games flair. He was just a "natural" ball player.'

Fred Castle was the son of the village tailor, one of the fellowship of businessmen in the village. The tailor's friend, the elder Ames, overcame the handicap of deafness to pursue a remarkable variety of working pursuits. Harold Ames was a rents and taxes collector, insurance man and the registrar for births and deaths. He was also a parish councillor, a man of substance and acumen. His responsibilities and the powers with which he was invested ensured that he was treated with a proper civility. At the family home at Chichester House he spent long hours meticulously preparing his accounts in his office adjoining the dining room. His fine handwriting gave an appropriate flourish to his labours.

It might perhaps have been expected that his total deafness, an affliction which beset him in his early twenties, would create problems, even friction within the family. Harold Ames negotiated a potential hazard as skilfully as he balanced his accounts. 'I cannot remember speaking to my father,' said Les Ames. 'I communicated with him by using the deaf and dumb alphabet. So did my mother and sister. If it was something tricky, you had to write it down. But he was very good at detecting your conversational drift. You might only be halfway through a sentence before he would take it up and finish it off for you.'

In Les's childhood there was the Saturday night social ritual of card sessions at the homes of the village elders. The hospitality was shared between the senior Ames and Castle and their friends, the butcher and the doctor. 'They used to play whist every Saturday night through the winter,' recalled Fred Castle. The stakes were a penny a game and there was much good-humoured banter if one or other of the assembly failed to settle up before the end of the evening. As their parents tussled for winning hands, Les and Fred shuffled their own packs at cribbage, until bedtime called a halt to the dealings.

As a young man, in later years, Les often enjoyed a game of cards with his mother and father on Sunday evenings. The custom had its dangers. There was always the likelihood of a swift abandonment of the game. Les's father was by that time in his fifties; however, he still had to exercise care, so as not to incur his own father's displeasure. Grandfather would come down to Chichester House for an exchange of the Sunday newspapers, Les recalled: 'As soon as we heard his rat-a-tat on the door there was a great rush to push the cards out of sight. Grandfather's arrival meant the end of that particular game.'

The restrictions also extended to cricket on Sundays, when ball games were strictly prohibited by Les's parents. Les had to attend church two or even three times on the Sabbath. As a respite from the sermons, there were walks—sedate processions with his mother and father—in the countryside after the afternoon worship. After the Sunday sporting fast, the boys of the village resumed their cricket play in high glee.

Fred Castle remembered that one venue for their games was a spacious area of the street beside the Rose and Crown, where the East Kent Hunt met on Boxing Day. Attached to the walls of the stables of the pub was a little box which held a water hose. This did service as the wicket in the intensely contested matches. At other times the boys simply chalked the wickets on the tarmacadam roads outside their homes. 'The surfaces were so true. I'm sure that they had a beneficial effect on my batting,' said Les Ames.

He cannot remember a time when he did not play cricket. 'The remarkable thing about those days is that there were about 10 boys at Elham as keen on the game as myself.' The cricketing throng included Bert Cole, the blacksmith's son (a brisk medium-pace bowler who later opened the Elham attack with Harold Ames); his brother, George; the Clayson brothers, Doug and Phil whose father was landlord at the Rose and Crown; Jack and Ken Hubble, sons of Lewis, the village grocer; and Don Wilcox, the school-

The Elham Boys' XI. Les (far right in middle row) pictured as a wicket-keeper for the first time (L. Ames)

master's son. The impromptu 'Test' matches were always England against Australia, with hero-worship compelling the inclusion of Blythe and Woolley in the home line-up. There were doubtless strong and insistent claims among the young pretenders as to who should play these exalted roles. Since he could not be Woolley, as a right-handed batsman, Les would usually assume the guise of Wally Hardinge, his own special Kent batting god. When the weather drove the boys indoors the passage-way leading to the Castle's family sitting room became the cricket wicket. Then they had to revert to under-arm bowling and temper their exuberance.

The affairs of the Elham boys' team, as old scorebooks retained by Bert Cole testify, were conducted with the utmost sobriety. The averages for the season were dutifully recorded. The gradings reflected a sort of elite. A batting average in the 20s was a mark of true excellence. Those boys achieving 10s with the bat and figures of 3s and 5s with the ball also enjoyed a certain esteem. The ground was a meadow called the Gore which was owned by the Rigden sisters, who also ran a private school in the village. Of this dauntless sisterhood, five lived into their nineties. Their names, Laura, Nora, Maria, Blanche, Alice, Trixie, Connie and Bella, are now laughingly yet fondly given to a set of poplar trees in the village.

The Elham boys travelled to away matches, involving distances of up to 10 miles, on bicycles carrying two but not made for two. Bert Cole, along with other older boys, placed the younger ones on cushions astride the crossbars. At home they made collections for their cricket equipment. The boys did not ask in vain. 'People were very kind; they did help us and gave as freely as possible,' remembered Fred Castle. 'But we also helped our-selves by mowing and marking our own cricket pitch on Saturday mornings before the start of play.'

Cricket ruled supreme among the boys of Elham but their enthusiasm spilled over into other sports. Playing soccer, billiards (on tables at the Hubble and Clayson homes) and table tennis entitled the youngsters to regard themselves as all-rounders. Les Ames was also an accomplished tennis player and this was one sport he shared with his sister Nell on the local courts. Quite early in their childhood Nell withdrew from cricket; she did not take kindly to having to do all the fielding!

Bert Cole related one telling story of Ames's cricket zest as a grammar school teenager. One evening Elham were due to play a match against Lyminge, a nearby village. 'Les must have dozed off on the train coming home from school; he missed his stop and didn't wake up until he reached Barham further down the line. The match started at 6.30 and it really looked as though we had lost him. But, no, he arrived in the nick of time. He told us afterwards that he had walked and run all the way back home, grabbed his bike and cricket gear and rode, with scarcely a pause for breath, to Lyminge.'

The stores of energy possessed by Les and his friends were boundless; the minutes and hours (except perhaps those at school) of the long summer days ticked by in a wonderful, action-packed playtime. As a country boy, Les would fill his home with collections of birds' eggs until his mother and father revolted and cleared them out. His response was to start all over again.

In the months of April and May the bushes and trees on the chalk downs and in the valley meadows hid a fascinating variety of nests. Bert Cole and Les Ames were the persistent foragers, each with collections of as many as 30 eggs. Entries from Bert's diaries of over 70 years ago reveal the extent of their industry. One entry reads: 'Best nesting day we've ever had. Six magpies, four rooks and about 20 blackies and thrushes.' Another entry comments: 'Found three more hen's eggs and scrambled them (for tea!) at Les's home.' Ames's adventurous instincts as a countryside predator also served him well in one prank at Harvey Grammar School. His sister, Nell, related one escapade: 'Les managed to capture a bird which had flown into the cloakroom. He concealed the bird in his pocket and took it into the school assembly. While prayers were being said, Les took the bird from his pocket and released it, much to everyone's amusement.'

At Christmas time the musical (and non-musical) boys of the village were more legitimately resourceful as carol singers. Bert Cole remembers singing in the hall at Acryse Place and raising the grand total of £18.15s.5d for a servicemen's charity on one exceptionally profitable series of carol nights soon after the First World War.

Francis Mackinnon, the Acryse squire with impeccable cricket credentials, was Les Ames's first cricket benefactor. 'A very upright old man and kind in deed,' in the memory of Mary Smith. Mackinnon, who succeeded his father as the 35th chief of the Mackinnon clan in 1903, played for Cambridge against Oxford in the famed 'Cobden's match' in 1870. This was the match distinguished by Cobden's hat-trick which enabled the Light Blues to triumph by 2 runs in a thrilling finale. Mackinnon also played for Kent between 1875 and 1885 and was a member of Lord Harris's team in Australia in 1878-9. 'He was an extremely graceful bat, very steady as an almost invariable rule, and a good long field,' said Harris of his fellow amateur. 'But he was very diffident of his own powers, and it was only with the greatest difficulty could I persuade him to take up county cricket.'

As a friend of the Ames family, Mackinnon was more venturesome in fostering the cricket ambitions of the young Les. After watching him practising outside Chichester House and on the village cricket field, the benevolent squire presented the three-year-old boy with his first cricket set. Mary Smith remembered that the kindness of the Acryse aristocrats was extended to all the people in the village. The Mackinnons drove down in their carriage and pair to present the prizes at Elham's annual flower show. Francis Mackinnon maintained his allegiance to Kent cricket until his death, at the age of 98, in London in 1947.

The annual visit to Elham of Jack Hubble, the Kent wicket-keeper (popularly known as 'Uncle Jack' by the village boys) was one of the highlights of the summer. Hubble spent Canterbury Cricket Week with his grocer brother, Lewis. Les Ames, along with the rest of his friends, revelled in the presence of the Kent star being only too keen to run errands for his mother to Hubble's corner shop. Such fleet-footed errands were really just an excuse to see the celebrated visitor. 'Jack and I were great friends despite the disparity in our ages,' said Les. Autographs were never in short supply during the Canterbury week. Hubble returned to Elham after the day's play with books filled with signatures of his Kent colleagues. He also had to cope with a barrage of questions on the events at Canterbury. 'The fact that Jack was in the village for a whole week meant a lot to the Elham boys,' said Nell Ashby. 'Jack, who was a friendly man, would always have a word or two to say to them.' Fred Castle also recalled those blissful days in August: 'Uncle Jack really got us going,' he said.

Francis Mackinnon, the Acryse squire, who was an early cricket benefactor (Kent CCC)

When Les Ames moved on, as a paid pupil, to Harvey Grammar School, he was deprived of the company by day of many of his Elham friends whose parents chose to send them to the Simon Langton School at Canterbury. Les, at the age of 14, registered his first century (104 not out in 90 minutes) for Harvey Grammar School against Dover County School at the Crabble Ground, Dover. He was presented with a handsomely inscribed bat by his school to commemorate the occasion. Ossie Ford partnered Les on the century occasion at Dover and shared the plaudits when their house won the inter-house championship at the Folkestone school in 1920 and 1921. He remembered how Ames, known for no apparent reason as 'Dicky' at school, often had to be cajoled to travel all the way from Elham to play in school matches.

Jack Godden was another fellow pupil at Harvey Grammar School and is a lifelong friend. Their friendship survived the wreckage of his Raleigh cycle, a new one, which Les borrowed and crashed during one school lunchtime. Godden told one story of Ames's loyalty to Elham and its punishing sequel. 'We were due to play Ashford Grammar School, great rivals at the time, on one Saturday. It so happened that the match clashed with a fixture at Elham. During the week Les tried to excuse himself by telling our headmaster, Major Denham, about a fictitious dental appointment. "That's all right, Ames," responded the Folkestone principal, "take the morning off—we must have you fit to play for us on Saturday."' Godden added: 'But Les was unable to avoid his school obligation. Major Denham discovered that Les had told a lie, so he was given detention as well as not playing for Elham that week.'

Bert Cole, one of the older boys of the Elham cricket clan, provided another memory of their schooldays. It is a recollection which still makes him glow with pride. On this occasion, as a pupil at the Simon Langton

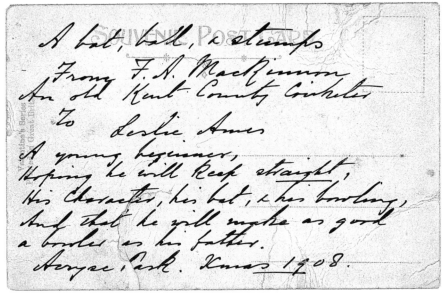

A Christmas postcard included with the present of a cricket set in 1908 (L. Ames)

9

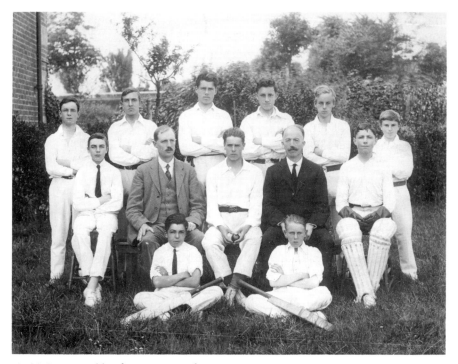

At 14, Les scored his first century—for Harvey Grammar School against Dover County School. In this school group of 1920 he is seated (left) on the grass in front of his headmaster, Major H. A. Denham (Harvey Grammar School, Folkestone)

School, he was opposed to his friend. 'I was fairly quick as a bowler at that level. I remember thinking that Les was a bit weak on the leg stump at the time. So I whipped one down—middle and leg. Les played forward and dollied me a return catch. Of course, I was nearly two years older and had a little extra experience. But it is a prized dismissal.'

Les was also one of his father's victims in the annual School versus Parents matches at Folkestone. Before one particular game he had vowed to show his worth as a cricketer against his father's bowling. Ames senior, impressed by his son's determination, offered the encouragement of a cash prize if Les scored 50. The incentive to augment his pocket money was irresistible. But the challenge went sadly awry for Les. He was bowled by his father for nought. Harold Ames, with his cunning left-arm slows, took 9 school wickets. In the following match against the Parents' XI Les achieved the goal of a half-century, but there was no financial reward that time.

After leaving Harvey Grammar School, Les began an apprenticeship as a grocer with his cousin, Edward Ames, at Brabourne, near Ashford. On his half-holidays he played for Smeeth, a local village club. A report in the *Kentish Gazette* (after Les had moved on to first-class cricket), recalled the promise displayed by Ames at Smeeth: 'I first saw young Ames while watching a village match when I was simply astounded to see, on an indifferent country wicket, the batsman making runs with an easy poise. He followed the ball with a quick eye and met it with the straightest of bats. If ever there was an embryo county cricketer, here he was playing for Smeeth.'

Ames, a reluctant wicket-keeper who only rarely kept at school, was perplexed by the indulgence of the Smeeth captain, a very good leg-break bowler. Catches and stumpings went begging as opposing batsmen groped myopically at his tantalising spin. The Smeeth wicket-keeper could not take advantage of his good fortune. Les told his captain: 'You're never going to get anybody stumped with that man behind the wicket. It's a wicked waste.' The village skipper considered that Ames was too good an asset as an outfielder, a position that Les preferred in his early cricket days, but he finally accepted that a change was necessary. Les took over the responsibility. 'I did not really regard myself as a wicket-keeper,' said Les. 'But I was good enough to stump three or four batsmen in every innings for the skipper.'

At Smeeth there was a productive harvest of runs by Ames to alert the county authorities. In 1924, when he was 18, his name was submitted by Smeeth farmer and Ashford captain, Bob Hobbs, to the Tonbridge headquarters. Hobbs arranged for Ames to be given a trial with Ashford against the Kent Club and Ground XI, captained by Gerry Weigall, at Barrow Hill. Ashford lost 4 wickets for 36 runs before Les put them on the revival path. 'Ames batted with the confidence of a veteran,' ran one report. 'He showed masterly form for his 46 runs, most of which were made in front of the wicket by clean, forcing strokes. He has a keen eye, keeps a straight bat and is quick on his feet. He played with great confidence and was not afraid to leave his crease to punish the loose ball . . .'

Gerry Weigall, a Cambridge blue and Kent player in the 1890s, played a major role in Ames's development as a cricketer. He was an unabashed and gigantic enthusiast. 'He was a very dear old boy although he was, to put it mildly, a little eccentric. He took a liking to me—and my son, John in later years,' remembered Les. Weigall's treasury of cricket jingles included: 'Never run to cover' and 'Never hook in May.' On his visits to Lord's, Weigall was mimicked unmercifully by one ace leg-puller, the Middlesex bowler, Jim Sims. 'Jerrah!' Sims would call out in the plummiest of tones from the players' balcony. Weigall would then pause as he made his magisterial entrance into the pavilion. The protestations of the MCC members would be ignored as Weigall sought the bearer of the greeting. The trick rarely failed, much to the amusement of the impertinent Sims, who chuckled unseen on the balcony.

Ian Peebles wrote of Weigall:

> He was loved for his indiscretions, his disasters, his sweeping and consistently erroneous prophecies, to say nothing of a warm and generous heart. He was one of the rich characters of a colourful age. He was a sturdy figure in his fifties, rather on the short side but erect and active.

Gerry Weigall (left), the Kent coach, who persuaded a reluctant Ames to take up wicket-keeping (L. Ames)

His hair was white, as were his shaggy eyebrows and heavy moustache. His eyes were a brilliant blue and his whole demeanour was fierce and majestic. He was loquacious, assertive and dogmatic and the target for leg-pullers of all ages. His good nature enabled him to brush their sallies aside with a fine condescension. He always rose but he never reproached.

His enthusiasm for cricket was as fierce and positive as a blast furnace, unquenchable, regardless of time and place. His umbrella, always unfurled, was a magician's wand, a conductor's baton, to be swirled into action at the drop of a hat. He was not a self-conscious man, and it was not unusual to see him wielding it on a traffic island in Piccadilly as he exhorted some embarrassed acquaintance to play 'sideways, sah.'

Weigall's powers of perception could not be faulted in introducing Ames to first-class cricket. Les had first to shake off his misgivings about wicket-keeping in the crucial debut for Kent Club and Ground XI against Hythe. Weigall had been impressed with Les's batting for Ashford, but he made plain the essential need to be 'double-barrelled'. 'There is little room for a lad who is just a batsman in first-class cricket—unless he is a genius like Jack Hobbs,' warned Weigall. Ames was later to be grateful for this advice. However, Les was ill-prepared to take on the mantle of wicket-keeping against Hythe. He said he was unsuitable for the job. Furthermore, he did not covet the role. 'I don't care, I want you to keep wicket today,' said Weigall. Les protested: 'But I haven't got any gloves or pads.' 'That's easily put right,' replied the Kent coach. The problem was overcome by calling upon Povey, the regular Kent Club and Ground wicket-keeper, to lend Les his cricket gear. 'There was no answer to that remedy,' said Les, 'and I was practically forced to keep wicket for the first time in a match of any importance.'

That game against Hythe still remains a vivid memory for Les, and 'not an unpleasant one either'. Weigall won the toss before a start delayed by rain. Ames, opening the innings, scored 22 in Kent's total of 180. Les was a little disappointed with his batting performance. 'I was convinced that my batting was not up to my normal standard, but I am afraid I could not concentrate fully. I was far too concerned about the ordeal that was to follow.' Sunshine broke through the clouds late in the afternoon and the wicket, drying nicely, provided perfect conditions for Kent's two left-arm bowlers, Sid Hearn and Harold Hever. They shared the 10 wickets and Hythe were bowled out for 92. Les was presented with four chances, three catches and a stumping, all of which he accepted with alacrity. The trial was an undoubted success. Weigall, his wise old eyes peering into the future, had given Ames his opportunity. Ames, as he never tired of saying, was in the right place at the right time. Povey, the displaced 'keeper at Hythe, was then aged about 40 and clearly not a candidate to succeed Jack Hubble in the Kent ranks. Gerry Weigall placed the seal on a satisfying day with the words: 'Not bad, young Ames. Not bad at all. We'll make a stumper of you yet.'

In 1924 Ames played eight innings and headed the Kent Club and Ground batting averages with 444 runs (average: 55.50). He also scored 500 runs for Smeeth to bring his tally in two seasons in club cricket to over 1,800 runs. His batting successes included 185 for Smeeth against Aldington and

A congratulatory postcard from Weigall on the award of the Kent Second XI cap (L. Ames)

another 100 for the Kent Club and Ground against Catford. When he graduated to the Kent Second XI, he made a fine half-century against Wiltshire at the Rectory Field, Blackheath.

There was another century for Kent Club and Ground in 1925, against St Lawrence, a match which also yielded two catches and a stumping. Playing under his future Kent skipper, Captain Cornwallis, against Weigall's XI at Bearsted, Ames stumped his boyhood hero, Wally Hardinge and took a catch to dismiss his coach and opposing captain. 'Ames is improving behind the stumps every day and his batting is more consistent than any of his colts team colleagues,' was the verdict of one observer.

Amid such glowing praise, it comes as a surprise to learn that Ames, at the age of 18, considered himself a better footballer than a cricketer. Playing soccer for Brabourne in the Ashford and District League he was described as a 'dashing centre-forward' and scored 53 goals in one season. Ames, the opportunist marksman, was also regularly on target when Brabourne, with 87 goals, won the second division championship and were beaten only once in the winter of 1924–5. Les moved on to Folkestone where his ball-playing skills and versatility as a footballer—he played in all the forward positions—attracted the attention of a covey of league clubs. Clapton Orient, then in the Second Division of the Football League, won the race for his signature much to the regret of a Folkestone club official. 'I am sorry he has left us', he said, after Orient had sealed Ames's departure with an increased cash offer. 'He is the best left winger in Kent and has the makings of a great player.'

Ames, in retrospect, believed that he chose the wrong club. 'The emphasis at Orient was on a quick dispatch of the ball, without much regard for the play. At Folkestone I was able to put on the style whereas at Orient there was no time for finesse. If you put your foot on the ball, you would be told in no uncertain terms to "get rid of it".' Ames conceded that he ultimately failed to measure up to the demands of league football. 'I wasn't really fit enough,' was his strongly couched personal assessment. His training was limited to one day a week, on his Wednesday half-holiday, at Orient, and the rest of the time at Gillingham where he had moved to set up a sports business in tandem with Jack Hubble (see page 25).

'My big football match was for Orient against Chelsea. I was in the cricket nets at Tonbridge when there was a telephone call inviting me to play. It was a mid-week evening match, the last of the season. Orient had to win to stave off relegation and Chelsea required the points to gain promotion.' The game was watched by a crowd of 45,000 and Orient defeated their London rivals 1–0. It would be nice to report that Les, in true story-book fashion, scored a spectacular winning goal. Les said that he could not claim the honour. 'Donald Cox, the brother of the Chelsea player, was our matchwinner.'

Soccer ambitions were perhaps better left unfulfilled as Ames's cricketing talents flourished mightily. In 1926 he topped the Kent Second XI averages and was also third in the Minor Counties averages with 763 runs. There was also a clutch of stumpings and catches to demonstrate that he had heeded the advice of Gerry Weigall. Les always defended his old coach against those critics who accused Weigall of talking nonsense. 'If this is true, he also talked a great deal of commonsense, for no one knew cricket and cricketers better than he did.'

One day, early in July 1926, Ames was playing in a Club and Ground match at Malling when a telegram was handed to him as he came off the field. He was requested to report to Tunbridge Wells on the following morning to play for Kent against Warwickshire. 'Well done, young Ames,' said Gerry Weigall when Les showed him the invitation. 'I am not surprised. I knew you would make it, and I know you will not let me down.'

Les Ames, ushered into his magical kingdom, never did let anyone down. His future exploits thrilled but did not surprise his friends back home at Elham. 'He hit the ball as high as our church tower,' is still recited in admiring tones. Reeling opponents, watching the ball climbing to the heavens, would testify to the aptness of this praise.

2
WEARERS OF THE GLOVES

Give me Kent cricket every time. I am content. There are several wicket-keepers deserving a Test match and may they all have at least one.

FRED HUISH, *uncapped by England but the standard bearer in a great tradition.*

One summer, after Fred Huish had retired from county cricket, he took up residence in a cottage in a Sussex village. To his new friends he gave no hint of his glorious partnership with the sensitive spinning master, Colin Blythe. The curtain had been lowered on a memorable era. How could they know that his hands had once tingled in unison with one of the most graceful and artistic of slow left-arm bowlers in Kent's serene cricket pastures?

The sporting identity of Huish, in this quiet Sussex retreat, was discovered in an amusing manner. As a gesture of welcome, the local club captain ventured to ask the newcomer if he would like to play in a match on one Saturday afternoon. Politely, he inquired of Huish if he had any preference as to a place in the field. Huish replied that he had done a bit of wicket-keeping. When the match started, the village fast bowler sent down a 'loosener', the ball hurtling erratically ouside the leg stump. Huish stepped across to gather it cleanly and tossed the ball back to the bowler. He was just as secure with the next wayward delivery. The local players began to stare hard at the recruit. The third ball was better: it was pitched accurately on a full length on the middle and off stumps. The batsman's stroke was too late as the ball rose off the wicket. His back foot strayed fractionally but fatally beyond the crease. In one smooth action Huish took the ball and nonchalantly removed the bails. He called out: 'How's that?'

Like the players, the umpire had marvelled at Huish's dexterity. He looked on in disbelief, quite unable to point the accusing finger and dispatch the batsman to the pavilion. All he could say, in an ecstatic cry of admiration, was: 'Damned wonderful.'

Fred Huish was born at Clapham, then within the borders of Surrey, in December 1869. He moved to Kent in his childhood and learned his cricket at Dover. It was somewhat ironic that his tutor and mentor, Harry Wood, the Dartford wicket-keeper, travelled in the reverse direction to achieve renown with Surrey. He was discarded by Kent after trials (a decision which Lord

Harris later conceded was a grave error) and swiftly welcomed at The Oval. Wood played for Surrey for 16 years, from 1884 to 1900, through one of their great periods. He was acknowledged as being in the front rank as a wicket-keeper, especially against fast bowling. In 1888 he played for England against Australia at The Oval. He twice toured South Africa, playing in the inaugural Tests in that country in 1888–9, and in 1891–2. On the second tour he scored his only first-class century—134 not out—for England at Cape Town.

Kent's wicket-keeping tradition goes back to the early-nineteenth-century; but Fred Huish, who made his county debut in 1895, can justly be described as the standard bearer in an illustrious procession. This is not to dismiss the clamour for attention by the worthies of former times: it would be remiss to forget the long stops and emerging wicket-keepers and their unflinching guard in pitifully inadequate gloves and pads on wickets hardly worth the name. Wicket-keepers are, by their nature and responsibilities, a resilient breed. The qualities of stamina and fortitude and unceasing cheerfulness gives them a special status. They are also, by and large, a race of long-serving cricketers. The nineteenth-century pioneers were no exceptions to this rule.

The wicket custodians of the last century were not subjected to the rigours of the daily championship rounds as are their modern counterparts. But, even allowing for less congested schedules, the length of service was remarkable. Tom Box, the Sussex wicket-keeper, played for his county from 1826 until 1856. In 24 consecutive seasons—from 1832 to 1855—he did not miss a single game. Edward Gower Wenman assisted Kent for the first time in 1825 and for the last in 1854. During his long career he kept wicket in only 61 matches and collaborated in 205 dismissals.

Wenman, from Benenden, was one of the great characters of Kent cricket. 'Many and many a match,' said Nicholas Felix, 'have we played in near silence, when we were under the superb generalship of Wenman. He had only to look, and we moved, like stars obeying the dictates of a great centre.' Wenman was a six-footer but he had two sons bigger than himself. One day he was walking with his boys across the green at Benenden. Their progress was watched by a small boy from a neighbouring village. The urchin could not resist a lusty shout. 'There goes a little 'un between two big 'uns,' he called out. In more respectful vein, Arthur Haygarth, in *Scores and Biographies*, said of Wenman: 'He was a cricketer much renowned, a true lover of the game itself, and one who could be trusted in his vocation, and every department of life.'

William Dorrinton, a tall, upstanding man from Town Malling, was Wenman's understudy. He played in 55 matches for Kent from 1836 to 1848, first as a long stop and then as a wicket-keeper, after Wenman had gone into semi-retirement. He was a prominent member of the Kent XI which enjoyed many successes against the All-England XI. Dorrinton's county batting average of 7.55 demonstrated that keeping was his *forte*. This strength was recognised by his selection, in three successive seasons in the 1840s, for the Players against the Gentlemen. Fuller Pilch was warm in his praise of Dorrinton. 'What a useful man he was: well-balanced everywhere: a fine field and a good wicket-keeper.' Pilch, either not wishing to tarnish his tribute, or be too censorious, added: 'He was a steady bat.' Dorrinton was only 39 when he died. He suffered a fatal chill, caught, so it was said, while 'fielding in the long, wet grass' with the All-England XI.

The health of Dorrinton's successor, Greenwich stumper, Henry Fryer, was not unduly disrupted despite losing the sight of one eye in a fall from his trap in 1862. He lived into the next century and reached his 90th year. Fryer's wicket-keeping was curtailed but he continued to play for the county until 1872. Edward Henty, from Hawkhurst, gained recognition in 1865. He played in 116 matches for Kent and dismissed over 200 opponents. Henty was described as a 'very persevering and plucky cricketer'. In his time, wicket-keeping gloves were just plain buff leather. They became very dry and hard unless they were constantly dampened. Henty was reputed to keep a sweet shop and he always had a reserve of 'jujubes' in the pocket of his flannels and sucked furiously on another behind the wicket. One Kent fast bowler did not appreciate the taste. He grimaced with disgust when Henty returned the ball via his sticky fingers. The ball was hastily dropped to the ground and rolled in the dust between deliveries.

Henty's retirement in 1881 left a gap which was not easily filled. Kent had to contend with an acute wicket-keeping problem. The emergence of two accomplished amateur 'keepers, Harrovian Manley Colchester Kemp and Edmund Tylecote kept the anxiety in check for a short time. Kemp played for the county in 88 matches from 1880 to 1895. In the latter stages of his career he was only available in August. Kent had to rely upon a Sussex man, John Pentecost, a kindly fellow but an indifferent wicket-keeper whose declining eyesight brought about his early retirement from the game.

Kemp was a redoubtable all-round sportsman, who also excelled at racquets, soccer and athletics. He was the Oxford University cricket captain in 1883 and 1884 and was awarded his blue in four successive years. Tylecote's pedigree was even better and it clearly swayed Lord Harris in advancing his claims above those of Harry Wood. With the departure of Wood to The Oval, Kent and Harris might have had cause to rue the preference had not Huish been so opportunely waiting in the wings.

Tylecote was a member of the Hon. Ivo Bligh's team in Australia in 1882–3. He also played for England against Australia at Lord's and The Oval in 1886. On Bligh's tour Tylecote made top score in each innings at Melbourne. At Sydney, in the match which decided the series, he hit 66 to help bring the Ashes back to England. 'As a batsman he is steadiness itself; a fine, free hitter and an excellent wicket-keeper,' related one contemporary observer. Tylecote's stylish batting was complemented by his quiet, safe methods as a wicket-keeper. He was the first batsman to score over 300 in an innings. His 404 not out, made in six hours out of a total of 630, was recorded in a house match at Clifton College in 1868. In 1883 he scored 107 in two and a half hours for the Gentlemen at Lord's against a Players' team with seven recognised bowlers. In 22 matches for Kent, from 1875 until 1883, he made 949 runs. His highest score was 104 against Sussex at Maidstone in 1881. This feat was surpassed in importance by his only other century—100 not out—against the famed Australian attack of Palmer, Garrett, Boyle and Giffen at Canterbury in 1882.

The emergence of Fred Huish, in the last years of Queen Victoria's reign, was to prove one of Kent's most important discoveries. His dominance as a wicket-keeper set an example for a tradition which was to thrust deep into the next century. Huish's arrival almost exactly coincided with the establishment of the Tonbridge Nursery under the inspired leadership of Captain McCanlis. Blythe, Woolley, Fielder, Humphreys, Jack Hubble (Huish's successor), Freeman and Hardinge were among the products of the Kent coaching camp. Here was a contingent of professionals—an immaculate fusion of talents—which enabled Kent to win the championship four times before the First World War.

Huish, most memorably in his association with Blythe, assisted in 1,310 dismissals (933 catches and 377 stumpings). He twice took 100 wickets in a season. In 1911 his tally was 62 catches and 39 stumpings. He overtook this figure with 102 dismissals (69 catches and 33 stumpings) in helping Kent to win another championship in 1913. Huish was undoubtedly a wicket-keeper of international standard, equally good at standing up to the spinners as he was standing back to the pace of Fielder and Bradley, and yet he never played for England. The explanation is that he was a contemporary of Warwickshire's 'Dick' Lilley. Lilley's superiority as a batsman coupled with his soundness as a 'keeper gave him the edge over his Kent rival.

It is, however, surprising that Huish was granted only one representative appearance for the Players against the Gentlemen at Lord's in 1902. Huish was content with this solitary honour. He did not, by his own admission, aspire higher than county cricket. 'There are several wicket-keepers deserving a Test match and may they all have at least one . . . Give me Kent cricket every time,' he said. His rule was absolute in the Kent ranks. Huish's prowess delayed the promotion of Jack Hubble, his excellent deputy, until after the First World War. Hubble played regularly for Kent as a batsman. Huish was never left out of the team, even though, on occasions, it meant that the recognised batting ended at No. 6. When Huish became the Kent senior professional, he was reputed to exercise firm control over his colleagues. It was alleged that, unless he appealed, no other fellow professional dared to ask for a catch at the wicket. They were left in no doubt that this was Huish's prerogative!

The writer of an article in the July 1906 issue of the weekly magazine *Cricket* cited Huish's methods as a model for a young wicket-keeper.

The manner in which he holds his hands could not be improved upon;

Fred Huish (above), the pathfinder in a great tradition, and four of his Kent wicket-keeping successors: Jack Hubble (above right), Howard Levett (far left), Godfrey Evans (far right) and Alan Knott (right, below) (Kent CCC)

the wrists are set close together, and the fingers, which point somewhat downwards, are spread apart, so that once the ball gets into his hands there is little room for it to escape.

In 1899 Huish took 74 catches in the county championship, a major advance on previous Kent wicket-keeping accomplishments. To mark this achievement he was presented with a handsome gold pendant displaying the county insignia of the white horse surmounted by a pair of wicket-keeping gloves. In this season Huish claimed eight catches against Nottinghamshire at Trent Bridge. He was to repeat this feat on four other occasions. In four innings in one week he did not concede a single bye. Six years later, in 1905, he again assisted in eight dismissals—seven caught and one stumped—against Gloucestershire at Catford. In three successive matches he dismissed 22 batsmen. In 1911 he enjoyed his greatest triumph, with one catch and nine stumpings in the match against Surrey at The Oval.

One of the most alert examples of his wicket-keeping occurred in the match against the Australians at Canterbury in 1902. Huish recalled:

Reggie Duff played a ball from Bradley towards point. As I was standing back to the fast bowling, he tried to take a sharply-run single. Not having time to pick up the ball, I kicked it on to the stumps at the further end before Duff could reach the crease, and he was run out.

Jack Hubble, the patient deputy, was 38 when he finally succeeded Fred Huish. Even then he had to surrender his place to the Blackheath amateur, George Wood, whenever the latter could take time off from his stockbroking duties in the city. Wood was a member of Archie McLaren's amateur team which astonished the cricket world by defeating the hitherto unbeaten Australians by 28 runs at Eastbourne in 1921. The Kent amateur also won an England place against the challenge of Strudwick. He declined an invitation to tour Australia in the winter of 1920–1 but represented England in three Tests against South Africa in 1924.

Jack Hubble stoically stifled his disappointment. The valiance of his cricket produced the not inconsiderable aggregate of 10,939 runs and 658 dismissals, including 221 stumpings, in the joint capacities of outfielder and wicket-keeper in a war-interrupted career. Hubble was an especially strong offside batsman, with a penchant for fast bowling. In 1919, at Canterbury, he came in to face Jack Gregory, the Australian, and one of the most vaunted fast bowlers of his day. Gregory, in the words of R. C. Robertson Glasgow, was 'tall, strong and raw-boned, like one of his native kangaroos.' He was an awesome opponent in his pomp. Batsmen were demoralised by the sheer speed of his bowling. Kent had lost seven wickets for 164 runs when Hubble stepped into the breach. He hit 71 not out in a partnership with Bill Fair-service, and the pair saved the day.

Two years later Hubble defied the combined might of Gregory and McDonald. He passed a test of courage in two innings for the MCC against the Australians at Lord's. But Jack Hubble, the veteran cricketer, knew that his wicket-keeping span had little time to run in the post-war years. Even so, Les Ames, as the hero-worshipping Elham schoolboy in the early 1920s, had little inkling that he would soon replace his idol in the Kent side. The prospect of a future enduring business partnership with 'Uncle Jack' was beyond his wildest dreams. By the end of 1926 the cricketing mission was not quite so impossible. Ames, while still a learner as a wicket-keeper, had announced his class. Hubble, his kindly adviser, realised that the time was ripe to step aside and leave the door ajar for his gifted successor.

It was, as Les said, a 'ready-made opening', but he did not squander the opportunity.

Wicket-keeping quartet: Ames and Evans (standing), Hubble and Huish (Kent CCC)

23

3
INHERITING THE LEGACY

*The rise of Ames has been phenomenal. It is not often that
a young player forces himself to the top of the tree so
quickly as this player has done.*

FRANK MITCHELL, *the Yorkshire-born sports
all-rounder and England and South
African Test batsman.*

A collusion of circumstances did aid Les Ames in his breakthrough into
first-class cricket. But he also exercised a single-minded determination and an implacable will to succeed. Nerve, heart and resource are
almost as great factors in the make-up of the international as prodigious
cricketing talent. Ames had an abundance of these qualities to impress his
jurors and place him, despite his youth, above more experienced rivals in
the exciting times ahead.

He came into a Kent team of buoyant attack, popular because of its attitude of going 'bald-headed' for victory given the remotest chance. Ames was
soon relentlessly stalking his own quarries. 'The danger is that someone of
influence will tell him not to take so many risks,' anxiously wrote one of his
early admirers. In July, 1926, amid the scents of rhododendrons bordering
the lovely Kent cricket arena at Tunbridge Wells, Ames made his county
debut against Warwickshire. Kent won by an innings, and Ames, batting at
No. 5, scored 35 out of 408. He helped Frank Woolley add 65 in 45 minutes.
It was a modest little overture to lift the curtain on their towering batting
feats for Kent. 'He possesses a good style; he gets to the pitch of the ball and
hits very hard', was the verdict of the *Kentish Gazette* on the county debu-
tant. The cares of wicket-keeping were still shouldered by Jack Hubble
against Warwickshire. Ames was able to note the practised ease of the
veteran from his position in the outfield (where he took two catches to
dismiss Norman Kilner and Len Bates). With Woolley absent on Test duty at
Leeds, Ames was retained in the side for the next match against Nottinghamshire at Trent Bridge. Larwood, a potentially nerve-racking opponent, was
also engaged at Headingley.

Kent gained another overwhelming victory by 201 runs but Les's contributions were limited to 8 and 22. As they changed after the match against
Notts, Cornwallis, the Kent captain, had words of encouragement for his
young colleague. 'Ames,' he said, 'you have had two fairly good matches.

Four generations: Harold Ames senior and junior, Les, and his son, John (L. Ames)

You have batted well and fielded splendidly, but now I want you to go back to the second eleven and continue with your wicket-keeping, of which I hear good reports. Perhaps next season you will find yourself a regular member of the county side.'

Jack Hubble, preparing to depart from the county scene, also perceptively acknowledged the potential of Ames. 'I think he thought I was going to make the grade and perhaps play for England,' said Les. Hubble placed the seal on their friendship with the offer of a sports business partnership at a shop which had just become available in Gillingham. Ames was delighted by the gesture but there was the problem of capital, of which he had none. His share was £750, a considerable sum of money in 1926. It seemed to bar him from the undertaking. After inspecting the Gillingham premises, Les revealed his dilemma to his father and grandfather back home in Elham. The Ames elders did not linger long over their decision; a loan was arranged; and by the end of the year the business had prospered to such an extent that Les was able to repay the cash advance. Ames never had cause to regret his investment. He had, in the words of one Kent colleague, a touch of the entrepreneur and a canny instinct in all his business ventures. His fruitful partnership with Hubble lasted nearly 40 years until the death of the senior partner in 1965. 'We didn't make a fortune,' said Les. 'But it did help to augment my cricket earnings. It also gave me something to do during those winters when I wasn't on overseas tours.'

In 1927, Cornwallis relinquished the Kent captaincy. He was succeeded by Major A. J. Evans, a former Oxford blue and captain who had represented

England against Warwick Armstrong's feared Australian team in 1921. His other claim to bravery was as the scourge of the Germans in his escapes from prisoner-of-war camps in the First World War. He wrote a book, *The Escaping Club*, about these experiences, a classic of its genre.

Evans, impressed by the reports he had received of the Kent colt, opened less forbidding gates for Les Ames. Ames took up his stance behind the Kent wicket for the first time in the opening match of the season against Worcestershire on his home ground at Folkestone. It was the first county fixture to be staged at this venue. Ames's wicket-keeping trial was preceded by the tumult of a batting display in which he was borne along by the reckless brilliance of Percy Chapman. 'His timing was so exact,' wrote one observer of the cavalier Chapman, 'that the fieldsmen had little chance to prevent a boundary unless they were right in line with the ball.' The surging power of Chapman's batting annihilated the Worcestershire attack. He hit 158 in two and a quarter hours. The Kent pair scored 155 together in 65 minutes, but Ames was frustratingly dismissed 10 runs short of a deserved century. It was, nevertheless, an innings of fine promise, demonstrating his ideal temperament for the big occasion. Once he had mastered the butter-flies, he peppered the boundaries with handsome shots. As a hint of his aggression and showing that he was not entirely overshadowed by Chapman, Les struck 19 runs, including a six and three fours, in one over off Bowles. 'He took care to get a good sight of the ball before attempting to force the game, but he then proved himself a punishing bat,' related one writer. This tribute was reinforced by another onlooker.

> Right from the start of his innings at Folkestone he faced the bowling of Root and company with the utmost confidence, and while exhibit-ing an almost impregnable defence, he revealed that he has any number of splendid scoring strokes at his disposal. He was dismissed by an uncommonly good ball, but if he maintains this form it cannot be long before he obtains the coveted three figures.

There were two stumpings off the wily Freeman and a catch for Ames as Kent coasted to an innings victory over Worcestershire. He had, as a pre-paration for his impending baptism as a wicket-keeper, been the recipient of kindly advice from Frank Woolley in pre-season practices at Tonbridge. In the nets, with Woolley batting, Freeman bowling and himself behind the stumps, Les had been quietly initiated into the mysteries of Freeman's leg-breaks, googlies and top-spinners.

In time Ames learned to 'read' Freeman's deliveries like the proverbial book. He would then amble happily up and down the wicket, with a nautical roll of his shoulders between the overs, as their conquests mounted. In his wicket-keeping debut at Folkestone he was just pleased to discharge his duties without undue blemish.

Hubble returned to keep wicket after the Worcestershire match, but he was now moving into retirement and played in only eight games for Kent in

1927. Ames established himself as a first-choice wicket-keeper. As a batsman, he steadily accumulated runs down the order. His first county century eluded him until the Whitsuntide match against Hampshire at Southampton. Had it not been for the charms which bestow their privileges at convenient times he might have had to wait a little longer. In the first innings the target was within range on an easy paced wicket. Phil Mead banished him with a catch at slip off the bowling of Jack Newman. Les had scored 70. Newman, with a charity that beggars description, gave Ames a reprieve in the second innings. He missed the simplest of return catches as the figure '13' appeared ominously beside Les's name on the scoreboard.

> It was Jack's slower ball, which he had disguised cleverly. I played much too soon, spooning the ball straight back into his cupped hands. Whether Jack was surprised I do not know; but he did take his eyes off the ball for a vital split second, and it dropped safely, and happily for me, to the ground.

The escape was an unexpected bonus but Ames still had to exercise the greatest possible caution against the tight bowling of Newman, Kennedy and Boyes. Newman bustled urgently into the attack in an attempt to make up for his lapse. Ames teetered slightly and understandably in the nineties before driving a ball from Kennedy to the boundary. The next ball was pushed firmly past short leg for 2 runs. Ames raised his bat in salute, gratefully rather than exultantly, for the first time as a county centurion. He had been at the wicket for just 10 minutes over two hours. There was an even greater pleasure in store at the end of the day's play. Les was awarded his county cap. Major Evans announced the award in a dressing-room ceremony. 'Ames has done all, and perhaps more than we expected of him,' said the Kent captain.

The century against Hampshire confirmed Ames as an outstanding prospect; his aggregate of 527 runs put him at the head of the Kent averages by early June; but he had achieved the status of a capped player after only six weeks as a regular member of the Kent side. The two Whitsuntide milestones ought to have been linked to a Kent victory. Ames's joy was only marred by finishing on the losing side. Phil Mead, as obdurate as ever, was undefeated after another century which

Les, the young county cricketer (L. Ames)

might have been carved out of granite. Hampshire, set a target of 375 runs, won by six wickets. But Ames, nursing his Kent cap, could reflect on a more important gain. He was now a recognised member of the Kent XI. His salary had leapt by £200 to £450, wealth indeed for a young man in the 1920s.

Another distinction, his first representative appearance, was delayed in this astonishing first season. Ames was prevented by a finger injury from coming under the scrutiny of the national selectors. He had to pull out of the Test trial between the North and South at Sheffield in June. The enforced withdrawal was regretted by H. A. H. Carson in the *London Evening News*. Carson wrote: 'Besides doing good work behind the stumps, Ames has made amazing strides with his batting . . . So far as his batting ability is concerned, the Kent 'keeper is streets ahead of his young contemporaries—but, of course, he must justify himself for the key position behind the wicket.'

On recovery from his injury Ames was selected for the following trial matches at Bristol and Lord's in July and August. At Bristol, playing for the Rest against an England XI, he was bowled by Larwood for nought. He improved on this summary dismissal in the match at Lord's, scoring 18 before becoming one of Freeman's four victims. He was in good company. Maurice Leyland, with whom he was to share many superb partnerships for England, was also dismissed by the Kent spinner. Greater satisfaction was afforded Ames, with two prized scalps, those of Sutcliffe and Chapman, when he took his place as wicket-keeper at Lord's.

In 1927, Kent won 12 games in finishing fourth in the county championship behind Yorkshire, Nottinghamshire and the champions, Lancashire. They twice defeated Notts, by five wickets and an innings, at Trent Bridge and Canterbury. At Nottingham Ashdown (104) and Ames (54) set Kent on the winning path with a fourth wicket partnership worth 107 runs. In the second victory at Canterbury, J. L. Bryan and Woolley led the way with a stand of 149 in 90 minutes. Ames consolidated the advantage in scoring 55 in 70 minutes. Freeman, encouraged by a plump cushion of runs, took 11 wickets for 91 runs in the match. Notts were twice dismissed in just over five hours.

Pelham Warner, in the *Morning Post*, wrote:

> With their present side, Kent are the best county team I have seen this season. Their batting, with Ames going in at No. 8, is tremendously strong. Freeman, Charlie Wright, C. J. Capes and Ashdown present a good variety of bowling, and their fielding and wicket-keeping are excellent.

After the triumphs over Notts, Warner added:

> On their present form I would match Kent against any county side with every confidence of victory. Three such left-hand batsmen as Chapman, Bryan and Woolley are a great asset on any wicket, and the side can and does score fast and make their runs attractively.

Les Ames topped the 1,000 runs, with the commendable average of 34.53, in 1927. 'He could hardly have done better in his first year as a regular member of the team,' reported the *Kentish Gazette*. 'His fine, forceful batting was always a delight to watch, his driving being remarkable for its splendid power and precision.' Frank Mitchell, in the columns of *The Cricketer*, added his voice to the growing chorus of praise.

> Ames is one of those refreshing batsmen who obviously prefers to score in front, rather than behind the wicket. He has a stroke that is not often seen nowadays. It is a pull-drive, a stroke played at a well pitched up ball that sends it high and to the right of mid-on.

Ames, now installed as Kent's first choice wicket-keeper, dovetailed his twin talents in a summer of subtropical temperatures in 1928. The barometer soared into the upper eighties and the searing heat produced a boom in early morning bathing on the South Coast. On the field Ames splashed contentedly in waves of his own making; his cricket sparkled on the fast wickets as the sun beat down with Mediterranean ferocity. He totalled 1,736 runs for Kent, an increase of over 500 runs on the previous year. There were four centuries—against Somerset, Warwickshire (twice) and Surrey—in a season of high endeavour. In one heady spate of run-making, he scored 375 runs for once out in four innings. At Maidstone he joined Frank Woolley in a day of spectacular batsmanship against Derbyshire. Woolley's innings of 198, once again, had cricket writers scrambling for superlatives. 'All were dwarfed by Woolley,' ran one report. 'He played with a lazy strength and knowledge of placings which makes a bowler feel that he is once more back at school.' Added the writer: 'Ames did not allow himself to be left behind in the pace of the scoring. He is at his best when forcing the game.'

In this exhilarating season of tall scoring Ames moved inexorably into contention for a place on the following winter tour of Australia. He was again a triallist for the Rest against England at Lord's. 'The only batting worthy of the occasion was provided by Ames, O'Connor and Nichols,' commented one writer. 'These three alone imparted the feeling that they were not hanging on for dear life.' The Rest's last four first innings wickets added 174 runs. 'The fine uphill game played by England's reserves furnished matter for satisfaction,' reported *Wisden*. 'Ames and O'Connor set to work in such refreshing fashion and with so much judgement that they added 78 in just over an hour.' But the celebrities, including Sutcliffe and Ernest Tyldesley, who both scored centuries at Lord's, were in no danger from unproven apprentices. Their names, along with Hobbs, Hammond, Hendren and Jardine, were already pencilled in for the Australian tour. The young recruits simply had to impress to gain even a foothold in this assembly.

Harry Smith, of Gloucestershire, was chosen for the first Test of the summer against the West Indies at Lord's. Harry Elliott (Derbyshire) and George Duckworth (Lancashire) were England's wicket-keeping representatives at Manchester and The Oval. All were being given the opportunity to display their credentials for the tour of Australia. Les Ames said: 'Unlike today, the selectors were searching for a wicket-keeper, and not a 'keeper who scored runs. I was exceptional in the sense that I was getting more runs than anyone else, and so my assets were as a batsman rather than as a specialist wicket-keeper.' Les added: 'I was good enough to play for England as a batsman, but not in 1928–9 with such an array of talent at the selectors' disposal.'

The cries for Ames's selection were, however, persistent and overwhelming as the summer drew on. 'Sooner or later the selectors will have to yield to the Kent player's claims for inclusion,' declared one writer.

> The day cannot be far distant when he will be one of the few men who may be regarded as a certainty for selection. At any rate, it will be something more than a nine days' wonder if he does not go to Australia with the England team this winter.

The predictions and prophecies, delivered in such a rousing manner by southern sports columnists, had the dangerous effect of raising Ames's hopes. The pundits had imposed a severe handicap on the Kent prodigy. The strain almost wrecked his chances. Amid the euphoria, Les suffered a disturbing decline. 'It may be that I tried too hard to impress, fearful of failing and spoiling my chance. Such a mental outlook is fatal in big cricket. My batting went to pieces for a while,' recalled Ames.

The turning point was the match against Surrey at the Rectory Field, Blackheath in July. A perspiring, shirt-sleeved crowd of 20,000, packed shoulder to shoulder, watched Ames regain his composure and self-belief. His double century, followed closely by 96 in the return match at The Oval, clinched his selection for Australia. 'The performance of the 22-year-old professional and the splendid Kent total were alike quite extraordinary, seeing that Ames went in just before 12 o'clock, when Hardinge and Woolley were out for 19 runs,' reported the London *Times* correspondent. 'Ames played well from the first moment, his confident defence and courageous driving accounting for the mastery obtained over the Surrey attack.' In an attempt to staunch the flow of runs Surrey called upon six bowlers—Gover, Fender, Peach, Garland-Wells, Gregory and Shepherd—at Blackheath. Ames found assurance in century stands with Chapman, who hit 58 in an hour, and Ashdown. Kent, after their early alarms, struck back positively to raise the siege. Ames hit 52 out of 91 in 85 minutes; 100 out of 193 in two and a quarter hours; 150 out of 289 in three hours and 35 minutes; and 200 out of 373 in four hours and 20 minutes. In a late flurry of runs, Ames and Geoffrey Legge added 133 for the sixth wicket in 65 minutes. The legions of Kent supporters, their faces burning with elation as well as sun, went home happy after the orgy of runs. Surrey were due to suffer further as Ames increased in maturity. His batting feats against them in 1928 and 1929 brought him 691 runs in eight innings.

L. V. Manning, in the London *Star*, was among those disarmed by Ames's revival at Blackheath. 'He was so sure of his timing that he never hesitated to lift the ball over mid-off's head,' wrote Manning. 'He has all the strokes and hits hard. Ames sailed well past the 1,000 aggregate for the season before he surrendered—not so much as the scorebook states to Shepherd—but to the heat.'

After Ames had been confirmed as a member of the MCC team bound for Australia, another observer enthused:

> Nothing has impressed me more during the last fortnight than the batting of the young Ames. I like the way he makes his strokes, the variety of them, and the absolute self-possession he shows at the wicket. To watch Ames bat no-one would imagine that he had fewer than two years' experience in first-class cricket. His physique and temperament are ideal for a big match player. Modesty is his keynote and he knows no fear.

The writer, perhaps distracted by Ames's panache as a batsman, added: 'Good wicket-keeper, as he is, I am inclined to think that he has a greater future with the bat than with the gloves.' He had forgotten, in his hasty reportage, other significant portents in Ames's momentous summer.

Fred Huish, watching his successor from the shade of the pavilion, had proudly announced that Ames, as a wicket-keeper, would be without equal in England in two years' time. Another man, 'Tich' Freeman, the enduring miracle worker of Kent cricket, had also watched, with pleasure and gain, the quiet efficiency of his accomplice behind the wicket. In 1928, at the age of 40, Freeman took over 300 wickets. These cricketing soulmates, in their maturity and youth, had come together in a marriage of merciless supremacy.

4
RECORDS AND FREEMAN

There was something grotesque in the way the little gnome of a man came rocking up to the stumps, and flicked one ball after another, all so nearly the same and yet so vitally different, until the victim would commit some act of indiscretion or, more probably fall to his own timidity.

E. W. SWANTON

I f Alfred 'Tich' Freeman was a liability at England level, the enormity of his achievements for Kent still place him as one of the truly great leg-spinners between the wars. Only Wilfred Rhodes (with 4,204 wickets between 1898 and 1930) exceeded Freeman's tally of 3,776 wickets in what was effectively 17 years in first-class cricket until his retirement in 1936.

In 1928, at the age of 40, Freeman took 304 wickets at 18.5 runs each to beat Tom Richardson's record of 290 wickets set up in 1895. It heralded a period of remorseless oppression. In four seasons the Kent maestro claimed 1,122 wickets. Les Ames, his adept young partner behind the wicket, profited from his sorcery to carve his own record-breaking niche. 'Freeman helped make Ames,' said Bob Wyatt, England's oldest surviving captain. 'Tich gave him the opportunities denied to other wicket-keepers of the time. But Les was also largely responsible for Freeman's successes. He didn't miss anything.'

Ames was indeed a model of consistency in the record-breaking summer of 1928. In his first 13 games he assisted in 48 dismissals, 26 catches and 22 stumpings, and the scorecards were embellished with notable scalps from England's top order batting elite. Sutcliffe, Ernest Tyldesley, Whysall, O'Connor, Carr and Hammond, on two occasions, were among the victims. Ames remembered one match at Bristol when he and Freeman combined to fox the great England batsman. Quite often Freeman would deploy his googly to the confusion of an incoming batsman. He decided on a change of strategy for Hammond. Freeman told Ames:

> Wally has a kind of walking shot which he plays to a leg-break on a good wicket such as this. He will be expecting the googly, Les, so I'll bowl him a leg-break instead, and you may have a chance.

Freeman bowled and the ball was well pitched up on the off stump. Hammond, as 'Tich' had forecast, played his 'walking shot'. The ball turned sharply away to defeat him, and Ames could scarcely suppress his glee as he removed the bails.

'His brilliant catches off fast bowling and quiet methods off others evokes great admiration,' commented a writer in *The Cricketer*, as Ames conscientiously and, in a typically businesslike manner, responded to the promptings of Freeman in his apprentice year. At Hastings, against Sussex in August, he achieved his 100th dismissal of the season when he caught Jim Langridge off Ashdown. It was an otherwise mixed day for Kent, without Freeman, who was playing for England against the West Indies at The Oval. Harry Parks and Arthur Gilligan both hit centuries off a weakened attack. An inconclusive match was buried in a surfeit of meaningless runs; but Ames found personal satisfaction in the finale. He stumped Cornford and caught Jim Parks off Marriott and then took another catch to dismiss Wensley off Woolley. This dismissal—his 103rd—enabled Ames to beat Fred Huish's record of 102 victims set up in 1913. It was only the third occasion on which a wicket-keeper had passed the century, and each of the feats were accomplished by Kent players. Ames went on to improve his tally to 121 dismissals and also scored 1,919 runs in 1928. George Duckworth, his future England rival, was thus deprived of a record which seemed to be within his grasp. Duckworth secured 107 dismissals (30 stumpings and 77 catches) in rather more vigorous style. He was generally acknowledged as the best wicket-keeper—to all bowling—in that summer. But, in the making of records, he did not have Freeman to bait the trap.

Kent, largely due to Freeman's excellence, were runners-up to Lancashire in the championship. The irrepressible 'Tich' moved from one triumph to another. He took 12 for 154 against Essex (at Leyton), 11 for 90 against Gloucestershire, 12 for 196 against Derbyshire, 13 for 168 against Northamptonshire and 14 for 181 against Essex at Canterbury, while in the second innings of the match against the West Indians he secured nine of the 10 wickets for 104 runs. Three times in the following three seasons—from 1929 to 1931—Freeman obtained 10 wickets in an innings for Kent. The hapless counties were Lancashire at Maidstone; Essex at Southend; and Lancashire again at Old Trafford.

Ames, however favourable the circumstances, alertly took his opportunity in 1928. He made history and perhaps, even more significantly, hastened his advance into England's ranks. *Wisden*, in naming him as one of its Five Cricketers of the Year, along with Duckworth, was responsive to his all-round qualities. 'Ames has a pretty style as a batsman and is not afraid to hit the ball hard, and he may become the best wicket-keeper batsman England has ever had,' was the verdict. 'Ames took Freeman very well indeed. He keeps without fuss or spectacular effect' (the latter view carried a different intent when aired by carping critics in later years: they tended to diminish Ames's value as a wicket-keeper). Much nearer the truth was *Wisden's* final judgement: 'It has been said of Ames that he makes wicket-keeping look easy, which appears to be true; it is the greatest compliment which can be paid to a wicket-keeper.'

The influence of Freeman brought many blessings for Les Ames. His all-round talents were burnished during the early years of their partnership. In 1929, he achieved another double of 128 dismissals and 1,795 runs. Three years later he recorded 104 dismissals, including what now seems a pre-posterously high record of 64 stumpings, and scored 2,482 runs. Only John Murray, of Middlesex and England, has matched Ames's double successes, and he did it only once, in 1957.

After his retirement, Freeman expressed the view that he was lucky in his association with Ames. 'A slow bowler without the support of a good wicket-keeper would probably find that half of his work was wasted,' he said. 'Les and I made the perfect combination. He knew everything I could do with the ball.'

Ames also cherishes his alliance with the reticent, unassuming little wizard. He does however, attribute the surge in the number of wickets taken by Freeman from 1928 onwards to the decline in the bowling powers of Frank Woolley. Woolley took over 2,000 wickets for Kent and England; and there were many people, including Wilfred Rhodes, who believed that he was a better slow left-arm bowler than Colin Blythe, in his heyday as an all-rounder before the First World War. By the mid-1920s Woolley had suffered a knee injury in Australia and his bowling was on the wane, hence Freeman was called upon more often. 'As a consequence of this Tich was increasingly having to bowl more overs,' said Ames. 'I was the beneficiary. I was getting the opportunities for catches and stumpings because Tich was taking so many more wickets.' At the risk of disrupting the argument, it could be said that Ames might have fared equally well with Woolley or Blythe in their pomp.

In the six years before Ames became Kent's regular wicket-keeper Freeman bowled between 1,000 and 1,300 overs each season and his wicket tallies ranged between 157 and 194. In 1928, when he exceeded 200 wickets for the first time, his bowling workload was 1,976 overs, an advance of over 750 on the previous season. In the following three years Freeman bowled 4,203 overs. In 1933, when he was virtually the Kent attack, he bowled 2,039 overs and took 298 wickets at a cost of 15.26 runs each. Like most slow bowlers of his era, he enjoyed being allowed the time to plot his stratagems. But his days of toil never eased. Frank Woolley once said: 'Whatever would we do if Tich fell ill?'

Freeman played in 12 Tests for England against South Africa, the West Indies, and Australia. The meagre total included only two Tests against Australia, under the captaincy of Arthur Gilligan on the 1924–5 tour. Freeman took 66 Test wickets at an average of 25.86. He headed the England averages with 22 wickets against the West Indies in 1928 and was summarily discarded the following summer after being heavily punished by

*'Tich' Freeman, Kent's tireless 'miracle
worker', and the second highest wicket-taker
in the history of the game (Kent CCC)*

FREEMAN'S WICKETS–ORDER OF BATSMEN

| | | BATSMEN | | | | IN REPRESENTATIVE MATCHES ONLY | |
| | | | | | | BATSMEN | |
Season	Tot Wkts	1–5	6–11	Season	Tot Wkts	1–5	6–11
1928	304	132	172	1928	52	20	32
1929	267	119	148	1929	53	25	28
1930	275	129	146	1930	15	2	13
1931	276	134	142	1931	19	7	12
1932	253	125	128	1932	27	16	11
1933	298	146	152	1933	36	16	20
Total	1673	785	888	Total	202	86	116

*The percentage of 1–5 batsmen whom Freeman dismissed was 41% in
representative matches and 42% in all first-class matches, and the only evidence
that he dismissed mainly lower order batsmen comes in 1930 when only 2 out of
15 of his wickets involved major batsmen.*

the South African batsmen in the Test at The Oval. Taylor and Deane put on 214 for the fourth wicket. Freeman's figures were: 49–9–169–0. Throughout the rest of his great county years he did not play for England again.

Ian Peebles described how Freeman would hitch up his trousers, run for five paces, and then deliver the ball with a neat rotary action like a 'spring snapping'. 'Tich's' cleverly flighted ball often resulted in a stumping or a skied catch. Only the truly adventurous player escaped the net and his top-spinner was an unexpected danger. Freeman would lull his opponents into complacency when he pitched a ball shorter than the others. It was often liable to be the top-spinner which skidded through to rap the batsman on his pads, or bowl him. Anyone with a penchant for the hook had to be suspicious of that ball.

'Bowling!'—a retiring victim of the googly is reported to have said—'Bowling! That isn't bowling. Them's just contraptions.' Freeman himself once claimed that he obtained many wickets by not bowling the googly—the ball that 'ought to but doesn't'. The description aptly reflects the embarassment of many of Freeman's victims. 'The batsmen knew I could bowl it and were always expecting it,' said Freeman. 'They often became fidgety trying to watch my hand in order to anticipate it and got out in some other way.' Denis Compton, as a young player, was unable to solve the puzzling conundrum. He was bowled by the leg-break after waiting for the googly that never arrived. Tom Pearce, the former Essex captain, remembers 'Tich's' disgust on those days when the googly did not deceive. 'If you edged his googly down to fine leg, it used to drive him mad. He didn't like being edged, unless the ball was in the air.'

Hedley Verity, the famed Yorkshire and England left-arm bowler, once told the story of an accomplished young batsman, with a reputation as a fine offside player, on his first appearance against Freeman. At the wicket he quickly produced a glorious cover drive for four. Someone in the crowd said: 'He seems to be at home.' The ball had been overpitched in the hope that the batsman would play back.

Verity continued:

> Freeman now shortened his length a fraction and the next two balls had to be played at the limit of the batsman's reach. The young player was playing into the covers correctly and well—and so survived, in fact, appeared to play them both easily. Up went the googly next ball and, still playing into the covers, the boy was beaten and bowled.

The theory still prevails that Freeman presented few problems to the world's leading batsmen. Those who did master him were players of the calibre of Hammond, Duleepsinhji and Hendren who came fearlessly down the wicket to him. But when the Australians came down to Canterbury in 1930, not having faced him all summer, they were just as baffled (at least in the first innings) as Freeman's county opponents. He took five wickets for

78 runs and his victims included Bradman, Ponsford, Jackson and Fairfax. 'Tich' had every right to be pleased at outwitting this illustrious quartet.

Herbert Sutcliffe was among those who doubted whether Freeman had been given a fair chance by the England selectors.

> Freeman has played so rarely in Test cricket that it is not possible to give a reasonable opinion on his qualifications. Judged by his record in county cricket in this country—he takes more wickets season by season than any other bowler—and with recollections of the success that has attended Australian bowlers of a similar type when they have visited this country, one is bound to say that Freeman ought to have been a valuable man for England all the time he has been such a valuable man for Kent.

Gloucestershire's irascible Charlie Parker, the third highest wicket-taker with 3,278 wickets, is the closest parallel in terms of neglect. Parker, judged as one of the finest slow left-arm bowlers in the history of the game, played only once for England—against Australia in 1921. His crime was a rampant dislike of the cricketing Establishment. Freeman's exclusion was manifestly of a different order and has never been satisfactorily explained.

Les Ames endorsed Sutcliffe's view and emphatically championed Freeman's skills as a bowler. 'I had a tremendous admiration for Tich. He was unfairly treated by the selectors. He was magnificent, the best leg-spinner in the country without any doubt at all. He should have played for England many more times'. 'Tich's greatness, said Les, lay in his ability to impart just the right amount of spin to fractionally beat the bat, or take the edge to produce a catch for the wicket-keeper or first slip. Freeman's age might have counted against him just as, ironically, Ames benefited in his youth from playing with him for Kent. There was also the question of Freeman's limited batting ability and his lack of a strong arm for stints at third man or fine leg. Les remembered 'Tich' fielding at cover for Kent—'his little feet would scamper along and he had a neat underhand flicked return to the wicket.'

The selectors, having brusquely cast Freeman aside, opted in the early 1930s for the all-round qualities of Walter Robins and Freddie Brown, and briefly flirted with Ian Peebles, the Middlesex leg-spinner, who teased Don Bradman into submission in the Old Trafford Test in 1930. But Ames's view differed:

> I suppose the reason for the selectors' choices was that Brown and Robins were good fieldsmen and capable of getting runs; but neither of them were in the same class as Tich as a bowler. He was also an absolute wizard at clearing up the tail from eight downwards. Mind you, tail-enders did not play as straight as they do today.

In Ames's time the roller was ready to be wheeled out as the late order batsmen flailed away in riotous abandonment. Orthodoxy would have been regarded as presumptuous and an irksome hiatus in the proceedings.

Ames agreed that Freeman was mastered at times on good wickets. 'Patsy Hendren and Wally Hammond used to give him some awful stick, but then the Australian spinners, O'Reilly and Fleetwood-Smith suffered similarly heavy treatment at the hands of our batsmen.' The accusations of Freeman's impotence against the best batsmen were stoutly denied by Ames. 'Wally Hammond was the greatest English batsmen between the wars and yet I must have stumped him perhaps half-a-dozen times off Tich.' Les remembered the bewilderment of the Sussex and Indian stylist, Duleepsinhji against the Kent bowler on a sticky wicket at Maidstone. 'Duleep was made to look quite silly by Tich. Then we went down to Hastings and Duleep got his revenge with a double century.'

Bob Wyatt had no doubts about Freeman's skills but he did believe that the Kent bowler wilted under severe pressure. Wyatt adopted the offensive approach, after initial discomfort, against Freeman in one match between Warwickshire and Kent at Folkestone.

> Kent batted all day on the Saturday and we went in on the Monday. The wicket at Folkestone was usually good but this time it did not last. When we batted it was rather like a gravel path. Percy Chapman put 'Tich' on with the new ball. He very quickly dismissed our first two batsmen. I went in, played forward, and was all but bowled. After that I made up my mind to attack him. I went down the wicket and hit him for six.

Warwickshire were bowled out for just over 100 and Wyatt's pugnacity left him unbeaten on 59. In the second innings, when Warwickshire followed on, Wyatt was again unconquered. 'It wasn't that I had played so much better than the other Warwickshire batsmen. I just didn't allow Tich to spin the ball to me as he had done in defeating my colleagues.'

In another match at Dover Wyatt was bowled by Freeman for 2. He was sternly rebuked by Bernard Quaife, who said: 'Couldn't you spot his googly?' Quaife went in and showed that he couldn't, and he was bowled for 1. Wyatt was dismissed by Freeman for 1 in the Warwickshire second innings. 'It may have been his googly. I couldn't play him anyway. Bernard again followed me in and was out for nought, so I was one up on him in that particular match.'

At Birmingham, Freeman's zeal cost his Kent captain, Geoffrey Legge, the sum of £20. Wyatt had hit a 100 in the first innings. Afterwards, in conversation with his fellow amateur, Ian Akers-Douglas, Legge asked: 'What will you lay me he doesn't get a 100 in the second innings?' A wager of £1, with odds at 20-1, was agreed. Legge seemed assured of winning his bet as Wyatt reached 94. 'Tich bowled me one a bit short of a length and I hit it—a real crack—past Akers-Douglas at square-leg. It went past his right ear for four,' recalled Wyatt. 'Ian went absolutely pale. I wondered whether he was thinking about his twenty quid.' Off the last ball of the over, with Eric Hollies as his partner, Wyatt advanced down the wicket to Freeman in an attempt to steal a single and retain the bowling. The foray failed as Wyatt just stunned the ball into the hands of Legge, who was fielding at silly point. 'We both thought it was a bump ball, but Tich appealed and I was given out. The interesting thing is that Geoffrey, by taking the 'catch', robbed himself of £20.'

It is now almost impossible to contemplate one authentic leg-spinner, let alone two, operating in English first-class cricket. In Kent in the 1920s and 1930s, Freeman was joined in the county attack during the summer holidays by the much-loved schoolmaster, Charles Marriott, affectionately known as 'Father'. There was even an instance much later of a trio of leg-spinners in action when Doug Wright rose to challenge his seniors. Marriott, who had previously played for Lancashire before transferring his allegiance to Kent, was one of the most accurate of English leg-spinners between the wars. His cricket, though, began and ended with his bowling. He was, by common consent, very nearly the worst batsman and fieldsman of his time. At the age of 38, Marriott was selected ahead of Freeman to play for England against the West Indies at The Oval in 1933. He claimed 11 wickets for 96 runs as England won by an innings. This led to an invitation to tour India in the following winter, but he did not represent England again.

R. L. Arrowsmith, the Kent historian, referred to Marriott's curious prancing action, the right hand hitting the small of his back so that the batsman heard the slap, and the left-arm thrown high to balance it. Marriott bowled at nearly medium pace with an accuracy that an off-spinner might envy. The googly he regarded with suspicion. He once impishly remarked that it could be more dangerous to the bowler than the batsman. He regarded the off-break, unusually for a bowler of his type, as a better investment, and this ball together with the more orthodox leg-break were his chief weapons.

Doug Wright, in his vastly different style, was, in the recent words of another great leg-spinner, Australian Bill O'Reilly, the finest spinner produced by England over the last 60 years. Wright's inimitable stiff-legged 'kangaroo' run-up—a movement of leaps, hops and bounds—is savoured in the memory. Les Ames believed that O'Reilly was closest to Wright in his bowling methods. 'Doug was rather quicker and a more vicious spinner of the ball, but he did not have quite the same accuracy as O'Reilly.' Discussing the merits of Wright and Freeman, Ames said: 'Doug had more bad days than Tich when his rhythm would desert him. But I would say that he was feared by the great batsmen more than Tich. However, day in and day out, Tich was a more effective bowler.' Wright, bowling his leg-breaks with a high arm action and at a much greater speed than any of his contemporaries, veered between the unplayable and the wildly erratic. He was undoubtedly a *tour-de-force* in a war-interrupted career; but the view has been expressed that his actual effectiveness was a little intermittent. Others regarded him as a magnificent but unlucky bowler. The enigmatic Wright was a finely tuned artist, a brilliant soloist when his extravagant spin was matched by unwavering length. That his majestic days far exceeded his mediocre ones are shown

C. S. ('Father') Marriott (Kent CCC)

by his career figures of over 2,000 wickets, including 108 in 34 Tests against South Africa and Australia. His figures included seven hat-tricks.

Jack Davies, the former Kent amateur all-rounder, referred to the fact that it was very difficult to set a field for Wright. It was a view shared by Les Ames. 'On a bouncy wicket,' said Davies, 'Doug would bowl his googlies to a ring of short-legs, and then he was really difficult.' Even at his best Wright was unfortunate, for the reason perhaps best expressed by the great S. F. Barnes, when he said of two tail-end batsmen: 'They aren't batting well enough to get out.'

John Arlott wrote:

> To watch Wright on his good days was to be aware of a great bowler. Possessed of his own rhythms, he seemed to bowl for the sheer delight of bowling, to spin for the sheer love of spin. Then, often beating both bat and wicket and fieldsmen because he is bowling almost too well, you would see a bowler, the measure of whose greatness is that six cricketing countries cannot produce a single passable imitation of him.
>
> Wright's great gift has only been maintained at the cost of constant

*Doug Wright, the brilliant but enigmatic
spinning soloist (Kent CCC)*

experiment, labour and disappointment: even, in 1949, 11 years after his entry into Test cricket, he was still experimenting with his delivery. No-one is more disappointed than Wright when he is out of form, no-one understands better than he does when he is taken off because he is not at his best. Then he will go away and practise with a fury of enthusiasm which is usually only found in a young cricketer.

Bob Wyatt provided a telling tribute from Don Bradman, one of Wright's greatest admirers. At Lord's, in 1938, Bradman was beaten and all but scuttled by the first three balls he received from the Kent spinner. 'Hammond unaccountably took Wright off and replaced him with Hedley Verity, a defensive bowler on that wicket. Wally was a lucky man that his mistake did not prove fatal. A few overs later Don pulled a wide one from Hedley on to his wicket.' Wyatt later met Bradman in the pavilion. He remarked that he was surprised that Wright had been withdrawn from the England attack. Bradman replied: 'I was jolly relieved.'

Doug Wright's wealth of spin entitles him to high rank in the Kent treasury. But the more consistent skills of 'Tich' Freeman still hold the attention. He was an enduring and endearing cricketer. He carried, like a pocket Hercules, as someone said, a monumental burden as the sole Kent match-winner. His supporters marvelled at his stamina. As he rested on the pavilion balcony after his bowling marathons at Canterbury, the brass band would play their own musical tribute. 'Little man, you've had a busy day', was a popular tune in the 1930s. It was a lullaby to chase away the cares of the cricketing hours.

Alf Freeman, like others of his spinning breed, was 'hit to blazes'. More often he would persist with an unruffled smile. At other times, perhaps at the end of an arduous, back-breaking summer, he would flinch at the batting assaults. He would grab his sweater, puff out his cheeks with indignation, and march to his place at cover. Schoolmaster Marriott, his spinning partner on holiday leave, would cluck sympathetically and prepare to take over. 'Let Father get the wickets,' 'Tich' would say, 'I'm done today.'

5
RIVALS IN HARMONY

I found everyone regretting that Ames could not keep like Duckworth, or that Duckworth could not bat like Ames.

P. G. H. FENDER, *at the outset of the*
1928–9 tour of Australia.

Les Ames and George Duckworth were not engulfed by the controversy which divided their supporters. Their friendship was strengthened in the cut and thrust of opposition. The two men, from Kent and Lancashire, took pride in each other's enterprises. 'It was a very friendly rivalry,' said Ames. He treasured his association with the exuberant and warm-hearted Lancastrian. 'I was more friendly with Duckie than any other cricketer during my playing career.'

Their wicket-keeping styles, though, were completely different. Discreet and disarming destruction, with his conjuror's hands, was the Ames method. 'Annihilation when it came was brief and painless; just a quick flick of the bails, a hopeless backward look, and from Ames, a tolerant, sympathetic smile. All very dignified, like the conferring of an accolade,' wrote Vivian Jenkins.

'He was the quickest executioner I ever saw,' said Bob Wyatt. 'Les would be looking the other way before the batsman realised he had been dismissed.' Ames's stealth contrasted with the shrieks of Duckworth whose appeals were said to vie with those of Doctor Barnardo. 'Quack, quack, quack,' was the mocking cry of the barrackers in Australia when 'Duckie' soared up the scales to his cricketing high 'C'.

Tom Pearce recalled the deafening roar of the Lancashire wicket-keeper when he was batting against Dick Tyldesley in one match. 'Duckie was standing up and appealed for a catch. I nearly jumped out of my skin. The shout was just behind my right ear.' Pearce said it would be wrong to suppose that Ames lacked voice behind the wicket, especially when he gave up keeping and stood at first slip alongside Howard Levett.

> These two used to talk all the time then. In one match Norman Harding, a quick bowler with a huge run, was bowling. Ames and Levett were chatting away. I turned round and said: 'Now then, Les and Hopper, I don't mind you talking, but would you please stop in the middle of his run-up.'

Les Ames, stockily built and 5 ft 9 in tall, did not fit the traditional image of a wicket-keeper, perched like a racing jockey behind the stumps. The cartwheeling acrobatics of the moderns and their histrionic gestures were alien to him. The trend back towards specialist wicket-keepers like Bob Taylor and latterly Bruce French and Jack Russell is a recent and welcome development. In the late 1960s and 1970s the all-round excellence of Alan Knott deprived Bob Taylor of many England caps. Knott, a zestful batsman in a crisis, often came to England's rescue. His consistency in both his roles was probably a factor in the later selection of far less accomplished 'keepers on the basis that they might contribute runs. The security of the wicket-keeping, in both one-day and traditional cricket, was put at hazard by this policy. In this connection it is interesting to reflect on the achievements of a post-war non-specialist, Jim Parks. Parks took up 'keeping in an emergency for Sussex in 1958 and made himself into a proficient wicket-keeper. He admitted that at first he was a 'long stop with gloves on'. In 46 Tests Parks was involved in 112 dismissals (101 catches and 11 stumpings). He shares with Ames, Langley, Grout, Taber, Marsh and Kelly (Australia), Lindsay (South Africa), Wasim Bari (Pakistan), and Lees (New Zealand) the distinction of eight dismissals in a Test. Bob Taylor has taken 10 catches and Marsh and Deryck Murray, the West Indian, nine each in more recent Tests. Jim Parks's career figures were 36,673 runs and 1,181 dismissals.

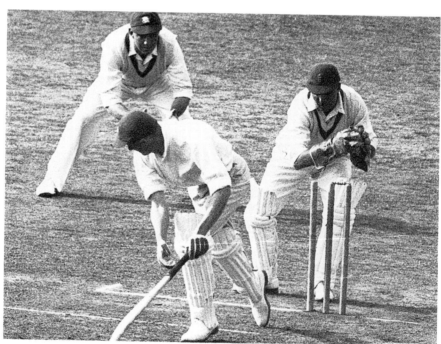

The rapid executioner: Wally Hammond, at first slip, looks on as Ames removes the bails (Kent CCC)

In the context of his time Parks was a formidable all-rounder. The proviso is the preponderance of catches, most, if not all, taken standing back. It is a vital statistic to be borne in mind in comparing wicket-keeping styles in two eras. In the 1930s, as Les Ames maintained, you would not have been looked at as an England wicket-keeper unless you could stand up. 'Wicket-keeping is no great art if you are standing back,' he said. Bob Wyatt and Wally Hammond, both excellent fieldsmen, kept to fast bowling in emergencies. Neither of them, as major England batsmen, would have presumed to intrude upon the province of the specialist.

Godfrey Evans, Ames's brilliant and marginally superior Kent and England successor, delivered the view that the style of wicket-keeping suited Les's technique.

> I idolised Les as a boy; his was the first name I looked for in the sports columns, and it was his example which inspired me to take up wicket-keeping. But I had to be different. In Les's time 'keepers did not believe in throwing themselves around as I did. If a throw was wide, they would leave it to the fielders to gather it. Les was no goalkeeper, but he missed very little.

In his great years Evans had an uncanny ability to move into top gear, often startlingly so, like someone turning on a battery of neon lights. He was, though, in his dramatic and topsy-turvy fashion, prone to unexpected lapses.

Jack Davies, like his fellow Kent amateur, Howard Levett, believed that Ames's reliability was the telling factor which edged him, ultimately, ahead of his rivals.

> Les was a conscientious man: he never eased up on the less important days, or when the state of the game did not perhaps warrant full attention. He would say: 'If you start doing that, can you guarantee to switch on full concentration when it is necessary?' Les was the right blend, not consumed with anxiety about his cricket as some people are, but there was nothing casual about him.

Bob Wyatt considered that Ames closely resembled the Australian wicket-keeper, Bert Oldfield, regarded by many observers as the best of his time. 'Les made it look easy; there was never any fuss about his work.' Wyatt was inclined to favour Duckworth in terms of keeping to fast-medium bowlers such as Maurice Tate and George Geary; but he insisted that the Lancashire 'keeper should be assessed below Ames in his skills against slow bowling.

Pelham Warner, writing in the *Daily Telegraph* in 1933 after Ames had established his place as England's first choice wicket-keeper, said:

> It is the reward for consistent success over many seasons during which his true worth as a 'keeper has not always been appreciated. A quiet and unostentatious method has hidden, for some, his combination of

Victor Richardson, the Australian batsman, dismissed by Ames's superb legside stumping, in the fourth test at Brisbane in the 1932–3 series (L. Ames)

safeness and efficiency. To slow bowlers like Freeman he is a veritable master, and G. O. Allen, Larwood, Clark, Voce and others will pay ready tribute to his sure hands when standing back.

Two years later, Ames rallied after lapses in form to regain his place against South Africa at The Oval. Frank Chester, the umpire in the Oval Test, said in the whole of his experience he had not seen better work behind the stumps.

Among his contemporaries there is no argument that Ames heads the list as the finest wicket-keeper batsman. His closest pre-war contender was the South African Horace ('Jock') Cameron. Cameron's career was tragically curtailed by his death through enteric fever shortly after the 1935 series in England. He was aged 30. E. M. Wellings, the Oxford blue and Surrey bowler and trenchant cricket writer, felt that Cameron could have rivalled Ames but for his early death. (Wellings also said that Godfrey Evans might have challenged his Kent senior as an all-rounder if he had fulfilled his early batting promise.) In 1935 Cameron demoralised the England attack at Lord's. He went on a batting rampage and hit 90 out of 126 in an hour and a half. His most famed exploit in an illustrious summer was against Yorkshire at Sheffield. He struck Hedley Verity for 30 in one remarkable over. Verity, typically, thought the assault on his bowling was a splendid testimony to the profits of calculated aggression. 'You should have seen that South African get after me,' he said. 'My, that was champion hitting.'

Cameron hit three centuries on the England tour in which he scored 1,458 runs and obtained 48 dismissals. In 26 Tests against England and Australia he hit 1,239 runs and gained 51 dismissals. Overall, in his short career, he totalled 5,396 runs and claimed 224 victims behind the wicket. He did, however, receive the

Good at either!

AMES   Kent County C.C.

Ames, as the finest wicket-keeper batsman, enjoyed his 'double-barrelled' status

highest commendation as a wicket-keeper throughout the world. His stumping of a batsman was, in one classic phrase, likened to the 'nonchalant gesture of a smoker flicking the ash from a cigarette.' 'Cameron's concentration upon his job was always evident,' commented *Wisden*. 'Some of his stumping efforts dazzled the eyesight.'

In the 1930s, a decade of top-class wicket-keepers in the English counties, Les Ames had to maintain his consistency to avert demotion. He may not, as Sir Donald Bradman has said, have been either the best batsman or keeper; but there was never any question of sacrificing one skill for another in his reign as England's wicket-keeper. Bradman and Bill O'Reilly, neither of them given to scattering compliments like confetti, rated Ames as the finest wicket-keeper batsman of all time. He earned widespread respect in his dual roles in Australia. Bill Brown, the former Australian opening batsman, remembered Ames as the complete craftsman. 'As a wicket-keeper, Les was efficient without any idiosyncrasies. He was not prone to appeal unless he felt the appeal was justified.'

Brown cited one example of Ames's enterprise in which the Kent wicket-keeper gave evidence of the footwork of his soccer days. It occurred during the Australian second innings at Nottingham in 1934. 'Hedley Verity was bowling and I edged a delivery down on to my pad. Before it could touch the ground Les shot out his foot, kicked the ball in the air, and promptly caught it.' Brown marvelled at Les's dexterity and the quickness of his reflexes. 'That was one of the fastest I can remember by a wicket-keeper. Although it brought my innings to a close, I was able to appreciate the flair which made Les far more than a tradesman behind the stumps.'

Another Australian, Keith Rigg, recalled Ames's all-round expertise as a wicket-keeper.

> Nowadays there are many 'keepers who can cope with fast bowling, but they are all at sea against the slows. Les was equally good with all kinds of bowlers—Gubby Allen, Bill Voce and Harold Larwood as representatives of the quickies, and Robins, Brown and Freeman among the slows. But I was especially impressed by the fact that Les stood up to Hammond and obtained stumpings from his medium-pace bowling. This was good keeping because the ball gathered pace off the pitch.

Sir Leonard Hutton provided another interesting verdict, which was endorsed by other contemporaries. He believed that Ames would have been England's No. 5 batsman for many years had it not been for the demands of wicket-keeping. 'It is most difficult to play as a wicket-keeper batsman in top-class cricket. The strain is considerable. I really did wonder how he sustained his remarkable ability over so many years.' Sir Leonard also commented that Ames was regarded by his Yorkshire opponents as one of the top six batsmen in the country in the 1930s. Ames himself, following the maxim of his mentor, Gerry Weigall, would not have welcomed selection purely as a batsman.

> I always felt happier because of having another string to my bow. If I got a duck, which made you feel pretty miserable, I could redeem myself behind the wicket. Similarly, if we fielded first and I took two or three important catches, then I was fairly content. This gave me the extra confidence when I batted. If you are solely a batsman, you have to shoulder a heavy burden.

P. G. H. Fender, the former Surrey captain and one of the shrewdest of cricket observers, was a commentator on the 1928–9 tour of Australia. At the outset of the tour he wrote:

> I found everyone regretting that Ames could not keep like Duckworth, or that Duckworth could not bat like Ames, but there were no two opinions, up to that stage, as to the greater ability of Duckworth as a wicket-keeper. More than once I heard it suggested that some of his form had nearly been as good as Strudwick at his best, and there were

few suggestions that England would suffer by comparison with her opposite number, Oldfield, in this important position in the field.

Duckworth confirmed his ranking as England's No. 1 'keeper in Australia. His collaboration with Maurice Tate was a major factor in England's triumphs. Clem Hill, a distinguished Australian of earlier years, described Duckworth's catch, which dismissed Woodfull off Tate in the fourth Test at Adelaide, as one of the finest in his experience. 'The ball was leg-glanced from Tate's bowling. It was his fast one but this young "jack-in-the-box" was there, and did the rest.'

Hill also praised the magnificence of Duckworth in the keenly contested and conclusive third Test at Melbourne. Duckworth's heroics, the spectacular tumbles of the showman, saved crucial runs for England. 'His exhibition of wicket-keeping was an outstanding feature of the match,' commented Hill. 'In fact, I have not seen anything better than some of his saves on the legside. If he could not reach the ball with both hands, he would dive across with one hand to stop it.' S. J. Southerton, writing in *Wisden*, also referred to the 'uniformly superb wicket-keeping' of Duckworth. 'He had to put up with a good deal of barracking from the crowds but remained unperturbed and his mistakes might almost be counted on the fingers of one hand.'

In the seesaw battle at Melbourne Hobbs and Sutcliffe came together in one of their great batting partnerships. It was a miracle of resource on a rain-affected wicket, and averted a rout. 'The wicket behaved as badly as it possibly could, brought out every trick in its bag, yet England's opening pair fought on without flinching in the face of tremendous odds,' wrote Fender. England escaped through the tenacity of two batting masters and moved on to a three wickets' victory to retain the Ashes. Australia's ageing team were not outclassed. Bradman and the ill-fated Archie Jackson were the emerging bright young stars, affording glimpses of majesty. Bradman was to wreak awesome revenge in 1930, and Jackson, had he not been cruelly struck down with a fatal illness, might have matched his compatriot in valour and deed.

Percy Chapman, the Kent cavalier and England's triumphant captain, was then at the peak of his popularity. He exulted in the honours bestowed upon his team. 'Chapman radiates enthusiasm,' declared one writer. 'He is not the ultra-correct Englishman of Galsworthy. He approximates more to the Elizabethan Englishman, happy, rollicking and audacious on the cricket field. He rules his team with charm and vivacity.' Chapman had, perhaps reluctantly, to relegate his Kent colleagues, Ames and Freeman to the reserves. 'My youth was against me on that first trip to Australia,' said Ames. 'Once Duckworth had been picked for the first Test there was no question of dropping him. He kept exceptionally well. England didn't want a wicket-keeper who might score runs. I was a little disappointed at not getting a Test place, but not unduly so. I thought I was fortunate to get on the tour so early in my career.'

Ames's batting in Australia was imbued with the zest of youth. One observer wryly suggested that he might have been well advised to suppress the fact that he could keep wicket. Ames, in fact, would probably have won his first England cap but for injury in the final Test at Melbourne. He had hit three centuries in a flurry of scoring before the match. His sparkling form seemed to have put him into contention. There was a vacancy in the team. Sutcliffe, incapacitated with an arm injury, and Chapman, recovering from influenza, were absentees at Melbourne. Ames's hopes of gaining a place were dashed in the state match against Victoria. He fractured the little finger of his right hand while keeping to Larwood.

Freeman's exclusion from the Australian Tests, after his memorable season in England, hurt Ames more. Percy Fender considered the selection of Freeman a gamble on the rock-hard wickets. He said the Kent spinner's figures compared unfavourably with those of the Somerset slow left-arm bowler, J. C. White, before the first Test at Brisbane. England fielded only four bowlers in the Test. White, as the only spinner, was selected ahead of Freeman, wrongly in Ames's view. England won by 675 runs and White, in one devastating spell on a treacherous wicket, took four wickets for 7 runs in 6.3 overs. Australia were dismissed for 66 in their second innings. In the fourth Test at Adelaide White performed less dramatically but equally valuably. He called upon tremendous reserves of stamina and accuracy to bowl 124 overs and take 13 wickets in the match. Ames conceded that White justified his inclusion. 'Poor little Tich couldn't get into the side after the events at Brisbane. Given the chance, in the conditions prevailing there, Tich could easily have had six wickets at small cost and made his place secure for the series.'

Ames's enduring friendship with George Duckworth was forged on the SS *Otranto* during the voyage to Australia in 1928. It survived a strongly orchestrated media furore on their respective merits in succeeding years. Les recalled how 'Duckie' soon revealed his sportsmanship. A bargain was struck at the start of their relationship. As they lounged on the deck one day, Duckworth said:

> Well, Les, only one wicket-keeper can play in each of the Tests, and that means you or me. If you are the lucky one, it will make no difference to our friendship, and I am sure you'll act the same if I am chosen to play. It is up to the one not selected to help the other in every way he can.

Duckworth retained his position as England's wicket-keeper against Australia in 1930 and in South Africa in 1930–1. Ames took over from his Lancashire rival in the three Tests against New Zealand in 1931. Duckworth gave proof, as the following story demonstrates, of his warm heart and generosity. On the eve of the Old Trafford Test Ames was involved in a nightmarish journey to Manchester. In London his luggage was mishandled by an irresponsible railway porter and loaded aboard an express train bound for Holyhead. Ames firmly instructed the authorities at Euston to send a wire to Holyhead and make sure that his equipment was transferred to Manchester as quickly as possible. He then caught the last train to Manchester and arrived there, feeling wretched and tired at 4.30 in the morning. He was only partially refreshed by a wash and breakfast when he eventually arrived at Old Trafford. Harry Makepeace, the Lancashire coach, was quick to aid Les in his distress. He telephoned Duckworth to explain Les's plight. 'Within half an hour Duckie was at the ground and offered to lend me his own cricket togs and wicket-keeping gear until mine arrived,' remembered Ames. The rains which fell in Manchester on that troubled day for once had the effect of restoring Les's cheerfulness. Not a ball was bowled, and his cricket bag and suitcase arrived without further mishap.

Ames had other cause to bless his friend, by then his deputy, on later tours of Australia. On the 1932–3 tour Duckworth was constantly at his side as he rested from his wicket-keeping labours against Larwood, Voce and Allen. At Duckworth's suggestion, slices of meat were placed in his gloves to save his hands from bruising.

By the time lunch came round, when it was 100 degrees in the shade,

The ebullient Lancastrian, George Duckworth, Ames's great England rival and friend (Nottinghamshire CCC)

the beef got a bit high. It had also been knocked to pulp by Harold Larwood's 'expresses'. 'Duckie' waited upon me like a valet. He would be the first person to greet me when I got back to the pavilion. He would wash out my gloves and, armed with a pair of scissors, he would cut up fresh slices of meat for my gloves before we went out again to field.

Ames recalled the soreness of his hands after their pounding by England's fast bowlers. It reached the stage where he could hardly take the ball without flinching. The slices of meat were the remedy. There was an amusing sequel in one Test on the tour. Les returned to the pavilion after a hot, tiring day in the field. He threw the gloves containing the meat under a chair in the dressing-room. He then took a shower, changed and enjoyed a refreshing drink before moving on to the team's hotel. 'I forgot all about my gloves until play restarted on the Monday.' The magnet of the rotting meat lured a battalion of flies over the weekend. Les was instantly reminded by the appalling stench pervading the dressing-room. His gloves, ruined beyond aid, gave off a stomach-turning odour. With a gesture of disgust, he pulled on a new pair before resuming his place behind the stumps.

On the 1936–7 tour Duckworth, with a finger injury, and Ames played together in one state match. Despite his handicap, Duckworth insisted upon keeping wicket. He said: 'It wasn't fair to let Les do it. Better have me smashed rather than risk him, too.' A writer in *The Cricketer* also described how Duckworth, far from being aggrieved at his loss of eminence, went to his captain, Gubby Allen, and begged him to give Ames more opportunities behind the wicket. 'Not only that, he actually coached his rival in certain details. Can there ever have been a finer exhibition of sportsmanship?'

The portrayals of gallantry convey the reasons for Ames's affection for his old cricket comrade. In his own county Duckworth had to contend with a major challenge from Bill Farrimond, another fine wicket-keeper who represented England in the 1930s. Ames, too, had a resolute deputy in Kent in farmer Howard Levett, who loved wicket-keeping and enjoyed days of inspiration. 'Hopper would roar with laughter when he made a catch. You could hear it all round the ground. The Kent crowds chuckled along with him, sharing his delight,' remembered Doug Wright.

Levett, one of the most engaging characters in cricket, represented the Gentlemen against the Players in four matches. 'He was easily the best amateur wicket-keeper in the country,' said Ames. 'What I especially admired about Hopper was his loyalty to Kent. He had several offers from other counties to qualify for them.' Levett, with his stores of nervous energy, was a tireless raconteur. He rarely completed one sentence before he started another. The stories he told, or were told about him, could have been incorporated into a Ben Travers farce.

Tom Pearce remembered one match between Middlesex and Kent at Lord's. Jim Smith, an unpretentious but fearsome hitter, was in rollicking mood as a batsman. 'Big Jim hit up a steepler, it went up many a mile,' said Pearce. As the ball swirled in the air, Levett cried out: 'She's mine; she's mine.' He cavorted frantically in a bemused fox-trot, moving ever further down the wicket. The ball, after what seemed an eternity, plummeted down from the skies. Before it descended Levett had arrived in the region of mid-on. Grim-faced, he first raised his gloved hands and then, with renewed hope, plunged forward into a headlong dive. He missed the ball. His Kent team-mates, watching this Chaplinesque pursuit, rolled on the ground. Their laughter verged on hysteria as the frustrated Levett roared with fury.

Ames's batting stature afforded the gifted Levett few opportunities to display his unquestioned expertise as a wicket-keeper in the Kent team. Similarly, this increasing prowess did much to press Les's claims to oust Duckworth at England level. Jack Davies, however, did not think that his colleague's dual talents as a youngster were a major factor in his selection. 'What is doubtful is whether he would have been picked as a batsman (at that age) but for his wicket-keeping.' In later years, Davies believed, Ames might have been played solely as a batsman. If statistics do not lie, little divided Ames and Duckworth. In 24 Tests Duckworth secured 60 dismissals (45 catches and 15 stumpings). Ames's aggregate in 47 Tests was 97 (74 catches and 23 stumpings). In all first-class cricket Duckworth's tally amounted to 1,090 dismissals (751 catches and 339 stumpings) compared with Ames's career record of 1,121 victims. Duckworth, after later careers as county scorer, BBC commentator and journalist, and a popular baggage master with touring teams, died in 1966. He was aged 64. 'He died too young, did George,' said Ames of his friend of many summers.

Ames, selected along with Kent colleagues, Woolley and Freeman, made his England debut against South Africa at The Oval in August, 1929. Sutcliffe hit two centuries amid a plethora of runs in a drawn match. Ames, never the happiest of starters, did not get off the mark. He was dismissed for a salutary duck, caught by Mitchell off McMillan. There were, however, two catches behind the wicket off Clark to send back Taylor and Morkel to bolster his morale.

There was a blaze of strokes to stun the South Africans when they came down to Canterbury on the weekend following the Test. Ames hit 145 in less than two hours; his partnership with Ashdown added 187 for the fifth wicket in 100 minutes. 'With a series of stinging drives and superb hooks, Ames raced towards his century,' reported the *Kentish Gazette*. Ashdown was equally aggressive at the other end. In 70 minutes before tea the pair added 118 runs. Subsequently the scoring rate became even brisker, with 69 runs accumulated in half an hour. 'Ames simply hit the bowling to all parts of the field, one grand six off Bell carrying the ball into the crowd at the Nackington screen,' continued the report. Ames was eventually caught by Cameron off another towering hit, the ball swirling high above the wicket. 'Despite the rapid rate of scoring, Ames gave no actual chances. In an innings, which contained every variety of stroke, his powerful, well-timed drives were a distinctive feature.' The South Africans, after Kent captain Geoffrey Legge had lost the toss for the ninth time in succession, led by 55 runs on the first innings. Dalton hit an unblemished 150 but he was missed five times in reaching three figures for the second time in the match. The tourists were perilously close to defeat at one stage, having declined to 113 for 6 in their second innings. Kent ought to have won. They were left to rue the spilled catches as the game dwindled into a draw.

Wilfred Rhodes and George Gunn were the veteran warriors on the tour of the West Indies in the winter of 1929–30. Patsy Hendren, then in his 41st year but eternally young, also accompanied Les Ames on his first tour of the Caribbean. The batting of Hendren of whom Neville Cardus said: 'One day he will be given out smile before wicket', excitingly commanded the attention. Learie Constantine, fiery in temperament and pace in those days, blinked with astonishment as the fearless Hendren hooked and pulled his bowling. Hendren enjoyed a remarkable season. In only 18 innings he scored 1,765 runs, with an average of 135.76. In the Tests he totalled 693 runs (average 115.50) and his feat in scoring four double centuries on that tour has been superseded only overseas by Bradman (six in 1930) and Weekes (five in 1950).

Ames was inevitably overshadowed by such gargantuan exploits; but he finished third in the tour averages with 855 runs, including four centuries, and he was more than just a foil to the rapacious Patsy. They were associated in two stands of over 200 against the West Indies, at Port of Spain in Trinidad and British Guiana in Georgetown. Les was missed first ball off Constantine in the Trinidad Test. He rode his luck to hit a century which was judged as fine as Hendren's double hundred in the match. The game coincided with Hendren's 41st birthday. As a tribute to the master and pupil, their hosts presented cheques of £50 and £25 to Hendren and Ames. There were also words of praise for Les's batting by a writer in *The Cricketer.* 'He has a good defence and any number of strokes. He is very nearly an England batsman already.' Of his association with Hendren, Ames says: 'Patsy was my ideal as a batsman. He had everything. He was a beautiful offside player, tremendous off the front foot, and he was one of the best hookers in the game.'

Ames and Hendren had rallied their team in the first innings at Port of Spain, adding 81 runs for the fifth wicket; and they again came to the rescue in the second innings. Hendren survived chances at 38 and in the forties; but thereafter both batsmen exerted their authority over the West Indian attack. They were especially severe on Constantine, who took four wickets but was hit for 165 runs in 40 overs. The batting spree did not end until the stand had realised 237 runs. During the match, Constantine and his partner, Griffith, employed a fast leg theory method of attack.

'Constantine brought most of his slips round to short and fine leg but Hendren and Ames dealt with the bowling on its merits, and the fieldsmen on the legside were lucky to escape injury,' related one observer. England were the victors by 167 runs; Bill Voce, at 18, furnished a glimpse of his future prowess with 11 wickets in the match; and Ames made one stumping and took three catches, including one to dismiss the forbidding George Headley off Haig.

The blossoming genius of Headley was unfurled in all its gorgeous colours at Georgetown, where he struck two centuries in the match to overwhelm the tourists. Headley followed this feat with a superb and defiant 223 before being brilliantly stumped by Ames off Wyatt in the final Test at Kingston, Jamaica. This match extended over nine days and was ended by rain in the manner of another cricket marathon nine years later in South Africa. England would surely have won at Kingston had not their captain, Freddie Calthorpe, inexplicably decided to bat a second time, after the tourists had amassed 849 in the first three days. The total

Patsy Hendren, an irrepressible batting partner on Ames's first tour of the West Indies in 1929–30 (Hulton Picture Company)

was a record for a Test match and the fifth highest in first-class cricket.

The innings was dominated by Andy Sandham, who scored 325 in 10 hours. Gunn, Wyatt and Hendren were his partners in the first course of a mammoth run feast. The England score was 380 when Ames came to the crease. The departing Hendren told him: 'Take no notice of the score, Les. This match is to be played to a finish, so don't throw your wicket away.' It was a signal of murderous intent which foreshadowed the greed of England's 903 against Australia at The Oval in 1938. Ames, thus instructed, did not show any mercy in scoring 149. Ames and Sandham put on 200 in just over two hours to place the match comfortably within England's grasp. The tourists led by 563 on the first innings but Calthorpe did not enforce the follow-on. 'It was not (as one report stated) a high compliment to his bowlers. The time wasted by the second innings might have been employed, probably with ultimate victory as a result, in dismissing the West Indies.'

Time was also a factor. The MCC party were due to sail for England on April 13, 10 days after the start of the match which had been specially arranged to decide the series. 'Both in this match and the third Test (not crucially for the West Indies, who won by 289 runs after also not ordering the follow-on) the side with an overwhelming lead seemed to be suffering from an inferiority complex,' added the report. The West Indies were finally set the ludicrous target of 836 runs, and with a nod to the skies to unleash their wrath, they reduced the deficit by 400 runs. Calthorpe's unenterprising captaincy, even allowing for the perfect wicket, was a culpable waste of the talents of Wilfred Rhodes. The Yorkshireman, with a rich cushion of runs at his disposal, would have relished measuring his wits against the conditions.

As a postscript to the tour, Les Ames recalled the amazing economy and stamina of Rhodes, then aged 52, in the heat of the Caribbean. Rhodes bowled over 500 overs on the tour, and one in every three was a maiden. He took 39 wickets at an average of 24.28 runs apiece. At Georgetown he bowled 91 overs for 189 runs and four wickets. 'In the first innings Wilfred bowled unchanged from lunch until close of play, despite the handicap of a frightful carbuncle on the back of his neck,' said Ames. 'I feel sure that many much younger players would have found intense discomfort merely sitting and relaxing in the shade of the pavilion. Wilfred bowled on without a break for four hours in a blistering sun and in considerable pain.'

Ames, after two tours and a continuous round of cricket, was less than certain on the rain-affected wickets of 1930. If there was a hint of tiredness in his play, he still quietly consolidated his position in the Kent XI. Duckworth deservedly retained his England place against the resurgent Australians, with Don Bradman, the young batting emperor, occupying centre stage. Ames's own summer ended on an adventurous note. He re-asserted his authority with a champagne century, his first of the season, against the Australians at Folkestone in September.

In 1931, Ames was selected as England's wicket-keeper in all three Tests against New Zealand. Duckworth, possibly, had cause for offence at being spurned at that stage. An editorial in *The Cricketer* commented that the Test selectors had acceded to the wish of the general public that young players should be given a chance. On the selection of Ames ahead of Duckworth, the writer said:

> Apparently, the selectors had their minds on the fact that too long a tail was to be avoided, so they have left out the better wicket-keeper for the better bat. It is to be hoped that the critics will cease to grumble and hold their peace.

Ames, as one of those young players and only too aware of the criticism, made the most of his opportunity. He could not be expected to entirely silence the grumbles of the Duckworth clique; but he did earn their respect. Apart from one critical phase in 1935, Les held the position until a recurring back problem ended his distinguished reign in 1939.

The series against New Zealand heralded a fruitful and influential associ-ation with Gubby Allen. The occasion was their (still unbeaten) record eighth wicket partnership of 246 runs in two and three-quarter hours at Lord's. The previous best stand for the wicket (against all countries) was 243 by Clem Hill and R. J. Hartigan for Australia against England at Adelaide in 1908. 'That morning at Lord's was a happy beginning to our friendship. It was the first time I got to know Les and enjoy his company,' said Allen. They

Sir George 'Gubby' Allen: the lifelong friendship of Allen and Ames began on a high note with their still unbeaten record stand of 246 for the eighth wicket against New Zealand at Lord's in 1931

came together after Ian Peebles, as 'nightwatchman', had been stumped off the New Zealand leg-spinner, Bill Merritt. 'Peebles was given the most frightful rollicking by the England captain, Douglas Jardine,' remembered Allen.

On the Saturday of the Lord's Test England lost seven wickets for 190 and trailed by 34 runs behind New Zealand. Merritt had weaved his spinning spell to take the wickets of Duleepsinhji, Jardine and Woolley as well as the hapless Peebles. Woolley had, in fact, been the only England batsman to show aggressive intent. Driving, cutting and pulling, he had scored 80 out of the meagre total.

As they walked out to bat on the Monday morning, Ames said to Allen: 'What do you know about this chap, Merritt?' Gubby replied: 'I don't think he likes the stick.' He remembers the broad smile which spread over Les's face as he relished the prospect. 'We both darted down the wicket to Merritt and really gave him a hammering.'

King George was at Lord's to watch the merriment of one half of his cricketing subjects. Merritt's length wavered under the onslaught of Ames and Allen. 'It was taken away from him by two precocious young men,' commented the *London Evening News.* 'Ames and Allen showed no mercy against indifferent bowling. Seldom have so many full pitches been seen in a match of this class.' H. D. G. Leveson-Gower, in the *Morning Post*, wrote: 'One thing that struck me forcibly about the batting of Ames and Allen was their "quickness of foot". They were always out to the ball.' The New Zealand captain, Lowry, switched his bowlers, making six changes in the first 40 minutes, but all were helpless and unnerved by the breathtaking riposte of the England batsmen.

'The professional and the amateur realised that their side expected much of them, and they did not let them down,' reported another observer. 'Ames was the more dashing and Allen the more watchful as the stand prospered.' Ames hit two fours and then a six and the 'experimental full-tosses', in one sardonic description, were contemptuously dispatched to the boundary. Seventy-five runs were struck in a tumultuous first hour to provide a momentum which never faltered. Both batsmen raced to their centuries before the stand ended at 436.

The record-breaking revels at Lord's brought together, as is the nature of cricket, two men from widely differing backgrounds. It sealed the friendship of the Etonian Allen and Ames, the village boy from Elham. Gubby and Les were to pool their collective wisdom in the corridors of cricket power in the years ahead.

6
BODYLINE AND BRADMAN

*The Don was the greatest hooker there has ever been in
the game. So I cannot think he was too frightened of the
English attack.*

LES AMES

———————

Les Ames was elevated to celebrity status in his season of reckoning in
1932. He was bracketed with the leading batsmen in the land. 'To
Ames came the batting honours,' enthused *The Cricketer.* 'Never had
he batted with such consistent skill and brilliance. Ames, Sutcliffe, Hammond and Jardine rank as the greatest quartet of the year.'

In Kent the triumvirate of Ames, Freeman and Woolley lifted their county
high up the slopes towards the championship summit. Ames achieved his
third 'double' with the ageless Freeman, who exceeded 200 wickets for the
fifth successive year. In all their history Kent had never had a wicket-keeper
to match the versatility of Ames. 'He is an iconoclast in world cricket,'
declared one writer. 'How long can he keep both irons hot in the fire?' The
munificent bounty of Ames and Freeman, in their argosies together, spun
Kent enticingly close to an elusive title. Kent won seven games, including
five by an innings, in less than two days; they headed the championship for
over a month; but the challenge faltered in July, and Yorkshire, with a greater
depth of talent, forged into the lead and pushed them into third place.

Ames, meanwhile, moved busily into contention for the tour of Australia
in the following winter. He far surpassed his previous batting accomplishments. His aggregate for the season climbed to 2,482 runs, including nine
centuries, at an average of 57.72; and he finished third behind Sutcliffe and
Ernest Tyldesley in the first-class list. His triumphant march was strewn with
garlands. 'He bats in the traditional Kent style. There are few men who hit
the ball harder,' was one of the many tributes. Ames's powerful off-driving
was considered reminiscent of another handsome stylist, Kenneth Hutch-
ings, the Kent and England batsman, who was killed in action in the First
World War. *The Cricketer* thought Ames's overriding claim for Test recognition lay in his batting.

> Even if he had never worn the wicket-keeping gloves, he must have
> been chosen for England for his run-scoring powers. But it must also
> be borne in mind that he was, statistically, by far the most successful

wicket-keeper in first-class cricket. He claimed 104 victims and thus created a new record.

At the beginning of July, Ames made three centuries in consecutive matches—130 not out, 149 and 120. In August he eclipsed the sequence with 130, 133, 52 not out, 180 and 101, a total of 596 runs for four times out, in the course of four matches played in 15 days. *Wisden* reported:

> He played equally well on soft or hard turf and often retrieved an unfavourable situation, indeed, more than once, scoring with an ease and brilliance when other batsmen experienced much trouble in withstanding the bowling.

One example of Ames's aplomb in difficult conditions was displayed against Middlesex at Tunbridge Wells. Woolley alone with 94—the fourth time he had been dismissed in the nineties during the season—averted a complete collapse against the spin of Robins in the first innings. Hearne and Hendren mastered Freeman in a stand of 152 runs for the fifth wicket, and Middlesex led by 200 runs. Kent, in their second innings, lost five wickets for 102. Ames had to summon all his patience to resist the Middlesex attack. He was becalmed to such an extent that his first 50 occupied an hour and 20 minutes. The restraint was uncharacteristic for a batsman who rarely tolerated delay; but it saved his side from defeat. 'Never taking the slightest risk, Ames showed a sound defence,' reported the *Kentish Gazette*, 'and when the bowlers, handicapped by a wet ball, erred in length, he pulled, drove and cut in grand style.' *The Cricketer* ranked Ames's 120 against Surrey on a constantly changing and weather affected wicket at Blackheath as his finest innings of the summer. 'His admirable 135, against Sussex at Hastings, was almost as valuable; and the way he dealt out punishment after his captain (Jardine) was out to the Indians in the Lord's Test match was an effort that gave intense joy.'

The expectations of Ames's Kent admirers were reflected in one earnest plea to the England selectors. 'Many consider that he should be given a place on the Australian tour for his batting alone and that Duckworth should be chosen as wicket-keeper,' declared the spokesman. Then, with a commendable show of loyalty, he added: 'A lot of rubbish has been talked about Ames not being a first-class 'keeper, but he misses precious few chances and concedes few byes, whether playing for Kent, or in representative matches. After all, mere showiness cuts very little ice from a practical point of view, and it is useless to carry a batting passenger when there is a man available to do all that is required.' In Lancashire, where George Duckworth held imperious sway, the argument was no doubt countered by the equally tenable view that their champion's proven wicket-keeping skills should take priority over even the most robust of batsman.

The decision ultimately taken, by more neutral judges, was that Ames was supremely fitted for both tasks. Later attempts to rehabilitate Duckworth foundered on this inescapable truth. In July Ames was named as one of the first six Australian tourists. The others were Jardine, the captain, Hammond, Sutcliffe, Duckworth and Duleepsinhji, whose illness later compelled him to withdraw from the tour. Jardine's all-out pace battle plan in Australia was to prove a decisive factor in Duckworth's exclusion from the Tests. Ames's swag of runs at home in 1932 undoubtedly tipped the scales in his favour. Equally, it could be said, that his proficiency in keeping to Kent's slow bowlers would have counted just as much had the accent been on spin.

At all events, Ames was deployed in a key role in Jardine's leg-theory plot. It is to his testimony to which we turn in assessing the claim that Don Bradman, the prime target, was defeated by the strategy. Ames was an alert witness behind the stumps on the controversial tour. He was adamant that the allegations of Bradman's frailties under the assault were unfounded. 'People may have misunderstood the reason for the way Bradman played in the series,' said Les. 'I am not saying that the Don did not get away from it a bit at times. But if he was funking the issue, he still "murdered" the ball through the covers.' Ames dismissed those critics who questioned Bradman's courage. 'No-one likes the bouncing ball, whether it is bodyline or not. No player likes it whizzing around his ears. Some play it better than others. The Don was the greatest hooker there has ever been in the game. So I cannot think he was too frightened of the English attack.' Ames was steadfast in his admiration of the magnificent Australian.

> He was streets ahead of anyone else. Really great players have perfect eyesight and see the ball just that fraction, perhaps 100ths of a second, before the average player. Don never seemed to make a mistake; if he went down the wicket he was always there, and the speed of his footwork made the ball into a half-volley nearly every time. He was either right down the wicket or right back on his stumps. Others have said that Bradman was always seeking to attack the ball. He hardly ever padded up or shouldered arms.

In three series against Australia in the 1930s, Ames gained great satisfaction in dismissing Bradman six times, off the bowling of Farnes, Verity, Hammond and Sinfield. Gubby Allen believed that the tally should have been seven and that Les was denied a catch off his bowling at Adelaide in the 1936–7 series.

> It was an extraordinary delivery. The ball was old. I had lost my run-up, so I reduced my pace. It swung a considerable amount. As it moved, Don tried to pull his bat away without success. The ball glided off his bat, turning perhaps two or three feet. Les made a quite magnificent catch. It wasn't going to carry to Hammond at slip, so he dived across and caught it one-handed. The umpire disallowed the catch.

Allen, in high dudgeon, snatched his sweater from the umpire at the end of the over. 'I'm sorry, Gubby,' responded the contrite umpire. 'I know he turned it, but I didn't hear anything.' Gubby, despite his indignation, had to accept the man's honesty if not his incompetence. Many years later he talked to Bradman about the incident. He described it as the worst decision in his experience. Sir Donald laughed and said: 'Well, I think it was the second worst decision.' He would not be drawn on the personalities involved in the decision which preceded it.

The phenomenal control of Harold Larwood was the pivot of Jardine's strategy in Australia in 1932–3; it won the series but left mental scars which were only partially healed in Gubby Allen's 'goodwill' tour in 1936–7 and not totally erased until after the Second World War. Bob Wyatt, England's vice-captain on the bodyline tour, regarded Larwood as the greatest fast bowler on plumb wickets.

> He had a perfect action and was so much quicker than anyone else. Accuracy was paramount in the method employed by Jardine. Harold's control of length and direction was ideal for the purpose. He could bowl at the off or leg stumps and he knew where he was pitching the ball, either short of a length or well up.

Larwood himself said that 'accuracy is my watchword. The effectiveness of leg-theory demanded it as the first essential.' He contended that if the accusations of bowling at the body were true, either he was extraordinarily inaccurate, or the Australian batsmen were exceptionally clever at avoiding the fast moving ball. Larwood did not play for England again after the Australian tour. He was, it is true, a casualty in physical terms; but his isolation was also the penalty he had to pay for his outstanding genius.

Ronald Mason's brilliant and penetrating sketch of Larwood stressed the magnitude of Australia's task against England.

> The very sight of his approach to the crease quickened the pulses. He moved so lightly and diffidently, cut such a modest, unassuming figure as he took his place in the field, that the energy and power generated in his run-up came as an unnerving surprise.
>
> He was stocky and wiry and presented a neat compact figure topped off by a shock of fair hair, and he walked quietly and meditatively back for about 20 yards before turning into a notable run-up. I call it notable because it had a quiet concentration about it that I have never seen matched; after the first yard or two it took on the quality of a purposeful and menacing sprint, contained, rhythmical, with a deadly, mounting acceleration over the whole distance. As he reached the wicket he climbed into a glorious whirling poise in which both arms circled at full stretch above his head and his run was hardly checked; then at the high climax of this exhilarating performance he released upon the batsman an offering of thunder and greased lightning. The wonderful revelation of glory and strength concealed cool-headed deliberation as much as it revealed the discipline and precision of the craft of a great bowler.

Bowling terror: 'The very sight of his approach to the crease quickened the pulses,'
wrote one admirer of Larwood (Sport-in-Print)

Joe Hardstaff, the former Notts and England batsman, described his county team-mate as the 'silent killer'.

> I used to field at cover point to him. He never had a mid-off but I still had the easiest job in cricket because nobody much tried driving Larwood in front of the wicket. As 'Lol' came up on that smooth, carpet-slipper run of his and I moved in towards the batsman, I used to pin my ears back and listen hard—to find out what kind of delivery he was going to bowl. If I could hear his feet tap-tapping over the turf I knew he would be well within himself. He would still be quick, mind you.

Hardstaff added:

> But when I couldn't hear him running up I used to look at the batsman and think: 'You're a split second away from trouble, son,' because I knew then that 'Lol' was coming in on his toes. That meant only one thing—he was going to let slip the fastest he'd got.

Frank Chester, the umpire, was unable to fault the 'amazing Larwood'.

> His speed almost outstripped the eye and his control over the twin essentials of length and direction was perfect. It was rather like releasing a thunderbolt to put him on to bowl and if his action had not been so beautifully balanced he would not have maintained so much accuracy at such speed.

In a series of articles in the *Daily Sketch* after 'the bodyline tour', Ames maintained that Larwood never did anything more sinister than concentrate on bowling on or just outside the leg stump, which he did with marvellous accuracy. 'So wonderful was his control,' wrote Ames, 'that he rarely, when bowling off-theory, bowled one ball outside the leg stump. When he switched over to leg-theory, he did not bowl one ball outside the off stump. That represents a wicket-keeper's dream of a fast bowler, and I know I appreciated his precision.'

Ames, at that time, thought the crowd, which threatened severe disruption in the ill-tempered Adelaide Test, was misguided in its barracking. 'The malice towards the English team was greater because they could not see what was really happening on the field.' His evidence seems to confirm the symptoms of uneven bounce. Bob Wyatt said that the dangerous ball on the tour was not the bouncer. The greater concern, in Wyatt's view, was the irregular bounce 'when you did not know whether you were going to play the ball up by your armpit, or down by your waist.' Ames continued:

> Often players ducked when balls from Larwood rose just over the middle or leg stumps. Sometimes they were hit by balls that were rising no higher than this. On some occasions I actually made perfectly legitimate appeals for lbw from deliveries which had hit the batsman in the back as he ducked low before the stumps.

One such incident occurred in the Sydney Test when the Australian opener Bill Woodfull ducked and the ball hit him on the thigh. Larwood and Ames both appealed for an lbw decision. The umpire, George Hele, ruled not out and then turned to Larwood and said: 'Harold, if that ball had been two inches lower, I'd have had to give him out.'

The anger of the Australian partisans rose to fever pitch at Adelaide. Larwood was subjected to round after round of bitter barracking after incidents involving Woodfull and Oldfield, who were both hit by the England fast bowler. Ames recalled:

> It wasn't a 'bodyline' field setting when Woodfull was hit. This occurred with the new ball and we always had a normal field for that. It was a nasty delivery and it reared up. The ball was hard and new and it may have swung in a bit. It was a fearful smack. But you cannot call it a bouncer when you are crouched and are hit in the chest. I don't think even Billy Woodfull himself would have criticised Larwood for what happened. He condemned our type of bowling, but not that particular ball.

Larwood took Bradman's wicket four times in the series and six times in all tour games. Bradman, with one century (an unbeaten 103 out of a second innings total of 191 in Australia's only victory in the second Test at Melbourne) was limited to an average of 56.57 in the series. His aggression was muted but such an average does not suggest that he was, like a stricken whale, harpooned by bodyline bowling.

In his earlier reflections on the Bradman–Larwood duel, Les Ames said that the Australian was confronted by a new proposition and tried new methods.

> Whenever he came in I used to study him closely. He was, so far as I could see, the same calm, imperturbable Bradman of the 1930 tour of England. Only in his batsmanship was there something different, something hurried. One thing is certain. It took a master batsman with a marvellous eye to score at all on the offside by stepping back against a bowler of Larwood's pace, with the ball rarely, if ever, pitching out-side the off-stump. The Don has not surrendered his place among the great batsmen of all time. After all, no-one else dared to try to solve the Larwood problem with such daring unorthodoxy.

There was, in fact, one other Australian, Stan McCabe, who did quell England's pace attack in the first Test at Sydney. In Jack Fingleton's words, McCabe 'took bodyline in his teeth and scruffed it as a terrier would a rat'. At Sydney, McCabe scored an unbeaten 187 out of 360 and, said *Wisden*, 'his daring and brilliance was not matched by any other Australian during the tour.' Australia were reeling at 87 for 4 when McCabe came to the wicket. Together with Vic Richardson, he put on 129 for the fifth wicket in just over two hours. McCabe scored 60 out of the 70 runs added by the last four Australian wickets.

Ames believed that McCabe's innings at Sydney and an equally dynamic 232 at Nottingham in 1938 were two of the finest batting displays of all time. 'It was an absolutely fantastic innings at Sydney,' said Les.

> But I think everyone would agree that Stan had to have a bit of luck to get 187. Everything went just right for him. He mainly hooked but occasionally stepped back to cut, although the attack was generally directed at the leg stump. We had two men right back on the fence and about five others round the bat. A few times he lobbed the ball over the inner ring and short of the outfielders. But if he made really good contact it was four and no mistake.

In an innings lasting four hours McCabe scored just 100 in boundaries. All but 16 of his runs came from onside shots.

Pelham Warner, the England manager in Australia, along with others, was high in his praise of Ames's wicket-keeping on the tour. It was said that Ames missed only one chance, and that a barely admissible one, off Larwood. Warner described Ames's legside stumping off Hammond to dismiss Richardson, in the fourth Test at Brisbane, as one of the best he had seen.

Ames, typically, discounted his work in keeping to Larwood. He maintained that this association did not present too many problems. 'It was certainly more difficult than if he had bowled in his normal orthodox style. You had, perhaps, to be a little quicker. You didn't get such a good, free sight of the ball.' His self-effacing analysis is refuted by one of his opponents in Australia, Leo O'Brien.

> I think one of Les's toughest assignments was in the 1932-3 series. He was outstanding. The fierceness of the bowling had to be seen to be appreciated. Day after day the attack was on the leg stump, which did not allow the keeper a consistent view of the path of the ball coming through at uneven heights. Les was jumping high and diving sideways most of the time. He must have been relieved when Hedley Verity came to the crease in his 'spelling' duties, and when the series was over.

Another Australian observer, in an angry letter to *The Times* after the tour, said the English tactics 'resembled the prize ring, not cricket as we know it.' 'The bowling of Larwood and Voce was on many occasions so short that it was not infrequent to see Ames taking the ball above his head and often with outstretched hands on the legside.' The outraged correspondent added: 'Larwood may have been bowling at the leg stump, but if he was he must have seen it suspended in mid-air.'

Many disparate and vexed voices were raised in the aftermath of the tour. Among them was the Hon. Lionel Tennyson, the buccaneering Hampshire captain. Tennyson, 'the brave basher', once said that he enjoyed fast bowling because 'it came on to the bat so damned sweet'. He is best remembered for his famous innings in the Leeds Test in 1921, when he withstood the might of the Australian fast bowlers, Jack Gregory and Ted McDonald. He recalled an assault as ferocious as that of Larwood and Voce in Australia.

> One would get a straight ball from Gregory and hit it to the boundary. The next ball, as likely as not, would be perilously near your eyebrows. Frank Woolley was hit all over his body in his two glorious nineties in the Test at Lord's. At The Oval I was struck over the heart by a ball from McDonald. My doctor assured me that if I had not been so well covered I would for certainty have been killed. It was six weeks before I was able to breathe normally. It is no mis-statement to say that every member of that England side was left black and blue from his knees up to his chin.

Tennyson added:

> There were no squeals of protests to Australia at that time about leg-theory or bodyline bowling. But now we have the fast bowlers who are making a success of the tactics adopted by Gregory and McDonald in 1921, the Commonwealth authority can have no cause for complaint.

The English leg-theory style of attack was first introduced by Bob Wyatt when he led the MCC against an Australian XI at Melbourne. He has rejected the view that it was a pre-determined plan.

> It was a very hard, fast wicket at Melbourne, and after Larwood had bowled a few overs with the new ball the shine had gone and the ball wasn't leaving the bat. It tended to come in a bit and the Australians, as mainly bottom-handed batsmen, played the ball on the onside. There was little chance for the slips, so I gradually moved the fielders over to the legside, not with a view to bowling bouncers, but simply to stop runs. Of course, every now and then the fast bowlers dropped one short. But this was a perfectly legitimate shock tactic.

England fast bowlers, Harold Larwood and Bill Voce (right) and Ames in relaxed mood en route *for the 'bodyline' tour of Australia (L. Ames)*

Wyatt said he afterwards mentioned the use of his leg-theory to Jardine. The England captain replied: 'That's interesting. We must pursue the matter.' Jardine was impressed by the discovery of a 'totally unsuspected weakness' on the leg stump by leading Australian batsmen who would be meeting England in the subsequent Test matches. Ames recalled that leg-theory was consistently used by Jardine during the series.

> He always started with the normal offside field setting for six overs and then, if nothing happened, he would revert to leg-theory. I can see him now—waving everybody over to the onside. When people like Bill O'Reilly and the other tailenders came in he didn't bowl it at them. He would get them out the other way just as quick. But I would say that leg-theory was regularly used against the first five or six Australian batsmen.

The unyielding Douglas Jardine was a cricketer vilified to a degree almost unprecedented in sporting post-mortems. Ames described his former England captain in the following words:

> He was a bit of a loner. He was never a man to let his hair down and have a few drinks. I never knew what his innermost thoughts were. He was a difficult man to understand, but when I met him again after the war he had mellowed and was charming company. It seems that his one ambition, and no-one could fault him for that, was to win the Ashes. I do not know whether he devised the 'bodyline' attack but I cannot think of anyone else who did. At all events, he pursued the tactics and, as far as they were concerned, they were successful.

By one of those strange quirks of fortune Ames rarely unfurled his batting gifts in Australia. On three tours there he did not score one Test century. The inexplicable lack of success defies explanation. Les confessed himself puzzled by the run famine, especially as he scored freely off the same Australian bowlers in England and also enjoyed huge batting rewards on similar wickets in the West Indies. It was suggested by Gubby Allen that the variable bounce of the Australian wickets might have contributed to Ames's disappointing form. Les discounted the theory, indeed he was sceptical of modern batsmen who attribute uneven bounce as the cause of their dismissals. In Australia, he said, this did not present any problem, apart from the isolated example of the Melbourne Test on the bodyline tour. At Melbourne England suffered their solitary defeat by 111 runs, curiously, in a tour dominated by pace, at the hands of Australia's spinners, Bill O'Reilly and Bert Ironmonger. Ames remembered that on his first tour in 1928 'you could almost go over to the legside with your eyes closed and the ball would find its way through the gap of its own accord.' The Australian wickets should have suited his style of batsmanship. 'I was predominantly a forward player, and with the ball coming through at a uniform height, the wickets should have been ideal for me.' The glare of the Australian sunshine reflected from the 'shirtfront' wickets has affected many England batsmen. Ames did regard this as a handicap.

> After sitting for a considerable time in the shadow of the pavilion, the brightness seemed intensified when the call came to bat. It happened to me quite often. Everything was all right if I stayed long enough at the wicket to attune my eyes, but more often than not I was back in the pavilion before that could happen.

Ames did fall below his high standards as a batsman in Australia; but on the 1932–3 tour he seemed to have exerted his authority over the formidable O'Reilly before the first Test at Sydney. Les, after a lean spell in the preliminary games, hit 90 as the MCC beat New South Wales by an innings. 'I had given Bill a bit of stick in the state game,' recalled Les. 'But then came the Test and he dismissed me for a duck.' Sutcliffe, Hammond and Pataudi each scored centuries in a massive opening to the innings. Ames was under no pressure; the opportunity was there to glitter as a batsman.

Les recalled: 'Bill Woodfull, the Australian captain, brought up Stan McCabe to silly point when I came in. I was a little hesitant at the start of my innings. I just pushed forward and McCabe darted in to take the catch. So I was out off the bloody first ball.' If he had reason to be peeved at this abrupt dismissal, Ames believed he had even greater cause for indignation about being given run out when he was well past the wicket in the final Test at Sydney.

Ames's batting dismay was countered by the certainty of his wicket-keeping in Australia. It pulled him out of the doldrums and refuted allegations that his claims for selection were primarily based on his run-scoring powers. As Jardine's juggernaut rolled invincibly over Australia, Ames had once again cause to rejoice in being 'double-barrelled'.

Ames, along with the rest of the English tourists, enjoyed the trust of his captain. Douglas Jardine, the cricket despot of so many accounts, was a leader whose Churchillian qualities were sadly discarded by the hierarchy in a mêlée of criticism after the tour. He was undoubtedly a man of war, but his refusal to compromise prematurely lowered the curtain on a distinctive career. 'His fighting power was a wonderful source of inspiration to us all,' said one of his most loyal lieutenants, Herbert Sutcliffe. 'He planned for us, cared for us, he fought for us on that tour, and he was so faithful in everything that he did that we were prepared on our part to do anything we could for him.' This praise came from a man who had thought Jardine was a 'queer devil' on the previous Australian tour in 1928–9.

Jardine underscored this faith in the retention of Ames amid his struggles for runs in Australia. Ames made amends for his batting failure in the first Test at Sydney by taking four catches to dismiss Woodfull, Oldfield and Wall (twice) off the bowling of Larwood, Voce, Hammond and Allen. Fingleton, Brown, Darling and Richardson, among the leading Australian batsmen, were other victims of his alertness behind the stumps on the tour.

Les ruefully recalled a rare error, a fumbled stumping chance, which allowed Australia to escape an innings defeat at Sydney. Australia, in their second innings, collapsed against Larwood who took 10 wickets in the match. Nagel and Wall provided unexpected resistance after eight wickets had fallen for 113 runs. Hedley Verity bowled the last ball of the day to Nagel, who forgot his circumspection and attempted a mighty blow off the Yorkshire spinner. 'He was yards out of his crease,' said Ames, 'and I could have stumped him with my eyes closed. With my eyes open, I missed the simplest of stumpings and Nagel, grinning broadly, scrambled back to safety.' The missed stumping meant that England had to bat again to score one run for victory on the following morning. A solitary spectator on the Sydney Hill, perhaps having slept there overnight, watched the final rites. The brief reappearance of Australia's last wicket pair was applauded by the lone partisan. His voice echoed around the ground. 'You'll never get 'em out,' went up the shrill cry.

Les Ames scored 604 runs at an average of 30.20 on the tour. It included a century against Tasmania at Launceston. In five Tests his aggregate was 113 runs, but it did include one substantial and important innings. At Adelaide he scored 69 in a fifth wicket stand of 98 runs with Verity. Their partnership ensured a commanding lead for England after five wickets had fallen for 295 runs. It was preceded by the astonishing dismissal of Wally Hammond. Don Bradman, pressed into the attack in the closing minutes of the previous day, bowled Hammond. It was reported that Hammond, looking first at the bowler and then at the clock, went down the wicket to his partner, Ames, and urged him not to take any chances. Ames recalled:

> Neither Wally nor I had ever seen Bradman bowl before, and as I was to take his first delivery I was determined to watch it with extra caution. Down it came, a rank long hop, which I promptly cracked for four. The next ball was a full toss, but I mishit it and scored only a single, bringing Wally down to face Bradman. Before taking strike, however, he called me down the wicket. 'There are only two more overs to go,' he said, 'so don't try to make a meal of Braddles. We don't want to lose another wicket tonight.'
>
> The Don's first ball to Wally was of a fair length, and he played it comfortably back. The next was a full toss, and Hammond, of all people, threw his head up and tried to knock the cover off the ball. He missed it completely and was bowled. I have never seen Wally so angry.

The careful resolution of Ames and Verity withstood the combined spin thrust of O'Reilly and Ironmonger, who each bowled over 50 overs in the innings. Australia were set an insurmountable target of 532 runs. 'Ames showed a welcome return to batting form,' reported one observer. 'He made some beautiful drives in his 69 which included six boundaries.' The ferocity of two thunderous drives off Bradman was surely not lost on the aggrieved Hammond in the pavilion.

Ames mixed caution and aggression in his innings, which lasted ten minutes short of three hours. Verity, after his 45 in the first innings, contributed another 40, with shots which were considered worthy of the great Sutcliffe. O'Reilly finally achieved the reward for his patient and potent skills by dismissing both the English batsmen. But the 'waiting game' of Ames and Verity, however irksome to the jeering crowds, had consolidated England's advantage. Both players knew that the longer they stayed there the worse the wicket would be for the Australian batsmen. Bradman's joyous and often outrageously adventurous 66 dominated Australia's reply. It was an essay in masterly footwork, a blast of defiance intended to salvage vestiges of respect in a forlorn cause. His captain, Woodfull, not equipped by nature or inclination for such extravagance, was undefeated on 73. He was more grimly resistant as Australia lost by 338 runs.

Les Ames, in the more relaxing environs of New Zealand, paraded his batting pleasures at Christchurch in a carefree finale to the tour. He stretched mightily, like a man released from the stocks, to score a century in a whirlwind partnership with Hammond. The pair gave a foretaste of their future alliances in a record fifth wicket stand of 242 runs against New Zealand. Sutcliffe and Paynter were both dismissed for nought in the first two overs and Hammond survived a chance at slip before the onslaught. Hammond and Jardine added 87 and, reported *Wisden*, 'there followed such fierce hitting that 242 runs came in two hours and 25 minutes. Ames rivalled Hammond in powerful driving; both men pulled hard and cut as discretion prompted.'

Hammond and Ames started by scoring 100 in 65 minutes, another 100 was put on in 45 minutes as 'the bowling was flogged all over the field.' Hammond was to eclipse his 227 at Christchurch with 336, then the highest score in a Test match, in the following match at Auckland. 'It was,' said Ronald Mason of the latter innings, 'a display of such devastating mastery that even he never equalled quantitively, and perhaps only once or twice in the matter of quality.'

Les Ames was the guest of honour at a dinner arranged by the Old Harveians Association at the Queen's Hotel, Folkestone on his return home from Australia. He was presented with a silver cigarette case engraved with his monogram and the coat of arms of his old school. His hosts welcomed a jolly, modest fellow. Les had added lustre to the school in the realm of sport which no other boy had achieved to such a degree. There was, said the Folkestone headmaster, Mr A. B. Downing with a gesture of pride, no danger of Ames requiring a bigger hat after his triumphs. The hero from Australia ducked his head in mock shame and shared the laughter of his friends when the principal said he had been looking at some of Ames's old school reports. 'No thank you,' replied Les when he was invited to read those dreaded messages again. The cricket examinations set by Larwood and Bradman were far less exacting than those of his schooldays.

7
ACCENT ON ADVENTURE

Les was temperamentally in tune with the Kent philosophy. He was always looking for runs.

J. G. W. DAVIES

A spirit of enterprise was the captivating mode of Kent cricket in the 1930s. Les Ames, along with his zestful batting companions, Frank Woolley, Percy Chapman and Bryan Valentine, were exhilarating entertainers. The tactics of the decade nurtured adventure. Ames emphatically championed this approach. 'We were never allowed to play for our averages. All our captains had the right idea. We had to get the runs quickly and attractively. In my time, scores of 400, even 500, in a day were commonplace.'

In 1933, a buoyant, free-scoring year, Ames achieved another milestone when he topped 3,000 runs. He hit nine centuries, including three over 200, and scored separate hundreds in one match against Northamptonshire at Dover. Only Hammond and Hendren scored more runs than Ames, who finished third in the first-class averages. *Wisden* acknowledged the maturity of his cricket. 'Overcoming his natural desire to punish the ball directly on going in, Ames often began with much care, but when set he enjoyed some dazzling hitting without being so prone as formerly to lift his drive.'

Pelham Warner, writing in the *Daily Telegraph*, enthused: 'No wicket-keeper in the history of the game has ever been such a fine batsman. Moreover, he gets his runs in a most attractive style, being a great lover of the half-volley, and ever ready to make a good length ball into one by his quickness of foot.'

In July, on his favourite home ground at Folkestone, Ames scored 295—his highest score in first-class cricket—in five and a half hours against Gloucestershire. Almost half his runs came in boundaries. It overtook the previous Kent record of 270 established by Frank Woolley against Middlesex in 1923. Woolley, the deposed record-breaker, praised his young colleague in the *Kentish Gazette*. 'Ames has a very upsetting influence on opposing bowlers. He makes a tremendous difference to our side when he is in form. His innings at Folkestone was a lovely effort, his perfect timing, driving and placing was an object lesson for any young players present at the game.' Kent totalled 592, out of which 368 runs were scored on the Thursday

*Bryan Valentine, a cavalier stylist and one of
Kent's outstanding amateur batsmen
(Kent CCC)*

before Chapman declared. Woolley and Ashdown were dismissed with only 24 runs on the board. Leslie Todd, with a century, and Ames manned the ramparts with a third wicket stand of 259. Arthur Fagg also aided the recovery in helping to add 91 for the fourth wicket. 'Ames all this time showed a complete mastery of the various bowlers brought against him,' commented the *Kentish Gazette*. 'He drove and pulled hard, getting a large proportion of runs (one six and 34 fours) in front of the wicket.' Bryan Valentine brought his own brand of aggression to the torrent of scoring. He reached his own century (out of 182) in 80 minutes. Two hours' play produced 204 runs. Ames and Valentine hit 113 out of the 218 runs added for the fifth wicket in 100 minutes. Chapman's declaration came after the innings had lasted six hours and 20 minutes. Goddard and Parker, the redoubtable spinning craftsmen, were startled into disarray. They carried the brunt of the attack, each conceding over 100 runs, in contrast to Freeman's subsequent command over the Gloucestershire batsmen. The Kent spinner took 11 wickets for 60 runs as the thoroughly demoralised visitors were trounced by an innings and 294 runs in two days.

Ames's chief memory of his innings against Gloucestershire was that he was told to 'get a move on' as he approached his triple century.

> The skipper intended to declare as soon as I got my 300. I needed five more and tried to get down to the other end with a quick single. I went to turn Charlie Parker to leg, the ball spun a little, and I was caught by Hammond. I had no regrets, though. When you saw the great Woolley still going for his shots in the nineties, you batted in like fashion. He set the standard and you were expected to follow suit.

The manner in which the runs were harvested could be likened to the urgency of hop-pickers in a Kent orchard. A good yield was, of course, important; but the ripeness of the product was diminished if it was not plucked swiftly from the richly laden plants. How could 'Tich' Freeman reap his own fruits if the batsmen lingered at the crease?

Les Ames blossomed in this atmosphere. He was always happiest on the attack. 'I was a quick scorer. Put it down to a lack of patience. I am an impatient man by nature. I got frustrated if I couldn't keep the scoreboard ticking over.' J. G. W. (Jack) Davies considered that Ames was temperamentally in tune with the Kent philosophy. 'Certainly, he was always looking for runs.'

Ames's batting was massive rather than spectacular; yet he matched the speed of the most flamboyant attackers. Twice before the Second World War he won the Lawrence Trophy for the fastest century of the season. His running between the wickets was revelatory; it was, as with all great batsmen, the means of acceleration without strain. It also had the additional merit of putting pressure on the field. 'I wasn't a big hitter in the true sense of the word,' said Les. 'I just scored fairly rapidly', was his laconic verdict on his own batting. Alf Gover has told an amusing story that illustrates his fielding deficiencies and Ames's alacrity between the wickets.

> It was at Blackheath and I turned from mid-on to chase his shot. I thought I would kid him to try for a second run, so I trotted after the ball, ready to turn round, whip the ball in and get him stranded going for the second run. It all worked out according to plan, except that when I turned round with the ball in my hand, Les had run three!'

Godfrey Evans remembered the fleet footwork of his Kent colleague.

> Les used to go yards down the wicket to get to the pitch of the ball. He enjoyed playing a low skimmer over cover point, like a three-iron golf shot. I used to call him 'twinkletoes', and I have never seen a major batsman play so far out of his crease.

Ames agreed that this swift plunder against slow bowlers on good wickets was one of the secrets of his success. 'But I wouldn't have dared to do it on a turning wicket against Hedley Verity. He would have left me high and dry.

On a good wicket, when there was not much chance of the ball beating the bat, I would adopt this offensive approach.'

Jack Davies stressed the emphasis on orthodoxy in Ames's batting. 'He was quick on his feet but he was also a good judge and did not make too many mistakes when he went down the wicket.' There was one particular aspect of Ames's play which Davies noted and admired. 'Once he was set he could hit the ball over the inner ring on the offside and not reach the long field. This requires great precision and Les was one of the best playing that shot I have ever encountered.'

As one of only two batsmen—the other was Australian Victor Richardson at Adelaide—to hit Harold Larwood for six, Ames was equally fearless against pace. The six-hit was made off the last ball before lunch during a match against Nottinghamshire at Trent Bridge. Les was staying, as he usually did, with Larwood at his home in Nottingham. There was a good deal of good-humoured banter and hints of dire assault before the game. Ames was batting, when Larwood was re-introduced into the Notts attack for a final burst before the interval. His expression darkened as he moved back to his bowling mark. 'I quietly patted the first ball back to him,' recalled Les. 'Look out,' said Harold, with a grin, as he prepared to deliver the next ball. 'I'm going to knock your bloody head off.' It was a wicked, vicious bouncer, bowled with all the venom Larwood could muster. 'I hooked it,' said Les. 'There was half-a-gale blowing that morning at Trent Bridge. George Gunn was fielding at deep fine leg.' The ball soared, like a crazy kite, in the wind towards Gunn. 'It was a beast of a catch. George was waving around and trying desperately to judge its direction. He missed it. The ball dropped over his head and beyond the ropes for six.'

Ames won, however fortuitously, that particular duel with Larwood. There was one other bowler, Bill Andrews, who exerted an unexplainable jinx over him as a batsman.

> I bagged a pair twice in successive matches against Somerset, and Bill was the bowler each time. Then came the sequel in a late summer festival match at Folkestone. He was bowling when I went into bat. I thought this will be my fifth duck, and it could well have been. He bowled one which nipped back from outside the off stump. I got a thick inside edge and it went down to fine leg for four.

From such perilous beginnings do great innings bloom and great batsmen often prosper. Les offered up a silent prayer for his good fortune and went on to score a century.

For all his magnificent work as a wicket-keeper, Ames gained more pleasure as a batsman.

> I enjoyed wicket-keeping but there is nothing to surpass batting when you are getting runs. Taking on the bowlers was my idea of cricket, not worrying about dropping a catch. You've no idea what it was like

keeping to Bradman, and thinking: 'I really can't afford to drop this chap.' It was much more fun when I let their 'keeper do the worrying.

Ames did communicate his joy as a batsman to the expectant Kent crowds. He revelled in run-chases against the clock. He was a committed professional but there was a panache in his play. Jim Swanton believed that Ames conveyed something of the spirit of the cavalier amateur in his attitude to the game.

After the 1936-7 series in Australia, C. B. Fry maintained, in his considered and respected view, that the MCC tourists included only three batsmen without obvious technical fault. They were Hammond, Wyatt and Ames. Fry regarded Ames as England's most dangerous batsman. 'Attack, attack, attack is his style and keep the odds always three to one on yourself against the bowler.' Bob Wyatt took pride in Fry's assessment, linking him with two other great players, by an outstanding judge of the game. Equally, by relating the verdict, he drew attention to his own high regard for his former England colleague. 'Les was a superb attacking batsman who always tried to gain the ascendancy over the bowler. He never liked being "bogged down"; on occasions he got out as a result of impatience.' Wyatt remembered Ames as one of the best on-drivers in his experience and placed particular stress on his correct footwork. 'His left foot would be pointing towards mid-on, not straight as is the case with some players. So the bat swung in a line—toe to toe—as he drove the ball wide of mid-on.' Bill Brown, one of Ames's Australian opponents, also recalled the neatness of his old rival's strokes. 'There were no frills to his batting but he was the complete craftsman. We always enjoyed watching Les, even when he was knocking us around.' Brown especially remembered Ames's cover drive 'hit sweetly and without fuss.'

In 1933, Les Ames asserted his authority to score 400 runs more than the next Kent batsman, Leslie Todd. The batting resources of Ames, Todd and Valentine did not entirely conceal the regrettable indisposition of Frank Woolley, whose absence from the team early in the season inevitably proved a severe handicap. Kent were never serious challengers for the championship; but they mined a rich seam of success from July onwards to finish third for the second consecutive season. In a dominant last month they won five county games, defeating both Yorkshire and Sussex, the champions and runners-up, and trounced the West Indians by an innings and 93 runs at Canterbury. Freeman carried the bowling burden yet again, and it hardly needs saying that he was the first bowler in the country to take 100 wickets. With 252 wickets, he beat his previous best return for Kent in the championship, and in all matches his 298 wickets was only six short of his record figures in 1928. Over six seasons he had taken 1,673 wickets. 'If at times he came in for punishment, he was blandly unruffled,' commented *The Cricketer.* 'An average of less than 15 runs does not suggest that too many liberties were taken with him.' C. B. Fry was another of Freeman's admirers.

'He is our nearest equivalent to Grimmett. Had he been an Australian and come over to England, he would undoubtedly have been written up as a terror.' Waiting in the wings in Kent was Doug Wright. At 18, he had demonstrated that he was a bowler of considerable promise. But three more seasons were to elapse before he succeeded Freeman in the county ranks.

Les Ames, now established as a Test player, emerged from his batting travail in Australia in the previous winter. At Lord's, in the first Test against the West Indies, he remained unbeaten on 83. His resistance averted a serious decline. England had lost four wickets, those of Sutcliffe, Hammond, Leyland and Walters, for 106 runs. They went in to lunch to ponder on a meagre total of 157 for 6. 'After lunch,' reported *The Cricketer*, 'it was Ames, a great Ames, with valuable and reliable support from Allen, Verity and Macaulay, who drove the overpitched fast ball hard and surely, gaining his runs with strokes all round the wicket.' England's final total of 296 was still not unduly formidable; but it was enough to ensure an innings victory. Oblivion descended like a merciful curtain on the West Indian batsmen. The resistance of Grant and the poise of George Headley, on a different plane to his compatriots, were the only morsels of consolation. Robins, Verity and Macaulay shared 17 wickets as the West Indies were twice spun out for 269 runs. 'The three short-legs stationed by Macaulay, the googlies of Robins and the flight of Verity, a monument of ease and steadiness, were as bad dreams to the West Indies,' commented *The Cricketer*. Ames conceded only four byes in the two innings.

Pride was restored in the drawn second Test at Manchester. Headley and Barrow gained distinction by becoming the first West Indian batsmen to score centuries in a Test in England. The game was sullied by another outbreak of fast leg-theory bowling employed by Constantine and Martindale for the West Indies, and Clark for England. Sutcliffe ran himself out after sharing a first wicket stand of 63 runs with Walters; Hammond was caught in the leg trap after having his chin cut open by a fast, lifting ball; and England lost four wickets for 134 runs. Douglas Jardine, displaying immense courage, did not waver under the assault. He might have chosen the occasion to score his first Test century. Ames, with 47, also defended doggedly. He assisted Jardine in adding 83 in an hour and 45 minutes. 'It was to the great credit of the England captain that he probably played the bowling better than any other man in the world,' commented *Wisden*. 'Jardine batted for nearly five hours and hit only five fours, but he gave a magnificent display against fast bowling, never flinching in the slightest degree and time after time drawing himself up to his full height and playing the ball down with a dead bat.'

Les Ames confirmed his growing status as a wicket-keeper in the Oval Test, a match in which his Kent amateur colleague, 'Father' Marriott spun his way into the record books. Marriott, then aged 38, claimed 11 wickets for 96 runs in his only Test. He toured India in the following winter; but the successes of Verity and Jim Langridge denied him further opportunities. At

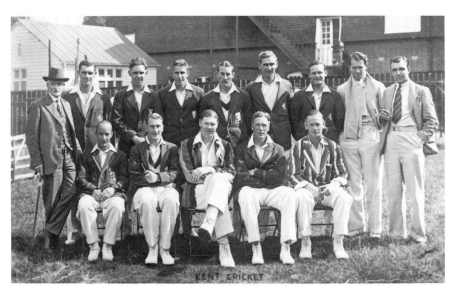

The Kent team, with Percy Chapman as captain, in 1934 (L. Ames)

The Oval the West Indies only just managed to avert defeat in two days; in their first innings they were dismissed for 100 in two hours and, following on, they lost eight wickets for 190 before stumps were drawn.

'The wickets of the West Indians tumbled like ninepins,' reported *The Cricketer.* 'From the start Clark bowled so well and fiercely that the batsmen shuddered, and when Marriott came on they turned to him with relief and were hopelessly deceived.' Ames conceded only one bye in the two innings and assisted in eight dismissals (six catches and two stumpings), a record haul by an England wicket-keeper against the West Indies. There were two stumpings to dismiss Headley and Griffith off Marriott and two catches off Clark and Nichols, with Barrow and Sealey as his victims, in the first innings. Barrow, Headley, Grant and Achong were his scalps in the second innings to provide further testimony of his alert guard against fast and slow bowling.

Freeman joined Marriott in another spinning conquest for Kent against the West Indians at Canterbury in August. They shared, equally and neatly, the 20 wickets, after Ames and C. H. Knott had added 156 for the sixth wicket in a match-winning partnership. Ames ended the season, still bristling with runs. For the Players against the Gentlemen at Folkestone he drove with unerring power to score 201 in four hours. The eager, rampant stylist hoisted his aggregate to over 3,000 runs. He wore the robes of a festive centurion in a crowd-pleasing finale.

This festive rapture was rarely absent from Kent's cricket in the 1930s. It did contribute to their fluctuating fortunes; but the fairground fervour, in victory and defeat, made them always a team worth watching. It would have been counted an act of betrayal by their admirers had they adopted a more cautious approach. Ames's affection for those adventurous years remains undimmed. 'It was a privilege to play alongside such wonderful people and tremendous characters as Bryan Valentine, Percy Chapman, Hopper Levett and Gerry Chalk.'

In his reflections on the professional–amateur relationships in Kent, Ames said: 'No side could have had a better type of amateur. Most of them were worthy of a place in the team. They were friendly men, full of humour and fun.' Monty Garland-Wells, the former Surrey captain, remembered that Jack Hobbs, even in his eminence as a professional, did not cross the line of authority appertaining in those times. Hobbs never addressed the Surrey amateurs by their christian names. The distinction was reinforced by the prefix 'Mr' and initials for the amateur and a perfunctory surname for the professional on scorecards. It persisted until after the Second World War. 'As professionals, we did defer to the amateur, always calling them "Mr" or "Sir",' said Ames. Away from the cricket field the discipline was relaxed and christian names were exchanged on the golf course. The one exception, in Ames's case, was Chapman. 'I always called him "Skipper", or "Mr Chapman". As a much younger player, I did not feel I had the right to refer to him as "Percy".'

The cricketing qualities of Kent's assembly of amateurs were immensely beneficial. Professionals in some other counties might have had cause to feel aggrieved at their exclusion when the amateurs came down to play in the summer holidays. Ames recalled that the Kent professional was paid £3 a week, plus match fees of £8 for home matches and £12 for away games.

Happy, charming and audacious:
Chapman, the enthusiastic leader
of Kent and England (Kent CCC)

Reunited with former colleagues,
Duckworth (right) and Ames
(L. Ames)

Out of these fees they had to meet hotel and travelling expenses. A player, who was out of the team for a month, lost as much as a fifth of his annual salary. 'It was very hard, especially for the professional on the verge of first-class cricket, if a less accomplished amateur came in to take his place.'

Ames rose above any threat to his livelihood. He could match even the most effervescent amateur in his approach to cricket. He delighted in the enchanted days of the 1930s, and the blissful extravaganzas in an unfettered time. He listened with amusement, and perhaps just a ripple of indignation, to those moderns who said: 'Of course, you wouldn't do it today. There must have been some rubbish bowled.' The validity of this criticism is open to question when one remembers the formidable talents of Bill Bowes, Larwood and Voce, Kenneth Farnes and Morris Nichols and the contrasting spins of Hedley Verity, Tommy Mitchell and Tom Goddard. These were not ordinary trundlers. They were also, as Bob Wyatt revealed, generally modest men. 'Their actions on the field demonstrated their quality, not only by what they did but the way they did it,' said Wyatt. Ames's response could not, therefore, be brushed aside as a piece of gloating nostalgia. 'Well, for the sake of argument, let us assume the sceptics are right. At least we got some entertainment. Artistry prevailed and if you went to see Wally Hammond or Don Bradman and they scored 250 you went home thrilled by what you had seen.'

One contemporary observer, watching one of those tall-scoring feats at Canterbury, said:

> I refuse to praise Kent for playing bright festival cricket. Surely, no side could do otherwise on this glorious ground, with its stately trees, its bunting, tents and flags; the dark green hops in the background, and, in the foreground, the colourful array of dresses amid which the scarlet tunics of the Buffs' band were like a giant geranium.
>
> It is here that one grand old lime tree is allowed to hold its unique position 20 yards inside the playing area, and to show how happy and unconcerned is the general atmosphere I watched the play for the greater part of the afternoon sitting under its welcome shade.

The fun was not just confined to Canterbury, Folkestone or Dover. On one extraordinary May day, at rural Brentwood in 1934, Kent actually scored 623 and went on to score 803 for four wickets in just over seven hours. It was the highest score in English first-class cricket since 1899 when Surrey scored 811 against Somerset at The Oval. Kent were lucky to win the toss on a superlatively good wicket with, according to *The Times* correspondent, 'an outfield as fast as glass and, judging by the difficulty the fieldsmen had in turning, just as slippery.' Essex, it must be said, were handicapped by the absence of Farnes and the fact that their other principal strike bowler, Nichols, was unable to bowl at full pace. In addition, they committed the unpardonable sin of dropping Woolley when his score was two. It was a straightforward, waist-high catch to Cutmore at square leg. At lunch the score was 153. Afterwards another 100 runs were put on in 45 minutes. 'There was such a deluge of boundaries,' said *The Times*, 'that it was difficult to tell one from another. The fieldsmen, almost entirely patrolling the deep were rendered as helpless as greyhounds chasing an electric hare on the race track.'

Tom Pearce was one of the hapless Essex fieldsmen at Brentwood. He ruefully recalled the missed catches of Woolley, and later Ames, but said this was not uncommon. 'We once missed 13 catches before lunch in a match against Sussex at Ilford.' The Brentwood venue was the original county ground in the last century; but the Kent match was the first to be staged there in modern times. It was a small field. At one end, said Pearce, you either scored a single or a four.

An extraordinary feat: Kent's record score against Essex at Brentwood (Kent CCC)

The sun beat down from a cloudless sky on the day of the batting massacre. Essex rang the bowling changes—first the two Smiths, Peter and Ray, then Nichols, Ashton, O'Connor and Cutmore—but Woolley and Ashdown swept remorselessly on. Two successive balls from Peter Smith were driven to the boundary, with Woolley doing little more than lean on the ball. In the over in which he reached his century, he cut a ball from Ashton through the slips, a stroke played so late that it deceived the eye. Woolley then lent variety to the plunder by giving chances off towering hits to Nichols at long-off and Pope at long-on in successive overs. Woolley was eventually bowled by Ashton for 172. His partnership with Ashdown had added 352 for the second wicket in just over three hours, and Kent finished the day on 623 for two wickets.

Les Ames, on the eve of his Test triumph against Australia at Lord's, hit a double century in less than three hours against Essex. Ashdown statistically surpassed him with a remarkable innings of 332, the highest ever achieved by a Kent batsman. One hundred and eighty runs were added in 65 minutes before Chapman applied the declaration. The run feast suggested, in one mistaken forecast, that if the match lasted until August the wicket would remain a staunch friend of the batsmen. The subsequent events, as confirmed by Tom Pearce, showed that the Brentwood wicket was a good friend for two days and then it crumbled in a most disloyal fashion.

Essex, in the friendliness still left to them, managed to score 408 in their first innings and then collapsed against Freeman in the follow-on. The contrast in the circumstances was emphasised by the fact that on the first two days 11 wickets fell for 1,169 runs and five batsmen scored centuries, while on the last day 13 wickets went down for only 245 runs. Freeman took 11 wickets in the match, including six wickets for 60 runs in 34 overs in Essex's second innings. Ames, untiring and unsated by his batting accomplishments, claimed seven victims behind the wicket, including four stumpings off Freeman.

Tom Pearce provided an interesting postscript to the staggering onslaught. He recalled that Jack Hobbs, due to play for Surrey in the following match at Brentwood, rang Bill Ashdown, Kent's triple centurion, to inquire as to the state of the wicket. 'Well, I suggest that you look at the scores, Jack,' replied Ashdown. Hobbs was reassured by the run tally, but the sequel was even more fascinating. Essex, as unpredictable as ever, beat Surrey by an innings and 192 runs, which was by exactly the same margin as in their defeat at the hands of Kent. In their first innings Surrey were dismissed for 115 in 90 minutes before lunch on the following day. Hobbs departed in the first over, with some reason to be puzzled that he could not obtain his usual quota amid the surfeit of runs. His conqueror was Douglas Read, a rejected triallist with Surrey in the previous season. Read, so often a wayward bowler, summoned deadly pace and accuracy to take seven wickets in the rout to complete an astonishing week at Brentwood.

The endearing caprice of cricket brings its pleasures and miseries, its balances to check euphoria. Les Ames and his fellow batting dictators had picked the right time to weave their spell of mastery. On another day, without conditions in their favour, they might also have been somersaulted into despair.

8
SETTLING A SCORE
AT LORD'S

It is a genuine pleasure to watch Ames's twinkling feet
and dancer's poise . . . He is a sort of troubadour
of a batsman.

C. B. FRY

T he impoverishment of a great batsman against Australia had to be
corrected sooner or later. Les Ames feasted happily in realising a
cherished objective—his first century against Australia in June 1934.
By a happy chance, it was achieved at Lord's, one of his favourite cricket
venues. It was registered in a crisis and executed in a manner at odds with
his natural attacking inclinations. In his own estimation it was his 'most
pleasurable innings'; and it was doubly welcome after his batting travail in
Australia in 1932–3.

At Lord's Ames found a kindred spirit on the England stage in the great
and genial Yorkshire yeoman, Maurice Leyland. They had been fledgling
tourists in the 1928–9 campaign in Australia. Leyland, capped by Yorkshire in
1922, was, unlike his Kent colleague, a seasoned county practitioner by the
time of the tour. It did not, however, quell a sense of outrage in some
quarters at his selection ahead of another left-hander, the revered veteran,
Frank Woolley. The choice of Yorkshire's 'cross-bat village-greener', in the
lamenting words of a celebrated Kent pundit, was not misplaced.

Ames, a strong contender for a place in the England team in the fifth Test
at Melbourne in March, was denied his chance by a broken finger. Leyland
was called up for his England debut against Australia. He hit a serene
century with unruffled poise, and another half-century in the second
innings. England could not profit from his valiant cricket. They were beaten
by five wickets on the eighth day, after squandering the apparent security of
a first innings total of 519. Leyland conquered at Melbourne, when the Ashes
were assured. Australia, aided by a major epidemic of fielding blunders,
gratefully and gallantly salvaged their pride.

Maurice Leyland was to demonstrate his dauntless qualities in less pre-
possessing times for England. 'Just to see him walk on to the field gave us
faith that all would come right,' wrote one of his admirers. R. C. Robertson-
Glasgow said of Leyland: 'He would have been a fit companion for Horatius

*Maurice Leyland, the genial Yorkshire yeoman, with
whom Ames shared many fine partnerships for
England (Nottinghamshire CCC)*

on the bridge. He has taken the view that to every bowler, every pitch and
every occasion, there is a more than equal answer.' Broad in physique and
rustic in appearance, Leyland was the exemplar of dogged North-country
resistance. He was feared as much, if not more than, Wally Hammond; and
he especially relished his duels with the Australians. His overall average in 41
Tests was 46, but against Australia it was 56.83. He scored 1,705 runs in 20
innings against Australia. In his last 11 innings against these opponents he
hit six centuries and averaged almost 70 an innings.

Bill O'Reilly, the fiery Australian spinner, with whom the Yorkshireman
shared many prolonged battles, said Leyland could have passed in the street
as a hard-working farmhand on his way to the market-place. 'He was ruddy-
faced, distinctly Yorkshire accented and splendid company. Maurice was
slow to talk but when he did he invariably improved upon silence. He was
often referred to as the canteen comic.' Leyland played all his cricket, even
in adversity, with a twinkle in his eyes. The humour was always bubbling just
beneath the surface. After the 'bodyline' series in Australia he said in
response to one questioner: 'I was bloody glad I was on our side.'

Leyland was loved and respected by all who knew him—from Gubby

Allen, his England captain in Australia, who prized his constant good sense and penetrating counsel, down to the raw, apprehensive Yorkshire recruits, who discovered the happiness and fun of cricket when they came under his charge in the Headingley nets. Leyland died, the sad victim of Parkinson's disease, at the age of 67 in 1967. At the funeral service in his home town of Harrogate, the Rev. W. Selby said: 'We shall remember Maurice not only for his achievements as a cricketer but for what he made of his life. He was a modest and kindly man, more prone to laugh at himself than others.'

Les Ames treasured his remembrances of a grand sportsman and a magnificent crisis player. 'Maurice and I were very fortunate. We had some good partnerships together.' At Lord's in 1934 their association was crucial to England's fortunes. The name on everyone's lips on this momentous occasion was Hedley Verity, the bowling architect of England's first victory over Australia at the headquarters since 1896. 'Without our runs Hedley could not have achieved his triumph,' said Les.

Ames and Leyland had sketched an outline of their Lord's alliance in the first Test at Nottingham, when they failed by only 10 minutes to save the match. Australia won by 238 runs and the spinning tormentors, O'Reilly and Grimmett shared 19 wickets. Percy Fender wrote:

> No praise can be too high for the great effort made by Leyland and Ames, for one has to remember that not only was the bowling of superlative quality, length, flight and spin, but the wicket was one upon which the spin took effect, and the ball turned and turned quickly. The bowling feats of O'Reilly and Grimmett overshadowed all else. I do not think I have seen finer bowling, especially when it is remembered that they were slow spinners and not on a wet wicket.

At Lord's Ames and Leyland halted the England decline in adding 129 runs in a stand of growing resolution. They came together after the loss of five wickets for 182 runs. Leyland scored his second Test century against Australia. Ames struck his first 100 against the old enemy to dispel the dispiriting bogy which had cast a shadow on his cricket in Australia.

The sporting placards of one London newspaper in the 1930s carried the compelling directive: 'C. B. Fry Says'. Fry's observations on cricket were delivered in the breathless, staccato style of Dickens's Mr Jingle. The old Olympian and autocratic commander was something of an oracle. His strings of firecracker words were both entertaining and wise. In his inimitable conversational manner he rejoiced in England's rally and Ames's timely batting renaissance at Test level. 'Leyland and Ames are at it,' he reported as the recovery gained momentum. 'You can hear a different sound as the bat meets ball. A quick musical crack quite unlike the sound of careful cricket.'

Fry enthused:

> A thoroughly interesting player is Ames. He has a silky, semi-Oriental ease and a delicate touch. He is quite an artist and one who likes

making nice strokes. Short beginning, late delivery, just in time, no body pull, long facile finish. A pleasant style to watch and not easily acquired. Ames has delivered at call one of the best innings I have ever enjoyed in a Test match.

Ames, in fact, was for a long time sorely restrained. The sense of adventure was kept in check to bolster England's cause. His century included 14 boundaries but it occupied four hours and 20 minutes, a span of time which allowed the weather to uncork its gremlins for Australia's discomfort. He did for the most part play a supporting role to Leyland. The Yorkshireman radiated composure and efficiency and produced the cutting edge to blunt the Australian attack. With Leyland's departure, yorked by Wall with the score at 311, Ames asserted his own command. The tail wagged in sympathy with him. Geary and Verity were intelligent and praiseworthy partners. England reached and passed what had earlier seemed an unlikely goal of 400 runs. 'Ames gradually began to show that quick footwork of his and from 50 to the end of his innings he was a joy to watch,' commented *The Times* correspondent. 'Without the fashionable shuffle across the stumps he was invariably in the correct position to make his stroke, driving the ball firmly past mid-off, cutting it, or hitting it hard and surely to leg.'

Ames, urgent and as decisive as ever between the wickets, moved to 96. He was then, incredibly, given a reprieve by the normally impeccable Oldfield off the bowling of Wall. From his sparring, anxious bat the ball darted high and wide but within reach of the Australian wicket-keeper. Oldfield, as eager to take the catch as Ames was to reach a coveted century, dropped it. As one observer put it, any batsman who was missed by Oldfield, the world's finest 'keeper, deserved his luck. The Australian made amends by catching Ames off McCabe on the brink of lunch. Before that happened the Kent man had gloriously square-cut Wall to the boundary in his best Canterbury style to reach his three figures. The defiance of Ames and Leyland had transformed the game. Their last-ditch counter-attack was applauded by Neville Cardus who, like others, criticised the temerity of England's front rank batsmen against Grimmett and O'Reilly on a perfect wicket. As the Kent and Yorkshire pair repaired the innings, Cardus wrote: 'Leyland's strokes cracked all over the field with his own jolly broad accent. "Ah've found thi out," he seemed to be saying to the weary Australian bowlers. "Ah've found thi out and ah can't think what our Herbert was thinking about."'

The acclaim for Ames and Leyland was inevitably dwarfed by Hedley Verity's subsequent triumph. The great Yorkshire bowler was irresistible after rain on the Monday when he took 14 wickets for 80 runs, six of them in the last hour of a memorable day. Verity's match tally of 15 wickets for 104 runs equalled the record of his mentor, Wilfred Rhodes, at Melbourne 30 years earlier. Don Bradman was twice the beleaguered victim of Verity's cunning at Lord's. His dismissal in Australia's second innings effectively settled the match in England's favour. The grotesquely miscued drive which lifted the ball high and straight above the wicket was the stroke of a batsman stricken by torment. For Les Ames, the downfall of Bradman fixed the match indelibly among his finest cricket memories. He remembered his palpitations as the ball flew from the top edge of Bradman's bat.

> Everyone was petrified to go for it. Hammond could have caught it easily as could Sutcliffe or Verity, moving into position from the bowler's end. The shout went up: 'Yours, Les.' I would have been quite happy if someone else had taken it. It was up there so long that there was time to think about it. If we hadn't taken the catch there could have been trouble. But I did take it at silly point, very silly point.

Cardus recalled that as Ames came forward to take the catch 'Bradman stood aside, exposed in momentary embarrassment, like a dejected schoolboy.'

Bill O'Reilly took three wickets with a replacement ball—those of Walters, Wyatt and Hammond—in one remarkable over in the drawn and ultimately high-scoring third Test at Old Trafford. England slumped from 68 for 0 to 72 for 3, but first Sutcliffe and Hendren restored the situation and then Leyland (153) and Ames (72) put on 142 for the sixth wicket in two hours and 10 minutes. Their partnership, admittedly in more propitious circumstances, was that of two batsmen blissfully in tune with each other. They had withstood the wiles of O'Reilly and Grimmett at Lord's and now, with heightened confidence, they played the same bowlers with the utmost certainty.

A moment of apprehension for Ames before he takes the crucial catch to dismiss Bradman off Verity in the second Test against Australia at Lord's in 1934 (The British Library)

'It looked for all the world as if the Lord's effort was to be repeated and Ames, having done the big thing in a partnership with Leyland, was to have to scramble for his own century after the Yorkshireman had left,' wrote Percy Fender. Ames, despite the reassuring presence of Gubby Allen, his record-breaking ally against New Zealand three years earlier, faltered as the century beckoned. He was dismissed by Grimmett to provide the Australian bowler with his only wicket in the match.

Bradman and Ponsford, both with double hundreds, imperiously and massively by turn, clinched the series for Australia at The Oval. Australia totalled 701 and it was said conservatively that eight catches were missed during the innings. The honourable exception was Ames who took two catches to dismiss Bradman and Grimmett and also conceded only four byes. Australia, after batting a second time, finally set England the mountain-ous target of 708 runs. Ames and Leyland, the England lionhearts, once again staged a rearguard action in the first innings. Leyland hit his third hundred of the series. Ames, with a freedom which belied the situation, more than once brought welcome cheer by darting down the wicket to drive Grimmett through the covers. 'We all felt that they might go on for a long time,' declared Fender. Jack Hobbs, in his watching brief, thought the tide was turning as the pair advanced the score by 85 runs. Then, without warning, the prospering stand, was suddenly shattered. The batsmen had run a single to deep third man. Ames turned sharply after running, staggered and held his back before being assisted off the field. The trouble was later diagnosed as an acute attack of lumbago. Hobbs reflected: 'It was a sad blow, for there are few better batsmen in the country, and while Ames remained with Leyland, we had a slight chance of saving the game.'

Les recalled the agony of a cruel setback. 'Maurice and I had just got going. I had reached 33 and was well set. I was never free of back trouble from that time.' The Oval Test had one dismaying, perhaps unnecessary, little footnote. Frank Woolley, at 47, was recalled by England and made an undignified exit from the international arena. He was, it is true, still captivat-ing Kent crowds with his artistry, his run-scoring powers not unquenched; but on this bigger stage he could no longer meet the challenge. He was dismissed for four and nought and was then called upon to deputise for the unfit Ames behind the wicket in Australia's second innings. He did his best for a player unaccustomed to the position, took one catch and did not miss another. The bye count was irrelevant in the context of the game and it could not be judged unseemly for a non-wicket-keeper and a veteran in the evening of his career. Woolley did not forget his failures at The Oval. Four years later, in his farewell season, he put the Australians to rout at Canter-bury.

Les Ames made his second visit to the West Indies in the winter of 1934-5. The MCC team, handicapped by an injury to their key fast bowler, Ken Farnes, and a loss of form by Jim Smith, suffered their first defeat at the hands of their resurgent Caribbean hosts. A major factor in the success of the West Indies was the towering ascendancy of their pace attack. Bob Wyatt, the England captain, described the bowling of Martindale, Constantine and Hylton as the best of its kind in the world. The trio claimed 47 wickets at a combined average of 15 runs in the series. Martindale's 19 wickets cost him less than 13 runs apiece. He earned the commendation of Jeffrey Stollmeyer, a fellow tourist in the 1939 series in England. Stollmeyer believed that Martindale, at his peak, was even more devastating than his successors in the West Indian attack.

In the 1934–5 series George Headley, the pathfinder in an illustrious tradition of West Indian batting stylists, invited comparison with Don Bradman. His dominance yielded 485 runs at an average of 97, and his 270 not out in the final decisive Test at Kingston, Jamaica, created a new record for his country in matches against England. At Kingston, as Les Ames recalled, England were overwhelmed by the ferocity of the West Indian bowlers, and lost by an innings. Martindale and Constantine took 13 wickets in the match. The decline was hastened by an injury of terrifying proportions sustained by Wyatt at the outset of the England innings.

Wyatt recalled:

> I had scored only a single when a ball just short of a length bowled by Martindale got up sharply and hit me full on the jaw. He was bowling at a terrific pace, in fact faster than I had ever seen him bowl. The ball just missed my wrist as I played a normal defensive stroke. It was like being hit by a sledgehammer and down I went like a felled bullock.

One England player, sitting in the dressing-room with the window closed, said it sounded like a revolver shot. Wyatt was carried off unconscious, with blood pouring from his mouth. Wyatt, with characteristic courage, revived as he lay on a stretcher in the pavilion and asked for a notepad. He then rearranged the batting order. At the hospital it was discovered that his jaw had been broken in four places. Errol Holmes, who had taken over the captaincy, went to see him in hospital. Wyatt was cocooned in bandages and unable to speak but he gestured to establish the score. He was told: '26 for 4' whereupon he grabbed the pad again and wrote: 'We must not lose.' To his anxious and unwitting assailant, Martindale, he sent a message telling him not to worry; it was, said Wyatt, a perfectly fair ball.

Wyatt's injury clearly had an unnerving effect on the rest of the team. Ames, Hendren and Iddon belied their plummeting hearts with resolute cricket. Even though he was in no position to judge at the time, Wyatt believed that Ames's first innings century revealed his true stature as a Test batsman. Les himself considered that it was his finest innings for England. Iddon helped him to add 158 for the sixth wicket and England totalled 271. Ames batted heroically for three and a half hours, did not give a vestige of a chance, and struck 16 boundaries in his 126. It took a brilliant catch by Constantine at silly mid-off from the bowling of the leg-spinner, Moodie, to dismiss him. Ames, it could be said with ample justification, had delivered his own credentials of courage, and brought some comfort to his stricken captain.

South Africa were the visitors to England in 1935. Ames played in four Tests, once as a batsman when Farrimond replaced him as wicket-keeper at Lord's, and he had to give way to his old rival, Duckworth, at Manchester. Ames was beset by criticism of his wicket-keeping in the rain-affected first Test at Nottingham. The 'White Horse' columnist in the *Kentish Gazette* wrote:

> A little junta of critics have found fault with Ames. The Kent player was supposed to have missed one or two chances and it was conveniently forgotten that he conceded only four byes. In view of his consistently fine form for England and Kent—work which is all the better for its lack of ostentation—I prefer to believe that Ames's displacement from the wicket-keeping position is due, not to any reflection on his ability behind the stumps, but to a desire to give him further opportunities to do justice to his great powers as a batsman.

After Ames had been dropped from the Manchester Test, the same paper again rose to his defence.

> In a recent match at Maidstone against Middlesex Ames kept magnificently and dismissed seven batsmen. He is in the prime of his cricket life. It would, indeed, be a lamentable thing for England if a few captious critics should succeed by their irresponsible clamour in ending his Test career.

The fears were exaggerated but they arose from inconsistent selections, a not uncommon state of affairs in England. Ames was, of course, sorely needed for his batting strengths as England vainly sought a winning combination to beat South Africa. The selectors, with the Lancastrians Duckworth and Farrimond, both fine deputies behind the stumps, at their disposal were juggling their options. There was also a bewildering sequence of injuries contributing to the confusion. England fielded four different opening pairs of batsmen; 10 players were selected for a single Test each; and altogether 25 players were called up during the series. Only Wyatt, the captain, and Hammond played in all five Tests.

England were baffled by the leg-spin of Balaskas at Lord's. The swarthy South African, on his debut, enjoyed his finest hour in Test cricket. He took nine wickets in the match as South Africa triumphed by 157 runs. It was to prove a conclusive victory despite feverish attempts by England to cancel out the reverse in the remaining Tests. The post-mortem following the Lord's defeat belaboured the selectors for choosing Farrimond ahead of Ames as wicket-keeper. It was not thought an improvement and Lionel Tennyson, the former Hampshire captain, Percy Chapman and Douglas Jardine were adamant that Ames's efficiency was unimpaired. Their verdict was that the selection of any other player would unnecessarily weaken England's batting.

In retrospect it can be seen that the attempts to separate Ames's two cricket identities were misguided. They were, in fact, complementary and indivisible.

Ames was reinstated as England's wicket-keeper for the fifth Test at The Oval. The drawn match meant that South Africa were the victors for the first time in a series in England. The decision by Bob Wyatt to put his opponents into bat has gone down in cricket annals as one of the most daring actions ever adopted in a Test match. The gamble did not succeed but it was considered by Wyatt and his fellow selectors to be the only means of achieving an outright victory necessary to level the series. In the event, South Africa batted until lunch on the second day, totalled 476, and, adding salt to England's wounds, the ninth wicket pair of Dalton and Langton put on 137 runs. Robins, with three wickets, was England's most dangerous bowler. The Middlesex leg-spinner was unlucky not to bowl Dalton on three occasions with his googlies, one of which beat Ames as well as the batsman and went for four byes. The England bowling, lacking the resource of the excluded Verity, disintegrated against the onslaught. In a late flurry of hitting South Africa scored 179 in two hours.

Les Ames, amid the distress, brought reassurance as batsman and wicket-keeper. 'Seldom, if ever, has Ames kept better and he has justified his inclusion to the hilt,' commented *The Cricketer.* 'He took the ball cleanly and splendidly on the legside to the occasionally erratic deliveries of Read, and accepted the only chances offered to him.' Ames claimed four victims in the match, two catches off Robins and Read accounting for Siedle and Mitchell in the first innings; and two stumpings off Robins to dismiss Viljoen and Cameron in the second innings. Out of 763 runs scored by South Africa he conceded only 12 byes.

The fluency of his wicket-keeping was matched by a memorable batting display. He renewed his liaison with Maurice Leyland in an aggressive fight-back by England. Both players hit centuries to build upon the foundations laid by the equally adventurous Hammond. C. B. Fry's voice again topped the chorus of praise.

> Ames and Leyland have pushed along with amiable freedom, making fair weather of some energetic and accurate bowling by Crisp and Langton. Ames is playing with distinctive charm, quick-footed and timing his drives and cuts to a nicety. A delightfully effortless player; a sort of troubadour of a batsman.

Fry thought Ames was the nearest rival to Hammond in style and technique, especially in his forcing strokes. 'It is a genuine pleasure to watch his twinkling feet and dancer's poise. His weight is always forward over the front foot, and he manages his shoulders with an easy aptitude.' Fry's invigorating reportage briskly communicated the excitement of Ames's century at The Oval. As the Kent man hove within sight of the milestone, he wrote:

97 at 12.30 precisely. He takes a single off Mitchell. He faces Crisp, just on again for Dalton. He lets a fast off ball go unplayed. Now he plays a semi-square cut to backward point and does not run. He places the identical ball next time a couple of yards wider; he takes one and then, with the fielder slipping and over-running, he hurries to another and his century.

Ames and Leyland, taking and giving attacking cues, established a fifth wicket record partnership of 155 runs in 11 minutes over two hours against South Africa. It beat the target set by Phil Mead and Percy Fender at Durban in 1922-3. Leyland's 161 was then his highest in Test cricket. Ames's 148 was one short of his best score for England. He batted for three and a half hours and hit one six and 14 fours. The six off Vincent hurtled into the pavilion and scattered the spectators. 'It was a superb innings, played at something of a crisis, after keeping us all waiting for a big score in representative cricket,' commented one writer. *Wisden* reported: 'It was a fine point as to whether his innings or that of Leyland was the better.'

The achievements of Ames and Leyland deserved a more fitting result. Wyatt declared with a lead of 58 runs. England fleetingly glimpsed a chance when South Africa lost three wickets for 67, and the absent Verity might have caused other flutters on a wearing pitch. Viljoen offered an unaccepted chance before the game was drawn and the South Africans departed for their celebrations. Bob Wyatt was criticised for his tactics in an ill-fated series for England. His pensive postscript dwelt upon the reasons for England's eclipse.

> If only we had been allotted four days for this series as in the Tests against Australia the year before there is little doubt that we would have beaten South Africa with something to spare. We had the better of all four drawn games, scoring more runs per wicket and taking more wickets per runs than they did. But lack of time defeated us—that, and the appallingly lifeless pitches on which our fast bowlers had to operate.

Ames's eminence as an all-rounder was confirmed against South Africa. His contentment was, however, abruptly dissipated by a reoccurrence of his back complaint in 1936. He had to retire from an early season match against Glamorgan at Cardiff. At first it was thought that he was suffering from another attack of lumbago. An examination revealed that the trouble was a displaced vertebra and he underwent a manipulative operation at the Middlesex Hospital. He made good progress throughout the summer, but was absent from the Kent team until August. After a recuperative holiday at Buxton, he tested his fitness with the Kent Second XI against Wiltshire and emerged from the match with no ill-effects. He returned to the First XI against Essex at Southend and conceded only four byes in a long spell behind the stumps.

At the end of August Ames celebrated his selection for the forthcoming Australian tour with tremendous hitting for an England XI against India at Folkestone. He had already established his recovery with a three-hour hundred against Yorkshire at Dover. Kent welcomed back the summer invalid. They totalled 406—the highest against a formidable attack since 1934—and won by nine wickets. Ames took three catches behind the stumps and looked as 'fresh as a daisy' at the end of his admirable innings. Sir Home Gordon, in *The Cricketer*, wrote: 'Ames will sail for Australia, having won the Lawrence Trophy and shown in the past month that he is a greater player than ever. There can be no doubt that his presence in the England side will have the effect of relieving Hammond of any undue sense of batting responsibility.'

In 1936, amid the joy at Ames's recovery, there was also sadness at the end of a distinguished career. Kent bade farewell to one of their greatest servants, 'Tich' Freeman. He was 47 and his powers were flagging if not entirely diminished. He was once again the country's leading bowler, with 103 wickets. He was presented with a cheque for £250 and, said a club spokesman, 'this action [to dispense with Freeman's services] is in the best interests of Kent cricket. Freeman's bowling has lost its accuracy and sting, and is at times expensive.' Freeman had missed several games at the beginning of the season as a result of a strain, and afterwards it was evident that the injury was troubling him. However, in the opinion of many people, it was considered that he should have been given another season to see whether the loss of form was permanent. The indignation of his admirers was an expression of regret and disbelief that the little wizard had run his course.

Meanwhile, the fortunes of Les Ames were given a severe jolt on his arrival in Australia. An unprecedented crop of injuries furrowed the brow of the England captain, Gubby Allen, on this 'goodwill' tour. Duckworth dislocated a finger in attempting to stop an erratic legside delivery from Farnes in the match against Western Australia at Perth in October. After the game Allen took his team out for practice and Robins split a finger on his bowling hand. The casualty list lengthened when Wyatt fractured a bone in his left arm in the third match of the tour and was unable to play in the first three Tests. Arthur Fagg, of whom much had been expected after an opening stand of 295 with Charles Barnett against Queensland, later contracted rheumatic fever and had to return home.

Les Ames would have been another absentee but for the resistance of Gubby Allen. Just when all seemed well Ames was plunged into deep gloom by excruciating back pains at Perth. The trouble flared again after a round of golf on a Sunday rest day. 'I couldn't move,' said Les. 'After being out of the game for over three months in England the previous summer, I was very depressed. I was certain that I would not be able to play on the tour.'

Gubby Allen remembered that he heard the news of Ames's relapse while he was visiting a mine at Kalgoorlie. A telephone call from Rupert Howard, the MCC manager, was the signal for urgent action. The call was relayed to Allen on his tour of inspection of the mine 6,000 feet underground. 'Les's back has gone and he is determined to go home,' said Howard. Gubby replied: 'Strap him to his bed. I'll be back as soon as possible.'

He rushed to the elevator to take him to the surface. His host, the manager at the Kalgoorlie mine, just as promptly drove him to the local airport. The manager's private single engine aeroplane, carrying the England captain, was speedily aloft and *en route* for Perth. Allen's journey was halted by a head-on gale. In the buffeting winds he was violently sick and told the pilot to land by the roadside. Down on the road he was recognised by a passing motorist, travelling to Perth as luck would have it, and given a lift. 'I went to see poor old Les who was lying flat on his back in his bedroom,' recalled Gubby. Les said: 'It's no good, Gubby; I must go home.' Gubby vigorously insisted upon Ames receiving orthopaedic treatment in Melbourne before making a decision. Arrangements were made for Les and Robins to travel by sea, independently of the rest of the team, from Perth to Melbourne. 'When we got to Melbourne Les was miles better. What is more, he played in all five Test matches and did exceptionally well.'

The success in restoring Ames's health and morale had another benefit for the two cricketers. 'I think it brought us closer together,' said Gubby. Les endorsed the efficiency of Allen's care in a trying situation. 'But for Gubby I would certainly have gone home. What was so comforting in the end was that I went through the rest of the tour without a twinge.'

Ames returned to his cricket duties against an Australian XI at Sydney in November. He batted for nearly two hours and hit 10 boundaries in scoring 76 to demonstrate that he had emerged from his crisis. 'Ames showed no signs of his recent indisposition,' wrote one observer. 'He drove hard once he got going and showed that the bowling had no terrors if tackled determinedly.' Ames's recovery was doubly fortunate in that it coincided with yet another injury. Duckworth broke another finger to return to the casualty ward. Ames was still unable to entirely break free of his batting chains in Australia; but his wicket-keeping earned the highest commendation. It was of such a standard that even the Australians admitted that Oldfield could not have surpassed him. Bruce Harris, a member of the English press corps on the tour, wrote: 'Once there were doubts about Ames's wicket-keeping in the sense that he would probably not have been chosen apart from his batting; now he is second to none as a 'keeper.' As an example of his alertness and concentration, Ames conceded only one bye in Australia's total of 604 in the final Test at Melbourne. Ames took a break from wicket-keeping to enjoy himself immensely as a bowler at Canberra. After battering the VIP tents with his six-hits, he took three wickets for nine runs with his leg-breaks. Not even the comment of one team-mate that 'you'll get some stick some day, Les' could temper his glee at the conquest.

England, depressed by injuries and unforeseen lapses in form by their young untried tourists, confounded expectations in winning the first two

Tests at Brisbane and Sydney. In the triumphant parade before Christmas Wally Hammond was at his immaculate best. He was, as events would prove, masking inadequacies in the batting. The majesty of Hammond's own batting did, however, provide a thrilling overture to the tour. For a while, before the weather intervened to England's disadvantage, he held imperious rule.

Hammond hit three consecutive centuries, two in one match against South Australia at Adelaide, followed by an unbeaten 231 to lead England to victory by an innings in the second Test at Sydney. Ames partnered Hammond in a stand of 104 runs for the fourth wicket in the Sydney Test. C. B. Fry described Ames's dismissal, caught off a long hop at cover with his score on 29, as a 'momentary inattention to time, place and propriety'. It was a vexing lapse. Fry added, with a hint of a rebuke: 'He might have scored a hundred had he received this Australian bowling, with the band playing the "Poet and Peasant" overture, on a lovely August day at Canterbury.' Of Ames's wicket-keeping in the match, Fry offered a more praiseworthy verdict: 'Please remember Ames when you talk of England's victory. He is a keeper of the highest class and as quiet as a nesting thrush.'

Gubby Allen, an ebullient and not an easily deflated man, was saddened by the subsequent events. His captaincy had carried England to the threshold of victory only for the door to be violently slammed in his face in the third Test at Melbourne. Australia were all but out for the count when torrential rain came to their aid to produce a wicket of demoralising savagery. Bradman, hitherto a forlorn and anonymous figure, rammed home the advantage with relentless batsmanship. He had scored only 133 runs in five innings before the Melbourne debacle: afterwards he made swift amends with 677 runs, including two double centuries, in four innings. At Melbourne, as the wicket eased, he scored 270 out of 564; and in the fourth Test at Adelaide (a match in which England briefly held the ascendancy) his contribution was 212 out of the Australian second innings total of 433. 'Sardonic imps fooled us prettily,' wrote Neville Cardus. 'Hammond began well and petered away; Bradman began as though riddled with infallibility, then at the right moment he displayed a precision even more inhuman than that which we saw in England in 1930.'

Hammond, in fact, played one of his finest innings at Melbourne. His 32 (out of England's 76 for 9 declared) was a miraculous miniature. 'The behaviour of the ball on this terrible Saturday went beyond all I had expected,' wrote Cardus. 'I could scarcely believe my eyesight. The pitch grew fiercer over by over.' Les Ames remembered the mastery of Hammond on this and other less hazardous wickets.

> Wally was the greatest offside player—he was so powerful off the back foot—in my experience. He was without doubt the most outstanding English batsman between the wars. I was an also-ran when Wally was batting. Everything he did bore the highest class whether batting,

The young Wally Hammond, another England batting associate, who was majestic and dominant between the wars (C. J. Barnett)

bowling or fielding. He was a more majestic player than Bradman and out on his own in English cricket.

Charles Barnett, as his Gloucestershire colleague, remembered the demoralising effect Hammond had on bowlers.

> Tommy Mitchell (the Derbyshire and England leg-spinner) couldn't bowl to him. He would retire to the pavilion with a real or feigned injury until Wally was out. Hammond was a great athlete. His strength lay in his eyesight. As a first slip fieldsman, he would observe bowlers. Wally had the great talent to use his assessments of them to advantage as a batsman.

Hammond was not quite so commanding on the onside and, in later years, his powers waned against fast bowling. O'Reilly and Grimmett, in an era in which spin held sway in Australia, did restrict him by directing their attack at his leg stump. 'They did pin him down, keep him quiet although they did not necessarily look like getting him out,' said Ames. At the pinch Hammond was becalmed and Bradman rampant when it mattered in the 1936-7 series. Ames remembered his own experience on the nightmare wicket at Melbourne. O'Reilly was bowling when he came in to bat. 'I received 23 balls from Bill and did not touch one of them.' He stressed that it was not a question of being perplexed by O'Reilly's spin. 'I was not likely to get out on that wicket against O'Reilly because the ball was doing too much.' Morris Sievers, at medium pace and observing a proper regard for line and length on a wicket on which the ball rose almost vertically, was the unplayable bowler. Sievers took five wickets for 21 runs to rout England in his third and last Test.

Even at the last the fates conspired against Gubby Allen after his much criticised decision to delay his declaration. His bowlers had to contend with a wet ball after they had taken five Australian second innings wickets for 97 runs. Bradman and Fingleton seized their chance to drive home their advantage. They scored 346 runs together and effectively won the match. At Adelaide, in the fourth Test, England tossed away their last opportunity to regain the Ashes with a batting decline after bowling out Australia for 288 on a perfect wicket. 'That's where we lost—at Adelaide,' said Allen after the tour. 'It has been our batting more than our bowling that has let us down in the Tests.'

Barnett scored a brave and disciplined century at Adelaide. Ames hit an equally defiant 52. The two natural attacking batsmen, conscious of a frail tail succeeding them, doggedly took root in a perilous situation. They added 64 runs for the fifth wicket. 'Ames played well, and when Fleetwood-Smith came back before lunch he pulled and drove him savagely for fours,' related Cardus. 'Ames throughout the season showed skill against spin and promised a long innings—a wicket-keeper who for years has had the opportunity to study Freeman on English wickets should have acquired a sense of the googly.' Ames, in the words of another observer, 'played O'Reilly with a fine confidence. A century had looked well within his compass. He had once again shown his partiality for the Adelaide Oval, with his side in a tight corner.' England collapsed with disillusioning speed as soon as Ames was bowled by McCormick, swinging stylishly but fatally at a ball on his leg stump. O'Reilly and Fleetwood-Smith took 15 wickets in the match and Australia won by 148 runs.

England were once again confounded by spin in losing by an innings in the fifth and conclusive Test at Melbourne. Australia, the beneficiaries of a winning toss and a spate of missed catches, made merry in the searing heat on the first two days. They topped 600 and Bradman hit yet another century to equal Jack Hobbs's record of 12 centuries in matches between England and Australia. Then a thunderstorm shook the heavens to deepen England's gloom. O'Reilly and Fleetwood-Smith blessed the elements in taking another 12 wickets in the match.

Among the more pleasing verdicts on an ill-starred series was the unanimous acclaim for Ames's wicket-keeping. For too long it had been regarded as simply an adjunct to his batting. 'His ease of style has deluded many into thinking him nonchalant and even careless,' commented one writer. 'That has always been the accusation against great artists who achieve the maximum of effect with the minimum of effort.' Les Ames was able to rest his case as he returned home to put bowlers to the sword and batsmen in a quandary on the cricket fields of Kent.

9
AMES AND WOOLLEY

It was a joy to be associated with such a great player.
I used to love batting with Frank.

LES AMES

———

The astonishing victory quest at Dover in 1937 began with a question put to Les Ames by Bryan Valentine. 'Can we win?' asked the Kent captain. 'I doubt it,' said Les. 'But it all depends upon whether Frank can give us a start.'

Woolley, then aged 50, still obeyed one of the cardinal principles of batting. 'If you go for them, they don't bowl so well.' He often created doubt where none should have existed. In the end, bowlers did not know where to bowl to him. A psychologist once ventured the theory that a similar domination could be obtained from the other end of the wicket. Was it not possible, he suggested, that given sufficient will power and determination even the greatest batsman could be overthrown. Arthur Mailey, the famed Australian leg-spinner and one of cricket's ace humorists, replied: 'Yes, I tried it once on Frank Woolley, and between us we lost the ball.'

At Dover, on a famous August day, Woolley won another battle of wits against another leading spinner, England's Tom Goddard. Gloucestershire had set Kent a target of 218 runs in less than two hours. It would have been impossible without the devouring flames of Woolley's stroke-play. The Gloucestershire second innings lasted until half an hour after lunch. A sedate finish to the match appeared the likeliest prospect. Woolley, first in as an unquestioned right in such a situation, hit nine off the first over. In 18 minutes he and Ashdown put on 51. Woolley was dismissed by a brilliant catch by Barnett in front of the sightscreen, but not before he had struck 44, with eight fours, out of 68 in 25 minutes. Ames eagerly followed the lead given by the Kent veteran. Driving and cutting with power and delicacy, he hoisted the 100 in 36 minutes. He hit Goddard for 17 in one over and scored 70, with three sixes and seven fours.

Kent, in an atmosphere of mounting excitement, rushed to 150 in 53 minutes. The scorers struggled to keep pace with the frenzy of hitting. It quickly became apparent that victory could only be threatened by delays caused by balls being buried in the pine trees at the bottom of the Crabble Ground. A sizeable band of club members was mustered to patrol the 150 ft stretch of trees. Even so, they had to mount a sprightly guard to keep the ball in play. An amazing triumph grew closer minute by minute. It was made certain by Valentine's decision to send in a fast bowler, Alan Watt. Watt rent the skies with a succession of hammer blows of awesome velocity. The pursuit of runs resembled a bacchanalia, hysterical and deafening in its tumult. In 10 minutes Watt scored 39 out of 51, hitting three sixes and three fours. Goddard was the hapless victim of the onslaught. The Gloucestershire off-spinner conceded 98 runs in 8.2 overs. Ashdown, with an unbeaten 62, played the sheet anchor role, as Kent rocketed to an eight wickets' victory. It had been achieved in just 71 minutes. The statistics reveal that Kent scored at the rate of 156 runs per 100 balls. More precisely, the runs were scored off 23.2 overs, or 140 balls. It is the fastest innings in first-class cricket.

The helter-skelter run rate against Gloucestershire eclipsed another tall-scoring venture at Dover four years earlier. Ames and Valentine were the match-winning partners, in scoring 205 in 95 minutes against Northampton-shire. Kent's barnstorming feat in 1937 is enshrined in cricket folklore. It was a happening which evokes a feeling of near disbelief among those who witnessed it. The two closest parallels were dominated by individuals, one a seasoned aggressor, Gilbert Jessop, and the other, Ted Alletson, whose day of glorious havoc is probably the only such deed to be recorded in a single book. Jessop's 191 in 90 minutes enabled the Gentlemen of the South to score 313 in 114 minutes at Hastings in 1907. Alletson's 189, which included 142 in only 40 minutes, excites more attention because it was unexpected and out of character. Alletson's dramatic assault was mounted against Sussex at Hove in 1911.

The attacking credo of Frank Woolley was maintained over 32 years, beginning in Kent's first championship winning year in 1906 and ending, with his talents still brightly unfurled, in 1938. He scored 58,959 runs, including 145 centuries, and only Jack Hobbs surpassed this aggregate. Woolley's tally of centuries might well have exceeded Hobbs's record 197 had he tempered his adventurous approach. He never dwelled in the nervous nineties; indeed he was dismissed 35 times between 90 and 99; and Bob Wyatt believed that there were times when he needlessly got himself out. Gubby Allen remembered one occasion, in a match against Middlesex at Canterbury, when Woolley adopted a sterner attitude. 'Frank played a marvellous innings of 270 and Kent still lost. After Woolley had reached his first 100, Nigel Haig said: "Oh, my God, look at this, chaps, Frank is taking guard again."'

Woolley, as a slow left-arm bowler, also took 2,066 wickets, the majority of them before the First World War. It is an almost forgotten statistic to strengthen his claim to be regarded as one of the greatest all-rounders of all time. His 1,018 catches, a record haul, completes the inventory of a spell-binding career. Gary Sobers, a majestic and unruffled batting stylist and a more versatile bowler, can be bracketed with Woolley. He is the nearest modern equivalent of Woolley as an all-rounder and in terms of box-office appeal.

All Woolley's great innings were invested with a charm, freedom and variety of strokes; and, significantly, as a measure of his genius, he never appeared to hurry. There was just a hint of frailty against top-class leg-spin; but he was a magnificent player against fast bowling. 'He was always an artist, never an artisan,' said Ronald Symond of Woolley. 'In his prime there was a zest and fire about his batting, yet all was performed with an effortless grace as though his whole body laughed in the joy of conquest. He was a handsome swashbuckler who would waken the game as if by magic and set spectators gasping with delight.' E. M. Wellings remembered Woolley's compelling appearance.

Woolley, the bright star of Kent cricket. 'There was an effortless grace as though his whole body laughed in the joy of conquest.' (L. Ames)

He was willowy tall and so upright that he seemed to lean slightly backwards. When he was in the mood he made the bowler feel helpless. He had such a tiny area on which to pitch the ball to curb Woolley's attack. Frank's great reach enabled him to attack almost everything either off the back or front foot, and one of his specialities was the six slashed over cover.

Bob Wyatt, in his first Test in England at Old Trafford in 1929, partnered Woolley in a record third wicket stand of 245 runs against South Africa. 'Frank made it look so easy; it gave me confidence,' recalled Wyatt. 'His technique was so perfect; his feet moved so easily; and there was a lovely swing and follow-through of the bat. Woolley was not only great; he was very great; and, in common with other gifted players of his time, he was also a modest man.'

Wyatt remembered one example of Woolley's prowess against fast bowling in a festival match at Folkestone in September 1928. The West Indian tourists, with Learie Constantine as their bowling spearhead, provided the opposition. Constantine had been stirred into furious action after watching a colleague suffer a painful assault at the hands of Hammond.

We went in on the Monday morning after a heavy dew had enlivened the pitch. My opening partner was the Middlesex batsman, Harry Lee. Constantine rushed up and the ball whistled past my cap and hit the sightscreen behind me first bounce with one hell of a crack. It was rather like a cannon going off. I thought to myself that it was time to get to the other end, so I played the next ball slowly to cover and we ran an easy single. Harry Lee decided he would do the same. He also hit the ball to cover, only much harder, and there was scarcely half a run. He just kept on running and was run out by yards. I've never seen a chap so pleased to get out. There was a huge smile on his face as he scampered back to the pavilion.

Lee's hasty departure brought Woolley to the wicket. Erect and unsmiling, he put Constantine to rout. 'In 90 minutes we took the score to 172, of which Frank made 95. He made Constantine look like a medium-pace bowler. Not one ball missed the centre of his bat.' Before his dismissal Wyatt had looked on with wonder at the explosion of strokes. 'Frank was quite magnificent. The faster they bowled the harder he cracked them to the boundary. I've never seen such an innings against really fast bowling. He finished up with 150 and he didn't make a mistake until he got out.'

Les Ames, by his own admission, was an admiring disciple whose own batting splendours never outshone Woolley's bright star. Woolley's career had still 10 years to run when Les joined him in the Kent team. 'I used to love batting with Frank,' recalled Ames. 'He was a fast scorer, faster than I was, but that didn't worry me.' One advantage of their alliance was that they could combat a right-left arm spin attack by dividing the responsibility. 'I would often stay at the right-hander's end and Frank would tackle the left-hander.' Jack Davies, in reference to the partnerships of Woolley and Ames for Kent, said: 'Frank, like Wally Hammond, liked to dominate the bowling. Everybody said you had to be ready to run off the fifth ball of the over. Les wasn't as spectacular as Frank and one would perhaps think he was dominating less than he actually did.'

According to Ian Peebles, there was one area of the collaboration in which Ames was unmistakably the master. Woolley, as an uncertain runner, generally allowed Ames to do the calling. 'Woolley had a most disconcerting habit,' recalled Peebles.

He would take off for a run and on reaching the further crease touch down and without pause return two or three yards, then stop dead. As he seldom called, the unaccustomed partner was subjected to the nervous disruption of a series of stop-go manoeuvres worthy of the worst run national economy. Les at a very early stage in their association took firm action. He did all the calling. His august senior took this in good part and, realising he had discovered an absolutely first-class pilot, implicitly followed his instructions.

Ames twice won the Sir Walter Lawrence trophy and the cash prize of 100

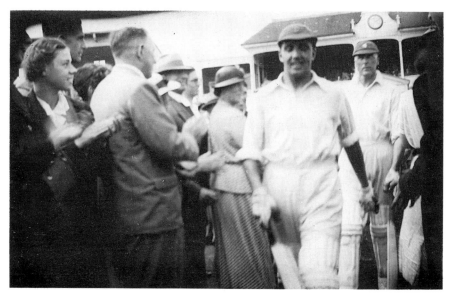

Applause for Ames (leading) and Woolley at Canterbury (L. Ames)

guineas for the fastest century of the season, in 1936 and 1939. On the first occasion, batting for an England XI against India at Folkestone, he reached his three figures in 68 minutes. Batting with him was Woolley, and Ames actually outscored his senior partner. Les had a major share of the stand of 169 runs in 70 minutes. He considered it a remarkable interlude. 'I scored the fastest hundred of the season and Frank was in with me all the time.'

Ames's ascendancy was, in fact, at Woolley's connivance.

> Frank helped me greatly. He would take a single off the first ball and let me have the other four or five. He was 40-odd when I went in. It wouldn't have happened normally, but I did have most of the bowling, loose I expect. Before I had time to look round I had caught Frank up. He reached his 50 and shortly afterwards I reached my own half-century while he had scored about five runs. It was most exceptional. Frank came down the wicket to me and said: 'You know you've only been here for about 20 minutes. You'll walk the quickest 100 if you don't do anything silly. I'll give you all the bowling I can.'

In 1937, his first benefit year, Ames retained his England place against New Zealand and batted with engaging verve. He scored 2,347 runs (at an average of 48.89) despite the indignity of being thrice dismissed without scoring in two consecutive matches, against Somerset at Bath and Gloucestershire at Cheltenham. His aggregate for the season included seven centuries. Against Worcestershire at Gillingham he hit a double century and was associated with Woolley in a third wicket stand of 161 in two hours. For the second time in his career he scored two separate hundreds, both 'gems of aggressive batting', against Surrey at Blackheath. Such a feat was always one to relish. From his earliest days Les had developed the habit of marshalling his most punishing form for Kent against the men from Kennington Oval. The habit was now well ingrained. In the first innings at Blackheath, Ames (119) and Leslie Todd alone stood firm to prevent a collapse, as Gover took seven wickets. In the second innings, after Ashdown had been dismissed cheaply, Ames and Woolley were in immaculate charge. They both hit centuries and trounced the bowling of Gover and Watts. In one overwhelming spell the score advanced by 120 runs in an hour. Altogether they hit 138 in only 68 minutes. 'Woolley was in majestic form,' reported the *Kentish Gazette*, 'The vigour of his innings may be judged from the fact that his 114 was made in 100 minutes.' A season of many blessings for Les Ames was flawed by lamentably small benefit proceeds. It realised only £1,107 and, said the Kent president, G. L. Mackeson, 'there is no doubt that this disappointing result was due to unfavourable weather on the Saturday of his match (against Hampshire) and to the reduced charges at Canterbury.'

In 1938, Australia were the visitors to England. In a preview to the tour, Bill Woodfull, the former Australian captain, wrote:

> One of England's great advantages over the Australians lies in the fact that wicket-keeper Ames is such a fine batsman. He has never been able to produce his batting form in Australia, but at home he has played brilliantly in recent Test engagements. His wicket-keeping, when last in Australia, was of the highest standard. He is perhaps the greatest wicket-keeper batsman in the history of the game.

Ames began his preparations for a series of mammoth scores in another batting extravaganza between Kent and Essex at Gravesend. The rate of scoring was phenomenal, even on a small ground and in tailor-made conditions for buccaneering strikers. In less than three days of an extraordinary match 1,422 runs were scored and five players hit centuries. The tally was only 53 runs short of the record aggregate achieved by Surrey and Northamptonshire in 1920. The prospects for the batsmen looked dismal when Essex lost five wickets for 71 runs. But the appetite was restored and the bowlers groaned when Nichols was joined by Peter Smith. The Essex eighth wicket pair both hit centuries and put on 184 runs, including 125 in an hour. Nichols, with 163 and last out at 450, played one of the finest innings of his career. Kent responded in kind despite the early loss of Fagg and Spencer, both caught behind the wicket by Wade. What followed was cricket on a carousel of sheer delight. Pandemonium reigned. Before lunch Kent scored 223 in two hours. Woolley hit 38, with nine fours, in an enchanting half-hour. Then Ames and Chalk, followed by Valentine, surged into a breakneck gallop. Kent hit 548 at the rate of 110 runs an hour. Ames and Valentine added 202 runs in 82 minutes.

'Ames, after a cautious start, opened out in dazzling fashion,' related the *Kentish Gazette*. 'Runs flowed from his bat in all directions.' Ames struck three sixes and 24 fours in scoring 170 in two hours and 15 minutes. He was especially severe on Eastman. He hit the Essex bowler for one six into the cars parked behind the spectators. Yet another six hurtled over the ropes to disperse the crowd as they frantically dived for cover. Valentine's 151 was just as exhilarating. He was at the wicket only 10 minutes longer than Ames. Kent led by 98 runs on the first innings.

O'Connor became the fifth centurion of the match as Essex sought equality. At lunch on the Tuesday Essex led by 143, with four wickets left, and a draw seemed to be the only option. Doug Wright had other thoughts on the matter; he swept the tail into his spinning net. Woolley and Ames briskly settled the issue. Kent won by six wickets in a game in which five bowlers conceded less pleasurable centuries.

The hundreds, seven in all, continued to flow in the first Test against Australia at Trent Bridge. This was a match distinguished by the brilliance of Stan McCabe whose 232 could not avert the follow-on but provided a heady counter to England's first innings run spree. McCabe's pyrotechnics were matched by Wally Hammond at Lord's. The gates were closed on a packed crowd of nearly 34,000 people—the largest crowd ever to assemble at the headquarters—on the Saturday of the second Test. On the previous day England had lost three wickets, those of Hutton, Barnett and Edrich, for 31 runs. McCormick, in the space of 25 deliveries, took the wickets at the cost of 15 runs. The stage was set for Hammond, at first aided by Eddie Paynter and then Ames, to play an innings which still produces a fascination and a tremble of excitement among those fortunate enough to have seen it.

Paynter, cruelly dismissed at 99, resolutely helped Hammond to establish a fourth wicket record against Australia of 222 runs in just over three hours. Hammond's innings of 240, soon to be exceeded by Leonard Hutton's marathon 364 at The Oval, was then the highest score by an England batsman in a home Test. *The Times* reported: 'He has never surpassed such grandeur. It was a combination of batting technique and cricket brain supported by physical endurance which was amazing.' Neville Cardus, calling urgently on his poetic muse, said: 'He drove almost nonchalantly. The swift velocity of his late cuts seemed an optical illusion. The wrists were as supple as a fencer's steel.'

Les Ames, exuding quality and promising another Test 100 at Lord's, was Hammond's partner in another record for the sixth wicket. Their stand of 186 runs beat the 170 made by Sutcliffe and Wyatt at The Oval in 1930. 'He is feathering the loveliest of off-drives,' wrote C. B. Fry of Ames at Lord's. 'He offers a caressing bat and the ball becomes a bullet.' Not for the first time, after Hammond had left, cheered all the way to the pavilion, Ames was compelled to hurry if he wanted a century before the innings ended. He had won his duel with O'Reilly, repeatedly driving the Australian bowler who whirled away like 'a giant starfish of waving arms and legs.' A deserved century eluded the Kent player; his innings ended at 83 when he leaned forward to Fleetwood-Smith's googly and was caught by McCormick at slip.

His ill-luck was compounded in England's second innings when a ball from McCormick fractured his little finger. He did not play again in the series. The intervention of war was to deny him further opportunities against Australia.

The finger injury kept Ames out of the Kent team for six weeks; but his recovery coincided with Frank Woolley's farewell appearance at Canterbury against the Australians. Woolley was run out without scoring in the first innings but his command was unrelenting in the second, as Kent battled to escape an innings defeat. 'Woolley obliged with a glorious swansong,' reported the *Kentish Gazette*. 'The veteran started with three dazzling drives off Waite to the tents. Attacking all the time, with superb drives, brilliant hooks and graceful leg glides, he made his 81 runs in 65 minutes.' Woolley seemed destined to grace the occasion with a century until Bradman took a catch off a low, skimming drive at mid-on. Ames and Valentine brought their own zest to an emotional day. They did not desert the tenets of Woolley. Ames hit a century and, in his partnership with Valentine, the runs came at such a rate that 96 were scored in 55 minutes, with both batsmen striking glorious sixes.

In 1938, music-hall's elegant duettists, the Western Brothers were among those who hungered for more of Woolley's artistry. In a rhyming curtain-drop song they yearned for an encore:

> Dreadful consternation is creeping over Kent.
> Heads are shaking to and fro,
> The cause of this repining?
> This show of sentiment?
> Surely they can't let Frank Woolley go?
> No more those flashing wrists.
> The cuts, the glides, the hooks.
> A gentleman of cricket, called a pro!
> Just a name to appear in reference books?
> Surely they can't let Frank Woolley go?

Kenneth and George were lamenting the departure of a legendary cricketer. Down the years his captivating spirit glows in the memory; and never more so than in the mind of Les Ames. 'It was a joy to be associated with such a great cricketer,' he has said. Woolley did provide one last encore against the West Indian tourists at Gravesend in 1939. Under Ames's captaincy, he showed that his freedom was still unchained. His opponents included the redoubtable Constantine and Martindale. Woolley's strokes rippled across the field. He always liked the fast men and the ball coming sweetly on to the bat.

10
FORTUNES BEFORE THE WAR

Again and again Ames went for the best attack and treated it with vigorously brilliant methods.

THE CRICKETER

T he tumbrils of war stopped rolling just long enough for Les Ames, along with his Kent colleagues, Bryan Valentine and Doug Wright, to tour South Africa in 1938–9. It was a series of massive aggregates accumulating to a point of tedium. In the end the uncompleted marathon Test at Durban toppled over into frustration and farce. England were set a target of 696 runs. 'Few people imagined they had a ghost of a chance of averting defeat, much less of scoring such a colossal total,' related *Wisden*. They came heartbreakingly close to achieving victory against the odds. England's sixth wicket pair, Ames and Valentine, both strikers of lusty renown, would surely have scored the remaining 42 runs had not rain resisted their ardour.

The torrential rains at Durban, unleashed at last as a kind of divine intervention after 10 days of cricket, allowed the weary players to discharge their obligations in a preposterous affair. The duration of the match exceeded the previous longest between England and the West Indies at Kingston, Jamaica in April 1930. A total of 1,981 runs were scored at Durban, South Africa's first innings total of 530 was their highest in Test cricket and lasted 13 hours. Ronald Mason thought the whole series was kinder to the record books than it was to the spectators, and remained a treasury of paper glories rather than of high achievements of courage or of art.

R. C. Robertson-Glasgow, in his report on the series wrote:

> The Test pitches had so far overstepped perfection as to be of little use to the bowler and to impose some inexplicable narcotic on the batsmen. They were plumb, but without pace. Yet the batsmen, with few exceptions, cannot be wholly acquitted of blame. Some of them nearly slept on the pitch, and it is recorded that the number of half-volleys played by the back stroke was quite dreadful.

The bizarre events at Durban exposed the futility of 'timeless Tests'. At the end of the tour the England captain, Wally Hammond, endorsed this view, and said: 'I don't think they are in the best interests of the game, and I hope that the last one has been played.' His wish was granted as saner counsels prevailed after the war.

Despite the Durban 'war of exhaustion', as one observer called it, Les Ames enjoyed his only tour of South Africa and the pleasures of a beautiful country. His batting retained its sureties of vigour and responsibility even amid the deadening tempo of the series. He kept wicket for the last time in Tests (the temptation, which he was not sure he would have resisted, of further wicket-keeping in Australia in 1940, was denied him); and he passed A. A. 'Dick' Lilley's record of 92 dismissals in international cricket. England, by virtue of their sole victory by an innings and 13 runs in the third Test at Durban, won the series.

This was a match dominated by Paynter's double century—the Lancastrian's third wicket partnership with Hammond yielded 242 runs—and the superb fast bowling of Farnes. Ames reserved his best batting performance for the second Test at Cape Town, where he again joined Hammond in setting up a Test record for the fourth wicket against South Africa. The Cape Town wicket, like the others, was so prepared as to resist the best that bowlers could offer. Hammond did not attempt to disguise the problem. 'Bowlers on both sides could break their hearts and exercise every guile in the calendar and still stand very little chance of getting a normally careful batsman out.' The England captain was both careful and lucky at Cape Town. He took 20 minutes to open his account and was twice nearly bowled before reaching 26. Gibb and Hammond shared a century stand and it was followed, reported *Wisden*, by 'a grand partnership between Hammond and Ames. Both were missed in quick succession, and the errors were costly indeed. Hammond drove and hit to leg beautifully, and Ames scored readily by powerful strokes all round the wicket; in two hours and 25 minutes the pair put on 197.' Ames, in hitting 119 with 13 boundaries, outpaced his captain. 'The Kent player, adopting forcing tactics, had two narrow escapes, but his batting was of a scintillating order,' reported the *Kentish Gazette*. Valentine also hit a century to crown a good day for Kent as well as England. His bombardment bordered on recklessness; but a thoroughly bewildered South African attack had to applaud an innings of merciless severity.

R. C. Robertson-Glasgow rejoiced in the 'old freedom of stroke-play, especially off-driving and straight hitting, that thing of joy which nature is always urging real batsmen to release' on English cricket grounds in 1939. Kent, and especially Les Ames, could never be accused of being affected by 'poisonous vapours and dunce-like inaction'. Ames's batting, before the world was plunged into disorder, touched a rich vein. He had relinquished his wicket-keeping duties to Howard Levett and, on occasions, to the 17-year-old Godfrey Evans, who was to capitalise on the endowment after the war. In May Ames was advised by his doctor that his back would be endangered if he continued to keep wicket regularly. 'By that time,' Les recalled, 'it was becoming pretty hard work trying to combine the two jobs. I was expected to get runs. It seemed sensible to give up wicket-keeping and just concentrate on batting.'

The choice, however hard for a man who had given enormous value in both his cricket roles, was indeed sensible. Freed of his wicket-keeping responsibility, Ames scored 1,846 runs, including five centuries, in a season curtailed by war. Gerry Chalk, sadly to be killed in action, was an enterprising captain and an improving batsman. He led a revival which carried Kent to fifth place in the county championship, their highest ranking since 1934. At Tonbridge, against Sussex, Kent won by an innings and totalled 580, the biggest county total of the summer. Chalk, forced by the lack of suitable candidates to go in first, put Kent on the winning path. He hit 198 in major partnerships with Fagg and Valentine. Wright brought the match to a dramatic conclusion by taking eight wickets in less than eight overs. He began a devastating spell of bowling by dismissing Sussex century-makers, Harry Parks and John Langridge, and Bartlett, Cox and Jack Oakes in 18 balls for three runs. Wright, at the peak of his powers in this last pre-war season, again bowled magnificently in another innings victory over Worcestershire. Ames scored a double century after Kent had been put in to bat, and he and Valentine were once again in merry mood. Their stand was only marginally less severe than the assault on the Essex attack in the previous season. They matched each other, run for run, in scoring 202 in just over two hours.

Bryan Valentine, a former Repton School cricket captain and Public Schools' lawn tennis doubles champion, was another of Kent's brilliant amateur batting stylists. In an era of illustrious batsmanship he did not represent England at home; but on his first tour to India in 1933–4 he scored a century on his Test debut at Bombay. He was a well-loved man, a cavalier stroke-maker in the county tradition; and as captain both before and after the war he followed Chapman's example of buoyant and adventurous command. 'Isn't it curious how Kent keeps finding class batsmen?' commented one writer, when Valentine joined his future great batting partner, Les Ames, in the county side in the late 1920s. 'If they were equally successful in unearthing bowling talent what a team we should have.'

As the war drew inexorably nearer in 1939, Valentine steered Ames to the fastest century of the season against Surrey at The Oval. As Woolley had done three years earlier, he graciously took a back seat to present Ames with a lucrative strike. E. M. Wellings was an onlooker as Kent won a race against the clock. 'Les enjoyed the right partner on that occasion in Bryan Valentine. Valentine himself was an exceptionally fast scorer, but at The Oval, with Ames galloping so well, he fed as much of the bowling to his partner as possible until the three-figure mark was reached in 67 minutes.' Ames finished unbeaten on 136 and scored 208 runs in the match.

Fishlock and Whitfield both hit centuries for Surrey in their second innings before Garland-Wells applied the declaration. It was a sporting challenge but not without precedent in those days of ambitious cricket. Kent were set a target of 231 to win in two hours and 25 minutes. Fagg was dismissed for nine and Ames, the next man in, very nearly followed him to the pavilion. 'I prodded my bat at the first ball from Alf Gover, got an edge, held my breath—and saw the catch missed at second slip,' recalled Les. 'I gasped with relief and sensed it was my lucky day, and from then on took all manner of risks.'

After the escape, Ames and Chalk flung caution to the winds. Parker was hit for 17 in one over, one steepling six shuddering the pavilion awning; and 14 was struck off another over from Gover. They scored 85 runs in less than an hour. 'Then came a riot of run-scoring by Ames and Valentine,' reported the *Kentish Gazette*. In 55 minutes the score advanced by 131 runs. Kent won in a canter by seven wickets, with 27 minutes to spare. 'Ames never relaxed until he finished a grand match with a magnificent drive,' reported *Wisden*.

From his earliest days Les Ames had exacted a severe toll as a batsman against discomforted Surrey attacks. His last pre-war batting revel, as a mature master, was a fitting finale. 'Ames batted most gloriously,' reported *The Cricketer* in its last appraisal of county cricket before the war. 'Again and again he went for the best attack and treated it with vigorously brilliant methods.' The bright candles of other burgeoning young talents spluttered and died, or were never fully rekindled after six years of war. Ames, improbably as the veteran campaigner, was to sound a clarion call of undimmed batsmanship, still brimming with adventure, when peace returned.

11
A CENTURY OF CENTURIES

Les was more interested in Kent winning than whether he got a particular record. He went for a win at Canterbury.

TONY PAWSON

T he sprightliest of Kent's old stagers had the chance to make his fourth tour of Australia under Wally Hammond's captaincy in the winter of 1946-7. 'Wally wanted me to go—and keep wicket,' recalled Les Ames, 'but after six years of war I was loath to leave my home and family again, and so I declined the invitation.'

Ames's decision meant that only six of England's last pre-war tourists— Hammond, Hutton, Yardley, Gibb, Wright and Edrich—travelled on what is now regarded as an ill-conceived tour. The success of the Victory 'Tests' between the Australian Services team and England in the preceding summer was a major influence in the decision of the MCC to undertake the tour. The frailties of England's cricket resources quickly became apparent. The party was composed of too many veterans, with their best years behind them, and other younger players as yet unblooded in Test cricket. England were beaten in three Tests, twice by an innings. A disappointing cricket venture did have merit as a gesture of gratitude to Australia for their loyalty and sacrifices in the war.

Ames served his own 'modest war' in the Royal Air Force in which he rose to the rank of Squadron Leader. His term of duty as an administrator, liaising with air crews, drew together the strands of leadership which were to flourish in post-war cricket. His service in the RAF took him to the lovely Yorkshire spa town of Harrogate. At Harrogate he captained the unit XI and on other occasions he assisted Windhill in the Bradford League. One correspondent, who lived in Harrogate towards the end of the war, remembered watching Ames jauntily cycling across the vast parkland of The Stray to his office in the Grand Hotel. Two other men, one a newly trained pilot and the other a renowned comedy actor, were taken to task by Ames at Harrogate. The pilot, home based after having completed his flying training in the United States, was admonished for losing his forage cap. He was then allocated the duties of orderly room runner and often had to visit the Officer's Mess to collect Ames's chocolate ration! Brian Rix, while playing in repertory at Harrogate, recalled how his cricket practice was abruptly terminated to allow Ames to take his place in the nets. The famous squadron leader asserted his authority on that occasion to eject the audacious actor. 'Since then, we have become good friends,' said Sir Brian. 'Les has never turned me out of any place again.'

On Whit-Monday, 1944, Ames made a nostalgic return to Lord's. Servicemen were admitted free to a match between the RAF and the Army. 'Hitler, please note. Our RAF boys are still winning,' reported the *Daily Express*. A crowd of 18,000 were entertained by glittering stroke play. It was an afternoon of festive cricket which struck chords in the memory. Ames rediscovered his old adventure at wartime Lord's. He was in buoyant mood in this carefree sporting interlude. He hit three sixes and 14 fours in his century, occupying just two hours, and the RAF won by five wickets. His eager forays rallied his team after Morris Nichols had dismissed Charles Barnett and Cyril Washbrook with only four runs on the board.

Ames returned to Harrogate by overnight train, an uncomfortable and taxing journey in a Britain at war. On the following day he captained an RAF XI against a scratch town side reinforced by a Lancashire League medium pace bowler. One member of the Harrogate team recalled that their bowling recruit did take two early wickets. 'Ames came in to bat when the shine was

Wartime service: Squadron Leader Ames, with fellow officer and another sports celebrity, Dan Maskell, the tennis commentator (far right) (L. Ames)

still on the ball. He took almost half an hour to play himself in and reach double figures. He then proceeded to demolish the Harrogate attack. He made an unbeaten century.' The ferocity of Ames's driving constantly pierced the field. As the hapless extra cover discovered, scampering to retrieve the ball rather than stop it, the Harrogate fieldsman was given an object lesson in offside driving. He wryly recalled: 'I came to realise that a ball does gather pace on its way to the boundary when perfectly placed.'

Before hostilities ended there was one brief period of alarm on the war front for Squadron Leader Ames. An imminent posting to the Far East loomed to give him pause for serious reflection. 'I was called up for inoculations prior to the posting. We were on 24 hours' notice. I was only too aware of the possible fate awaiting me in India or Burma where we were bound,' he recalled. Then came the announcement that the ship carrying an earlier batch of RAF personnel had been torpedoed and sunk. Ames's anxiety was dispelled by the cancellation of his posting. 'I had the luck of the draw in that episode,' he said.

A happier summons came in July, 1945, when Ames was reunited with other cricket celebrities at Lord's. Two former England captains, Flying Officer Wyatt and Lieutenant-Colonel Allen, captained the RAF and Army XI's in a keen struggle. Ames hit 93 (out of the RAF total of 195 for 8). He shared a stand of 56 with Wyatt after the RAF had lost three wickets for 34 runs. The victory target of 225 looked well within range until Ames was out to a superb running catch by Donald Carr. The Army bowler was Lieutenant Douglas Wright, who took three other wickets at a cost of 43 runs in 14 overs in the drawn match.

The fervour which accompanied the exploits of the Australian Services team in England was a harbinger of peace in 1945. Their impact on English cricket was likened to that of their predecessors after the First World War. Keith Johnson, the Australian manager, considered it an honour and a privilege to have assisted in the rehabilitation. In the 1946 *Wisden* Johnson wrote: 'There was something about the games of last season. Something carefree and refreshing, which I hope has come to stay.' Lindsay Hassett and Wally Hammond were the rival captains in a series which was hastily arranged as a sporting celebration of VE (Victory in Europe) Day in May. Five three-day 'Victory' matches were played at Lord's, Sheffield and Manchester. The honours were shared, with two victories to each side and one match drawn. In the first match at Lord's Keith Miller gave evidence of the flair which was to make him a box-office personality in Test cricket. He struck an elegant and emphatic century as Australia won by six wickets. Cecil Pepper, one of the mightiest of post-war hitters, made the winning hit off the fourth ball of the last over. Les Ames, although on the losing side, responded to the spirit of the occasion. He was England's top scorer, with 57, in the first innings. It was a neat and fitting prelude to the resumption of his association with Kent.

Ames, together with other Kent colleagues returning from war service, was welcomed back to Canterbury for a charity match in August. There was an especially warm greeting from Les's old cricket mentor, Francis Mackinnon, then aged 97, but still alertly attentive at the homecoming. The ranks of the two teams included two future county captains, David Clark and Bill Murray-Wood, and pre-war stalwarts, Arthur Fagg, Jack Davies and Howard Levett. The St Lawrence ground had escaped serious damage despite the fury of the aerial bombardment of East Kent. The official report of wartime experiences said that 135 incendiaries had fallen on the playing area 'with negligible effect; in fact the ingredients appeared good for the grass!' Athletics meetings as well as cricket matches had been staged at Canterbury throughout the war. The programme had also included two baseball matches featuring American servicemen. This activity was considered a sacrilege by the Kent head groundsman, Joe Murrin.

Murrin was involved in an amusing interlude prior to the Bank Holiday match at Canterbury. Gerald Hough, the Kent manager, recalled the confrontation with a runaway cow. 'On the day before the match the cow broke loose from the market, outdistanced all pursuit up the Old Dover Road, came in at the gates, made a beeline for the pitch and proceeded to walk up and down it. Joe's horror when he spotted it had to be seen to be believed.' Murrin, who could only walk with the aid of a stick, entered his car and tried to dismiss the cow with a series of frantic gestures coupled with raucous blasts on the horn. 'The cow was a humorist and a tactician,' said the Kent manager.

> Having discovered that the car could not compete with clever dodging, it remained on the pitch for about 20 minutes until its drover appeared. Why it stayed there so long when it had the whole of the playing area and surrounds of the ground to choose from has always been a mystery to me, unless it thought this was a new game. Joe must have used a considerable amount of petrol as he was repeatedly changing gear and backing every 22 yards.

Murrin did not take kindly to Hough's laughter, or his remark, after order had been restored, that it was good fun to watch. The groundsman's anger was not a whit abated by the view that a few hoof marks and droppings might help to produce a result in the following one-day match.

The capers of the cow were certainly appreciated by one fast bowler, Norman Harding. On a sporting wicket he took all 10 wickets as Kent beat the Rest by 104 runs. Seven of his victims were clean bowled; six failed to score; and he conceded only 32 runs in 15 overs and four balls. In less friendly conditions Harding was to give promise of becoming a major striking force. Harding's early death in 1947, through infantile paralysis, was a sad loss. It deprived Kent of a menacing arm and a player who could have bolstered their attack in the threadbare years after the war.

In the golden summer of high-scoring accomplishment in 1947, Les Ames belied his advancing years as a batsman. He hit 2,272 runs, including seven centuries, to finish fourth in the national averages behind the record-breaking Denis Compton and Bill Edrich, and Cyril Washbrook. Ames was to score over 9,000 runs in five seasons before his retirement in 1951. Many of his post-war contemporaries have expressed their astonishment that he was passed over by the England selectors. Jim Laker and Tom Graveney were among those who believed that Ames maintained the thrust of his pre-war batting. 'I couldn't believe it when I first saw him,' said Graveney. 'He gave our Gloucestershire bowlers some fearful hammer. I envied his footwork and confidence.' Laker added his own tribute. 'I think perhaps he couldn't pick my flight, but it made no difference to the way he attacked me. He would take a chance, dart down the pitch, and crack me all over the place.'

In 1947, with Ames, Fagg (returning as a regular opening batsmen) and Todd as their premier batsmen and Doug Wright at his mesmeric best, Kent finished fourth in the county championship. The batting trio shared 17 three-figure innings between them and Wright matched their prosperity in taking 136 wickets at less than 19 runs apiece. Kent, led by Bryan Valentine, still adhered to their traditional enterprise. Tony Pawson was one of Kent's engaging young amateurs after the war. He remembered the enthusiasm engendered by Valentine and Les Ames. 'Despite their years in cricket, they were not blasé about the game. Through their example, you always felt that cricket was something to enjoy. We didn't do too well in the late-1940s and early-1950s, but we had a marvellous time.'

The vivacity of Kent's cricket in 1947 excited the praise of *Wisden*.

> Their final record of 12 victories and eight defeats, with only six drawn games, conveys something like an accurate idea of how Kent always strove to bring about a definite result. For this reason their cricket vied with Middlesex (the county champions) for producing the brightness which gives the fullest enjoyment to players and spectators.

Ames, almost always in the batting vanguard in a prolific season, was in scintillating form in one tremendous week at Gravesend. He struck a double century to compile a match aggregate of 265 runs without being dismissed against Nottinghamshire; and hit another century in the following match against Northamptonshire. Wright took 11 wickets, including seven in the visitors' first innings, to place the seal on a nine wickets' victory.

The enterprise did not lessen but the chasm opened in the following season when Kent declined to 15th place in the championship. From then on they scrambled to retain some dignity, with only fleeting glimpses of the old panache to sustain them in the hollow years ahead. Ames, Fagg and Todd, all in the twilight of their careers, carried a heavy burden as the guardians of batting respectability; while Wright and Fred Ridgway had to persevere as bowlers with minimal support.

Ridgway took 1,069 wickets between 1946 and 1961 and represented England in five Tests in India in the 1951–2 series. The former Royal Marine instructor was sadly deprived of an ally as Kent's opening bowler by the death of Norman Harding. Ridgway and Harding had briefly demonstrated their potential as a formidable combination. Vain attempts were made to secure a partner of substance for the ill-supported Ridgway. Derek Ufton was Godfrey Evans's deputy as Kent wicket-keeper after the war. He remembered that Ridgway and Ray Dovey, a tidy off-spinner and an accurate if unremarkable seam bowler, were often Kent's opening attack in this period. 'Fred was a very good quick bowler. He wasn't very tall for a fast bowler. He was only about 5 ft 9 in tall but he was lithe and very fit. He had a long run-up and a fabulous last stride from which he generated his power. He used to move the ball very late off the seam.'

Ufton recalled that a bowling rota was strictly operated by the Kent captains in his time. It was commonplace for 24 overs to be bowled in an hour. Ridgway, perspiring and rapidly enfeebled, had to complete his stint of 12 overs as a matter of course. It was all done by the clock. To add to his distress Dovey moved in off a few paces, allowing his partner very little time to rest between the overs. 'Fred, after his first over, would trudge down to third man, and by the time he arrived there the over had been called. Back he would come for his second over at the end of which he wouldn't even reach third man before it was his turn again. As the morning progressed he gave up the walk and settled for third slip.'

By this time there was a barely concealed conspiracy among the rest of the team to speed up the overs. Amid mounting merriment, the ball would be returned to Dovey as promptly as possible. 'After about eight overs Fred would say: "I can't bloody well bowl anymore. Don't throw the ball back to Ray so quickly."' Tears of laughter would stream down the faces of the mischievous fieldsmen. Ridgway would pull out his handkerchief to mop the perspiration which ran in rivulets down his own face. His appeals to his captain were unavailing. 'Come on, Fred, it's only twenty minutes past 12,' was the response to his entreaty. 'You've got another 10 minutes yet.' There was, of course, a more serious lack of acknowledgement by the Kent committee of Ridgway's plight. They disregarded his unceasing toil. In later years he might conceivably have won a case for more sympathy. But, in a more autocratic era, he would have been sternly rebuked had he rebelled against his labours. 'Ridgway, you are employed to bowl. Get on with the job,' would have been the committee's reply. As was inevitable, Fred was a weary and devastated man by July. 'The committee couldn't believe it when Fred broke down, or lost his snap, and failed to take any wickets,' said Ufton.

Les Ames remembered Ridgway as one of the quickest bowlers on the county circuit. Don Bradman, on his farewell visit to England in 1948, was still a fearsome hooker of the short-pitched delivery. Ridgway was at his fastest at Canterbury. In his second over with the new ball he bowled Bradman a bouncer. It was dispatched in a trice into one of the tents beyond the boundary. 'Ridgway stood aghast, staring at Bradman as though he could not believe his own eyes. Then, as if to prove it had not really happened, he released another bouncer. It was given the same treatment as the first bouncer.' Ames, who was fielding at short-leg, called down the wicket: 'I shouldn't bowl any more of those, Fred, if I were you.'

Bryan Valentine was succeeded as Kent captain by David Clark in 1949. It was a position which Clark believed should have been occupied as a matter of right by Les Ames. Ames had, in fact, already received a signal from Valentine in a dressing-room talk at Southampton in the previous season. He was told that the county committee were prepared to offer him the appointment if he reverted to amateur status. He declined the invitation on the grounds that he was not going to change course at that stage in his career. Others have said that Ames would have regarded such a move as an affront to his integrity as a professional.

David Clark had made his Kent debut against Yorkshire at Canterbury in 1946; he had been a schoolboy cricketer of distinction at Rugby and had represented the Lord's Schools against the Rest in 1938; but he was, by his own admission, lacking in first-class experience for an onerous position. On Clark's retirement in 1951 to concentrate on his farming interests, Gerald Brodribb said: 'He has led the side with skill and popularity, and always set a fine example by his excellent fielding in close-in positions.'

Clark never entirely departed from the view, expressed to the Kent committee, that it was wrong in the interests of Kent cricket not to utilise Ames's acumen as a cricketer. 'I was a very ordinary club cricketer although I had played quite a lot for the Kent second team. By contrast, Les was enormously experienced and very knowledgeable about the game.' Before agreeing to accept the captaincy Clark had discussed the matter with Ames. He re-emphasised his stance on the question. Les replied: 'David, you are wrong. As a professional cricketer, I would always feel that I had to advance the players' point of view. If it came to a showdown, with my living on the line, I would not be able to take the same tough line as I would expect you as an amateur to take.' Clark had to concede the argument and accept, as he put it, that he had a 'pressure point', which was denied to a professional.

Clark later described Ames as 'God's gift to any young amateur coming in to captain a county side with very little experience.' He did, however, more than once reflect on his senior professional's retiring disposition. As an example, he cited a match in which one of Kent's opponents registered a century in the first innings. In the second innings Clark stationed an extra short-leg for the centurion and was rewarded with the early dismissal of the batsman. 'Les came across from gully and said: "Well played, skipper, we nearly always get him out there."' Clark thought the information might have been relayed to him earlier. He expressed his puzzlement at the late advice. Les said: 'You'll learn much more by working things out for yourself.' Apart from decisions regarding the toss and occasional reflections on younger players, mostly gleaned at Clark's instigation, Ames maintained a reticent posture. 'This was one of the extraordinary things about Les's character,' said Clark. 'He was intensely anxious not to interfere.'

Ames, remembering the early reserve of his own seniors, would often remonstrate with the Kent captain for 'making too much fuss of the young boys.' Clark believed that his encouragement was necessary in a difficult period, and that it was also, possibly, attributable to his own inexperience. Such benefactions assisted him as well as the rest of the team. In the changing social climate, in cricket and other spheres, he was building a bridge over the divide which had existed between the old and young in the 1930s. 'I'm sorry, Les, if they didn't talk to you,' he observed on one occasion. 'But I hope this means that life is a little better for youngsters than it used to be.'

Ames was not as uncaring as his reserve might indicate. Alan Shirreff provided an anecdote of sympathetic coinage. The occasion was Shirreff's county debut against Northamptonshire at Northampton in May, 1950. Shirreff had hero-worshipped Ames as a boy. At Northampton, to his considerable embarrassment, he was involved in a batting misunderstanding with his idol. Before the game he had been earnestly enjoined by Godfrey Evans and Leslie Todd to be very circumspect in his dealings with the great man. The young amateur had been told that his future with Kent would be jeopardised if he put a foot wrong.

'Northants batted first and made 347,' recalled Shirreff.

> Then Kent made a poorish start. When I got to the wicket we had lost our first five batsmen. But Les was still there, batting like a master. You can imagine my trepidation. Things ticked along quite nicely for a while, and then suddenly Les, tapping one in to the covers, called me for what I thought was an impossible run, and set off.
>
> My immediate cricket instinct was to shout: 'No, get back,' forgetting momentarily to whom I was addressing such an imperious command. Alas, while turning to regain his ground, Les slipped and fell full length on his stomach. He was run out by a mile.

Shirreff, in fact, batted on pluckily to save the follow-on; but he was inwardly quaking at the enormity of his folly. The words of the ragging Kent professionals raced through his mind. On his return to the pavilion Fred Ridgway said: 'Toddy has packed your bags and the next train to London is the 7.52.' Shirreff was overcome with a dreadful fear.

> As I walked into the dressing-room, you could have heard a pin drop. I sat down disconsolately and slowly unbuckled my pads. Les was sitting nearby and I leaned over and said softly: 'I am terribly sorry, Les. I don't know what possessed me to send you back.'

To his amazement and joy, Ames replied: 'Dear boy, if you had responded to that crazy call, I wouldn't have thought much of your cricket judgement.' At tea Les made a point of sitting next to the discomforted Shirreff. 'It was entirely my fault,' he said. 'I should have known better. Forget it.' Shirreff never forgot the generosity of the Kent veteran. 'I wonder how many international cricketers of Les's stature would have been so humble and considerate to a youngish new boy in his first county game.'

In 1949 Ames hit 2,125 runs, including seven centuries. *Wisden* reported: 'At the age of 43, Ames, in a vulnerable batting line-up, set a grand example of cultured batsmanship.' David Clark remembered a masterly century against Surrey and the testing spin of Jim Laker on a rain-affected wicket at The Oval. Laker took 12 wickets in the match and was only countered by Ames, who hit 131 (out of the Kent first innings total of 224) in three and a half hours. 'It was one of Les's best innings and produced through superb footwork,' recalled Clark.

At Bristol, on another challenging wicket for batsmen, Ames again demonstrated his skills against the Gloucestershire spinners. Clark remembered taking Les out to inspect the wicket. 'You could almost pick it up in lumps.' He went to see the Gloucestershire secretary, Lieutenant-Colonel Henson, and asked if the wicket for the match could be changed. Henson told Clark to choose any wicket on the square. 'Go and find one which is better,' he said. The Kent captain and his senior professional made a further inspection to confirm that the selected wicket was as good as any other. Ames's response was to visit the groundsman's quarters and borrow a big, heavy mallet. He carried it to the Gloucestershire dressing-room, exchanged greetings with several of the home players, and then turned to his old spinning rival, Tom Goddard. He brought the mallet down with an almighty crash on a table, 'That is what I've got for you, Uncle Tom,' he said. Ames hit a six and 11 fours, mostly off Goddard, in scoring 79 in Kent's second innings. Clark recalled that the turning wicket at Bristol, along with others at the time, was an integral part of the game. 'Batting technique was put to the test. Les shone in those circumstances.'

Ames revelled in his duels with Goddard and Charlie Parker, a superb slow left-arm bowler. Reg Sinfield, another Gloucestershire rival, recalled one match against Kent in which Les was caught in the deep field off Goddard. 'Les walked past me, and said with a rueful smile: "Well, I'd rather be caught out there than at short-leg."' Ames invariably relied on the aggressive approach against Goddard. 'It was either me or Tom who would win. I reckoned that if I stayed in the crease he would dictate the length to me. Tom didn't like the long handle at the best of times and I loved to see his reaction if I got hold of him. Mind you, he made a fool out of me on more than one occasion.'

Ames led from the front as a batsman and carried the burden of the captaincy just as lightly and skilfully when called upon to deputise for the indisposed Clark during Maidstone Week in 1949. The match against Warwickshire brought Ames into opposition with another respected tactician, Tom Dollery, one of the first professional captains in modern times. It was an absorbing contest in which both players carried the batting honours and scored centuries. Dollery failed by only five runs to score two separate hundreds in the match. Warwickshire gained a lead of 24 runs on the first innings. Ames then hit a superb 160 on a wearing wicket. Pritchard hastened a Kent batting decline by performing the hat-trick in dismissing Phebey, Crush and Ufton. Ames set Warwickshire a target of 277 in three hours. Dollery took up the challenge in exhilarating style. He scored 118 in less than two hours. The surge seemed irresistible until the Warwickshire captain was caught behind the wicket by Ufton off Martin.

Eleven minutes of the match remained when Dollery left at 262. Wolton, Pritchard and Grove were dismissed for the addition of one run. Warwickshire, with two wickets left, needed five runs off the last over. In an exciting finale Taylor was caught off the first ball, and from the next one Bromley survived a stumping chance. Bromley and Spooner each took a single off the third and fourth balls and scampered a leg bye off the fifth ball. Spooner, forced on to the defensive by the accuracy of Dovey, was denied the winning runs. The match ended in a draw, with only a single separating the teams.

Derek Ufton, who made his county debut in this fluctuating struggle, was the guilty wicket-keeper who missed the crucial stumping. 'I did the good thing in catching Dollery on the legside, and then failed to stump Phil Bromley off Ray Dovey in the last over.' Ufton remembered the kindliness of Ames which helped to dispel his disappointment. 'This was the beginning of another phase in my hero-worship of Les Ames. He was generous in praise of my catch and forgiving about the stumping error.'

In what was to prove his last season in county cricket Ames departed the stage in the grand manner in 1950. Amid scenes of wild excitement he reached the coveted milestone of 100 centuries at Canterbury. Ames, the only wicket-keeper to achieve this feat, joined an illustrious list. Among the 11 players who preceded him to the target were Grace, Hobbs, Woolley, Sutcliffe, Hammond and Bradman. Ames arrived at his own landmark in 915 innings, and the tally included centuries against all the first-class counties. 'If I hadn't got a move on at Canterbury, I might have had to settle for 99 hundreds,' said Ames. He did not know at the time that the two hundreds he had scored for the Commonwealth team in India in the preceding winter would later be given first-class ranking.

Ames's progress to his ultimate triumph was strewn with feats of high accomplishment; and his enterprise rarely faltered. Against Gloucestershire at Bristol in May he scored centuries in each innings for the third time in his career. In July he travelled to Nottingham to hit his 98th century, a match-saving effort, after Kent had followed on. Ames and Evans were the county's saviours, unflinchingly resolute in an unbroken partnership of 188 in just over two hours.

Ames, Hearn and Pawson each scored centuries in another tall-scoring extravaganza against the sorely tried rivals, Essex at Maidstone. For the Smiths, Ray and Peter, it was yet another tormenting experience at the hands of the Kent batsmen. The Smiths, to be fair, constituted what was virtually a

CANTERBURY CRICKET WEEK
KENT v. MIDDLESEX

WEDNESDAY, THURSDAY and FRIDAY, AUGUST 9th, 10th and 11th, 1950

‡ Captain   † Wicket Keeper

MIDDLESEX—1st Innings

	1st Innings		2nd Innings	
1	**Robertson J. D.** st Evans b Wright ...	40	b Dovey	54
2	**J. G. Dewes** c Evans b Wright	60	c Pawson b Dovey	32
3	**Sharp H.** b Dovey	62	c Clark b Wright	21
4	‡**W. J. Edrich** b Ridgway	6	not out	77
5	**Brown S. M.** b Wright	19	not out	51
6	†**Compton L. H.** b Wright	7		
7	**Titmus F.** c Evans b Ridgway	9		
8	**Sims J. M.** c Fagg b Ridgway	13		
9	**J. J. Warr** b Wright	4		
10	**Young J. A.** b Dovey	14		
11	**Moss A. E.** not out	7		
	B 4, l-b 4	8	B 6	6
	Total	249	Total (3 wkts. dec.)	241

RUNS AT FALL OF WICKET—
1st Inn. 1—99, 2—106, 3—114, 4—142, 5—156, 6—179, 7—207, 8—212, 9—242, 10—249
2nd Inn. 1—80, 2—89, 3—126

ANALYSIS OF BOWLING—1st Innings

NAME	O.	M.	R.	W.			O.	M.	R.	W.
Ridgway	31	9	86	3		Ridgway	22	8	59	0
Mallett	20	5	58	0		Mallett	27	8	65	0
Dovey	19.5	4	36	2		Dovey	20	4	64	2
Wright	30	8	61	5		Wright	11	2	47	1

KENT—1st Innings

	1st Innings		2nd Innings	
1	**Fagg A. E.** run out	88	c Compton b Warr	0
2	‡**D. G. Clark** c Compton b Warr	6	run out	3
3	**Ames L. E. G.** c Compton b Warr ...	4	c Moss b Young	131
4	**Hearn P.** st Compton b Sims	17	b Young	30
5	**H. A. Pawson** not out	103	b Warr	57
6	†**Evans T. G.** c Sims b Warr	6		
7	**Woollett A. F.** c Young b Warr	10	not out	0
8	**A. W. H. Mallett** not out	15	b Warr	9
9	**Dovey R. R.** did not bat		not out	5
10	**Wright D. V. P.** ,,			
11	**Ridgway F.** ,,			
	B 4, wd 1	5	B 4	4
	Total (6 wkts. dec.)	254	Total (6 wkts.)	239

RUNS AT FALL OF WICKET—
1st Inn. 1—18, 2—34, 3—77, 4—183, 5—197, 6—232
2nd Inn. 1—0, 2—16, 3—125, 4—211, 5—234, 6—235

ANALYSIS OF BOWLING—1st Innings

NAME	O.	M.	R.	W.	Wd.		O.	M.	R.	W.
Warr	26	8	67	4		Warr	11	1	57	3
Moss	21	4	76	0	1	Moss	5	2	18	0
Sims	16	2	53	1		Sims	14	1	53	0
Young	14	8	15	0		Young	19	3	90	2
Titmus	11	2	38	0		Titmus	0.5	0	4	0
						Edrich	1	0	13	0

UMPIRES—J. T. Bell and H. Elliott   SCORERS—E. Hoskins and J. Murrell

Kent won by 4 wickets

The century of centuries scorecard

two-man Essex attack. Kent totalled 532 and Ray and Peter between them bowled 124 overs and conceded 392 runs.

Tony Pawson, who scored his first county 100 against Essex, was strongly involved in the spectacular denouement at Canterbury. The portents on the dramatic last day of the match against Middlesex offered the slimmest of victory hopes. Les Ames was so far convinced of the inevitability of a draw that he dissuaded his 75-year-old father from travelling by train from his home in Ramsgate. It did seem a futile journey for the old man; but he was to be denied the pleasure of witnessing one of his son's finest innings.

The preliminaries to this tumultuous affair did not cause flutters of anticipation. The declarations by Clark and Edrich were chivalrous in their intent; but practically forlorn gestures. As always, in matches between the two counties, the motions were exemplary in their purpose. Middlesex won the toss on the Wednesday and scored 249. Doug Wright, content in the harmony of his bowling rhythms, was not flattered by his figures of five wickets for 61 runs in 30 overs. Kent lost the wicket of Clark, caught by Leslie Compton behind the wicket off Warr, before the close of play.

On Thursday a developing stand between Fagg and Pawson was abruptly halted by a run-out. In his first season with Kent after the war Pawson had found himself at odds with his professional senior. 'Arthur was a fine bat but a ponderous runner, who hated being called for a short single, which was a

Canterbury, in the 1930s, and the scene of Ames's ultimate triumph in 1950 (L. Ames)

key element in my scoring technique.' In one match Pawson had called for several quick singles, all of which were loudly refused by Fagg. At length Fagg came down the pitch and said: 'Now, Mr. Pawson, you've only come into the side in August. I'm tired out. I've been playing since May. If you call me for any more quick singles, I'll make sure you are run out.'

The run-out which did happen against Middlesex at Canterbury had the usual elements of farce; but it also conveyed Pawson's readier appreciation of the amateur-professional code of conduct. 'We were both in our eighties when I cut a ball, very hard, from Titmus into the covers,' recalled Pawson.

> It was either four or nothing. The shot was brilliantly stopped, and I instantly realised that the fielder was very interested in the prospect of a run-out. Suddenly there was an expletive in my ear—it was Arthur Fagg, who, for some reason best known to himself, had charged down the pitch. For a minute or so we glared at each other. Then I thought: 'Oh, well, the amateur does the honourable thing on these occasions,' and so I walked. I got halfway to the pavilion before I was recalled by the umpire on the right grounds that I had not left my crease. So poor Arthur had to go, and I was able to continue and reach my 100.

Pawson's century enabled Kent to gain a lead of five runs on the first innings before Clark applied the declaration. Middlesex began their second innings just before four o'clock. Edrich and Brown, initially steady and circumspect, were aggressive and bold on the last morning. They shared an

Always happiest on the attack: Ames, the fleet-footed batting adventurer (Kent CCC)

unbroken stand of 115 runs. Middlesex advanced their score to 241 before the second declaration of the match. Kent went in to bat at 12.20, requiring 237 to win in two and a half hours, including the half-hour extension. They made the worst possible start. Fagg was caught behind the wicket off Warr before a run had been scored, and Clark was run out with only 16 runs on the board. Ames was quickly into his stride and Peter Hearn, playing in more dogged fashion, stayed with him until lunch. The target was then 165 runs in 80 minutes.

David Clark recalled his lunchtime instructions to Hearn. 'If runs aren't coming reasonably well, I will wave a handkerchief. This will mean that you must have a slog and either get runs or get out. If we are going too slowly, Les will have to take unnecessary risks.' With Hearn's departure, bowled by Young at 125, Kent were still well behind the clock. Pawson, next man in, bustled to the wicket with the reminder, if he needed one, from his captain 'to run every possible single to get Les going.'

Ames, supported by a partner who responded to every call, produced an astonishing acceleration in the scoring rate. Hurricane hitting rendered the Middlesex bowlers as impotent as net trundlers. Jack Young, a slow left-arm bowler of established skills, conceded 90 runs in 19 overs; and his spin accomplice, Jim Sims, was subjected to only marginally less harsh treatment. When Warr took the new ball Ames struck him mightily for three fours

The three Kent centurions: Colin Cowdrey, Frank Woolley and Ames (Kentish Gazette)

into the Nackington Road end in one over. Jim Swanton watched the run revel as a broadcaster. 'Les was in his favourite role, chasing runs against the clock. He went yards down the wicket to Young and Sims and hit them sweetly past extra cover.' Ames scored 131, including two sixes and 17 fours, out of 211 in exactly two hours. He and Pawson, in an ecstasy of power, added 85 runs in 35 minutes. Kent, incredibly, won by four wickets, and Dovey made the winning hit with seven minutes to spare.

Tony Pawson marvelled at the precision of Ames's batsmanship on this glorious August day at Canterbury. 'The Middlesex bowlers started with one deep mid-off and Les peppered the onside. Then they had one fieldsman on each side, and he hit straighter between them. Eventually they put three men out, and Les was still finding the gaps.'

Pawson also recalled his run-stealing rapport with Ames. 'In such a situation you had to take short runs. Even at his age, I was happier going for them with Les than with certain other batsmen. He was such a good, balanced caller. Either he would respond or stop you straightaway. We were right for each other at Canterbury.'

The lure of the 100th century, however beguiling, was clearly not uppermost in Ames's thoughts in the helter-skelter run gallop. 'Les would always be more interested in Kent winning than whether he got a particular record,'

125

said Pawson. 'At Canterbury we were lost in the race for victory. It was a great occasion for Les, but it was improved by the fact that we beat Middlesex.'

Ames's own version of the events dwelt upon the initiative of Bill Edrich. He maintained that Edrich's intervention (the Middlesex captain bowled one over for 13 runs) at a crucial stage in the Kent innings was the catalyst that sprung open the doors to victory.

> We were well behind the striking rate and a draw appeared inevitable. Bill was never a man to let a game dawdle and he deliberately gave us some runs to help us get up with the clock. He did bring his regular bowlers back; but we didn't stop going. We just played straightforward, uncomplicated cricket. Without Bill's help the match would certainly have fizzled out into a draw.

Tony Pawson, Ames's effervescent ally at Canterbury, was the victim of a jape by the Middlesex players. 'In the way of those days, when Les reached 99, Jack Young offered him a gentle full toss. Les responded in the same manner, pushing it for one rather than hitting it for four.' Pawson completed the run and then went down the wicket to congratulate Ames. A loud appeal went up behind him. Leslie Compton had removed the bails and the umpire's finger was up to signal his dismissal. Pawson, his eyes blazing, returned to his wicket and shook his fist in anger. The Middlesex players rocked with laughter. 'It was only a joke,' they said.

David Clark remembered the tumult of an historic day. After Ames had been dismissed, caught in the deep going for another towering six, the Kent members paid him the signal compliment of standing to applaud him all the way back to the pavilion. The Kent captain had to make a hasty order of champagne to celebrate Les's feat. He had been carrying two cases in his car for some time in hot weather. The century had seemed likely to elude Ames against Middlesex. 'I'm not taking the champagne to Canterbury today,' Clark told his wife. 'It's just being ruined.' At the ground, as it increasingly became clear that he had misjudged the situation, he rang a city caterer to make an urgent plea for a new consignment. The caterer had run out of supplies; but he responded with alacrity when told that a vintage occasion required champagne to toast Kent's hero on his happy day.

Les Ames ought to have retired to the adulation of the Canterbury crowd. Instead, it ended on a note of anti-climax on a bitterly cold day at Gillingham at the start of the 1951 season. 'David Clark persuaded me to play against Notts when I wasn't really fit,' recalled Ames. 'I had stood for most of the Notts innings at square-leg, doing very little running. My back stiffened up.'

Kent's old cricket warrior then stumbled in to bat, scarcely able to place one foot after another. 'I tried to hit a ball round to leg and collapsed in a heap.' It was an undignified exit for a batting adventurer who had caught so many opponents on the hop.

12
A Marvellous Second Innings

*Les was my hero as a kid; he was my hero as a player;
and he is still my hero.*

DEREK UFTON

An admiring assembly of disciples cherish the virtues of Les Ames. In their memories of a wise counsellor he exudes an aura of kindness and commonsense. His qualities as an administrator, it could be argued with some conviction, transcended the bounty of his cricket. The uncompromising perfectionist, in his post-war role of Kent manager, he arrested the decline in the fortunes of the club, and powered it into an era of majestic command.

Ames had, as perhaps his most precious and enduring quality, a rapport with the emerging and ultimately triumphant Kent youth. He did not linger in his illustrious past. The slate had been wiped clean for new challenges. Bridging the generation gap was the keynote of his leadership. There was a smile in his eyes which betrayed the reserved, private man; and he shed the weight of his years in the cut and thrust of banter with boys young enough to be his own children. To his great joy, the barriers were down in a swelling tide of affection and respect. The fact that he could readily accept a joke, often against himself, drew him into the camaraderie of the dressing-room. It endeared him to his young charges, who swung happily but carefully on the leash of his levity. The noose was tightened on other more serious occasions, when he did mount his pedestal, and his seniority was unquestioned.

'Les could join in the fun and be one of the boys,' said one ardent admirer, Colin Page, Ames's assistant manager in the 1960s. Discipline could be relaxed because the Kent players—and later the England tourists under Ames's management abroad—did not abuse the trust placed in them. 'We knew without being told about the perils of taking advantage of Les's good humour,' said Page. 'It was the mark of a great leader that he could be accepted as one of the team and yet remain indisputably the boss.' Alan Knott, another of Les's 'boys', endorsed Page's assessment of Ames. 'Les enjoyed enormous respect from members of our great teams in the 1960s and 1970s when a lesser man doing his job might have been overshadowed by top-class modern cricketers.' Derek Underwood commented: 'Having been a player himself, Les knew enough about people to understand the personalities involved. He was very open, very straight, and, at times, quite hard.'

Graham Johnson was one of the ragging juniors in the interludes of fun. In one match, the West Indian bowler, Joel Garner was jarring the fingers of the flinching batsmen. Johnson, as one of Garner's vanquished opponents, was in impish mood. He ventured to question whether Les would have taken adventurous steps to counter the West Indian. 'I suppose,' he said mockingly, 'you would have gone down the wicket to him.' Ames rose to the bait, his piercing voice was withering in its scorn. He summoned an equally mocking reply. 'Yes, of course, I would. That's the way to play him.' At a time when his sartorially handsome pupils paraded like peacocks before a looking glass, Les would often arrive at the Canterbury ground in one of his old suits. It was a matter of some glee among Kent's young men that he cast a bleak eye on their flamboyance. The preening youngsters cut a splendid dash in their finery; but Ames was defiantly and comically unperturbed. Johnson would roguishly appraise his chief and start the day with a joke. 'I see you've got the new style on today, Les. Is it coming back into fashion?'

Ames roared with laughter at the sally, as he did on another occasion during his playing days. Then he might, with justification, have severely rebuked his tormentor, Peter Hearn. In 1950, his last season, Les was twice dismissed by Cliff Gladwin for nought, against Derbyshire at Derby. 'Peter was the arch clown,' remembered Colin Page. Ames returned disconsolately to the dressing-room for the second time, with the dreaded pair against his name. Hearn maddeningly tapped the table with two soup spoons. He lifted the spoons to his eyes as if wearing spectacles. 'Amo, a pair,' he shouted, with scant regard for the distress of his aggrieved senior. The comedy was aimed to tease rather than offend. Les shrugged off his dismay and joined in the general mirth. 'It was then that I saw a marvellous man who could share a joke even at his own expense. He never showed bad feeling,' said Page.

Ames is widely credited as being one of the few people able to control the ebullience of his Kent and England wicket-keeping successor, Godfrey Evans. In 1950 Evans was at his zenith as a wicket-keeper, breathtakingly acrobatic in his swoops behind the stumps. Les was captain in one game and he watched Evans plunge into a dive to attempt an impossible catch. The ball just eluded his fingers as he sprawled in front of Arthur Fagg at first slip. Evans picked himself up as Ames, standing at second slip, looked on with disdain. 'Gawd,' said Les, 'another one put down. I don't know.' The deadpan humour was not without purpose. As Colin Cowdrey related, Ames could be startlingly direct in his response to a situation. 'He was a hard judge on himself and others. He would never let Godfrey get away with anything.' Les would often disarmingly mingle jest and truth. He was not unduly impressed with Evans's spectacular but abortive dive. 'If you are going to put it down,' he told Godfrey, 'I should let it go to first slip.'

David Clark, the chairman of the Kent cricket committee when Ames was appointed county manager in 1957, considered that Les's astute business brain contributed most to his success in this capacity. Ames, with other commitments, was a reluctant convert to the Kent management, a post unknown in county cricket at that time. The offer of the appointment, at the instigation of the newly installed captain, Colin Cowdrey, did involve a serious appraisal. Initially Ames was recruited to bring his vast experience to guide a faltering team. The challenge, with Kent trudging glumly in the foothills, was of Everest-like proportions. It was, of course, irresistible for a man of Ames's temperament. He was ideally fitted to combat the crisis. Colin Cowdrey was the immediate beneficiary: the presence of Ames at his side brought comfort and reassurance during a difficult apprenticeship as Kent captain.

Cowdrey, at 24, was a prodigiously talented cricketer; but he faced potential hazards in his relationship with senior and ageing players. 'The fact that Les was around meant that they wouldn't take me to the cleaners,' he said. During the early years of the Ames-Cowdrey association it was Les who bore the brunt of the disciplinary tasks. 'Colin was very good tactically on the field; but he hated ticking off a player,' remembered David Clark. By contrast, Ames could be imperious, the steel of his nature fairly but unswervingly bringing offenders to attention. 'Les was tough', recalled Clark. 'If an individual or the team had had a bad day, he would use the appropriate strong language. But he would do it.'

Cowdrey remembered the ease of their alliance on team selection issues. Les generally took a relaxed view on such matters, not wishing to obstruct or dissuade his young captain in his choices. In games which went awry there was never any question of the Kent manager hovering at his shoulder and expressing the concern which comes with hindsight. There were, however, times when Ames would emphatically present the claims of a promising second team player. This would be discussed amicably over a drink; but Les would not countenance any reluctance. 'He has got to play in three or four games and we must give him our full backing,' was the instruction. Les would add: 'If it doesn't work out, we will at least possess knowledge of his ability at first team level. Then we will be able to make a judgement on his future at the end of the season.' 'You would never disagree,' said Cowdrey. 'If he wanted his way he would insist but he did not abuse this prerogative.'

David Clark and Colin Cowdrey both remembered the fusion and unity and sense of purpose as Kent began the long haul to prosperity. Stuart Chiesman, as the zestful chairman of the county committee, was the fourth member of an industrious group. 'Nearly all the work, apart from major policy decisions, was carried out by us,' said Clark. 'The day-to-day running of the club was really done by Les. If he wanted advice or help he would ring one or other of us. Our regime did work: it was quick and so much better than having long meetings and discussions when 60 per cent of the people present wouldn't know what we were talking about.' Clark, as cricket committee chairman, smoothed the progress of Ames and Cowdrey in his dealings with the club committee. 'They had to liaise with David,' said Cowdrey. 'If they felt strongly on some matter, he would relay their comments to Les and myself.' Cowdrey stressed the vital importance of this consultative process. 'I don't think a captain should be isolated or on his own. It is too difficult. You need support and help. Certainly, I needed Les Ames if I wasn't on the right lines.'

There was an early gain in the tight control of Kent's financial budget when Ames became secretary-manager in December, 1960. Deficits, some caused by implausible and inept reckoning, were speedily erased. Within a year Ames was able to announce to an astounded Kent treasurer, Leslie Cremer, that he had not only balanced the books, but had made a profit of £9,000. Les admitted that his fiscal prescription, involving as it did some severe weeding, had to be pursued with a degree of ruthlessness. 'I was never one to throw money away; I cannot bear waste.' His business instincts, sharply honed outside cricket, served Kent well in this transitional period. He instantly relished his new role. 'The club was in a financially parlous state. I had to make a bit of a success of the job. There was only one way to go—and that was up.' At Les's side in the rescue operation was the meticulous Bert Crowder, a former Army major of a loyal if fiery disposition. 'He was an absolutely first-class assistant. I couldn't have done all I did without Bert,' recalled Ames. 'He was so good at dealing with mundane tasks such as writing up the minutes. He would make copious notes and enjoyed the exercise, which I found irksome when he was away on holiday.' Les could also rely upon Crowder to efficiently run the Canterbury office when he was absent at cricket weeks at Folkestone, Tunbridge Wells and Maidstone.

During his onerous assignment as Kent manager Ames was never too busy to extend the hand of hospitality to all who came to Canterbury. One man, then living in London, travelled to Kent to watch a match against Middlesex. He had not booked accommodation for his visit and called in to the county club office to seek advice. Les spent more than half an hour on the telephone, trying unsuccessfully to obtain lodgings for the supporter. 'I'm not going to be beaten,' said Ames. 'You've come down from Middlesex to see the cricket and it is the least I can do to see that you get a decent place to stay.' Eventually he had to admit defeat in his quest and expressed his apologies. The visitor did find bed and breakfast accommodation near Canterbury railway station. On the following morning he returned to the ground. Ames had not forgotten the needs of his caller. He had discovered a hotel with vacancies and a room had been provisionally booked for the next two nights. 'Les Ames was involved in everything and genuinely interested in people. Nothing was too much trouble for this likeable and kindly man,' recalled the cricket follower.

In his term as manager, Ames was happy to delegate the coaching responsibilities first to Derek Ufton and then Colin Page. But he always kept a fatherly eye on the emerging Kent players in the 1960s. Derek Underwood was the last of Les's 'boys', when he retired in 1987. Underwood, interestingly and probably later to Surrey's chagrin, was recommended to Kent by one of his early tutors, Tony Lock. 'Les stood behind the net at my trial. He thought I was quite a promising batsman.' In his apprentice years Underwood was aware that there was a 'powerhouse behind the scenes'. 'Les was always wandering around the nets and keeping a close eye on our progress.' Alan Knott, like his great bowling ally, Underwood, was a member of the Kent Schoolboys' XI. Both players had boyhood allegiances to Surrey's magnificent team in the 1950s. Ames at first advised Knott to concentrate on his off-spin bowling. The advice was more specifically aimed at keeping options open, as Knott embarked on a distinguished career. Les watched Knott keep wicket, standing up, in a junior match at Canterbury. Knott made one especially outstanding catch, which elicited a surprised reaction from Ames. 'However did you get to that one, young man?' was his typically guarded commendation. Even so, it was a tribute to treasure. A whisper of praise from Ames was worth more than a gush of gratuitous compliments from anyone else.

Knott was one of the most enterprising improvisers, notably when England were in the doldrums. He was spared the perils of over-coaching in Kent. He was encouraged, in the manner of his illustrious mentor, to use his feet to the spinners. The maxim of grasping the initiative as a batsman was an early and profitable lesson.

Ames, in common with many of his Test contemporaries, had won his spurs through natural ability. His cricket background, coupled with an impatient nature, made him both distrustful of the fruits of coaching and ill-equipped to deal with the wide-ranging aspects of the development of Kent's young cricketers. 'I was never interested or much in favour of coaching,' he recalled. 'You can make a mediocre player into a goodish cricketer; but you need a certain temperament and mental toughness to succeed in the first-class game.' Ames strongly maintained that the key to progress was to play in better class cricket.

Such reservations, as Ames gratefully accepted, did not extend to the productive nursery of the Association of Kent Cricket Clubs. This was first mooted by Bryan Valentine and it flourished through the devoted service of the secretary, Jack Overy. Claude Lewis, later to become the county scorer, brought his zeal and kindly influence to bear in his post-war years as the Kent coach. Les Ames watched and encouraged the rigorous scouting and coaching campaigns, which yielded a crop of outstanding prospects. Many of these young men were to usher Kent into happy times.

Derek Ufton was Godfrey Evans's deputy as Kent wicket-keeper in the 1950s. A shoulder injury in 1958 led to his displacement by Tony Catt and he resisted an offer from Sussex before being offered the captaincy of the county second eleven in 1959. He occupied this post and that of Ames's assistant for 18 months before being restored to the first eleven. Ufton remembered how the blow of being dropped from the first team was softened by his close association with Ames. 'Les wanted the second team to be run on more professional lines. He was always fair and honest and superb to work for, and supportive in every way.' Ufton provided a tribute which emphasised the uniqueness of a special man. His boyhood hero did not have feet of clay. 'With complete honesty, I could say that Les was my hero when I was a kid; he was my hero as a player; and he is still my hero today.'

Ufton, who also played football for Charlton Athletic, was encouraged by Kent to develop his wicket-keeping after the retirement of Howard Levett in 1947. He kept regularly in Army cricket during his National Service. He ousted his Kent rival, Catt, to succeed Evans as the Kent wicket-keeper in 1960. He played in 60 successive games and was third in the national wicket-keeping averages with 90 dismissals, one behind the then England wicket-keeper, John Murray, in 1961. As a young cricketer Ufton had no aspirations towards wicket-keeping and played as a left-handed batsman. His model was another left-hander, Leslie Todd, a punishing batsman on occasions. In the view of Kent historian, R. L. Arrowsmith, Ufton, who scored nearly 4,000 runs in a chequered career, was good enough to have been played frequently as a batsman alone. Ufton recalled his term as deputy to Evans. 'Godfrey was quite unique as a wicket-keeper. He did fantastic things behind the stumps. He was not all that consistent at county level in a poor Kent team. But it was very hard for him to raise his game on his return from Test match duties. However, when Godfrey did turn it on, he was absolutely unbelievable.' Ufton's retirement in 1963 coincided with the emergence of Derek Underwood and in the following season Alan Knott moved into the limelight to quell any doubts about the wicket-keeping succession in Kent.

Colin Page succeeded Ufton as the Kent Second XI captain and served as assistant manager before assuming overall charge on Ames's retirement in 1974. Page described Les as his 'cricketing father' and recalled how his idol had directed him along a new administrative career path. 'Les was a pillar of strength and a great delegator. If you needed help, he was always there to guide you. He did not interfere with my running of the Second XI. But I never neglected to advise him of my plans. It was a privilege to spend so many years with a person of his calibre.' Page said Ames was a quiet man as a manager. 'When it was necessary he could cut people down to size. Les was perfect for the job because he had the complete confidence of everyone in Kent.' Derek Underwood also considered that Ames's strength of character transformed the administration of the club. 'A successful club is a happy club, and Les played his part there. He was very shrewd and sensitive in his dealings with people. Only eleven of us could play for Kent. He was keenly aware that those left out had to maintain their morale and be kept on top of the situation.'

Colin Page also reflected on the paradox of a retiring man, who, on first acquaintance, appeared austere and aloof. As his relationship with Ames grew he came to realise that this was a shy facade which masked a genuine spirit. Utterly unpretentious, Ames was equally at home, swopping yarns in the public bar, as he was conferring with his cricket peers at Lord's. 'He is never out of place in any company,' said Page.

Through the barren years in Kent, Ames was drawn inexorably into the struggle to restore the county's pride. The corner was turned in the 1960s when Kent moved steadily up the championship ladder to finish as runners-up to Yorkshire in two successive seasons (1967 and 1968). In 1967 they won the Gillette Cup for the first time, beating Somerset by 32 runs at Lord's. The victory heralded a remarkable run of successes in one-day competitions. Kent won the Gillette Cup again in 1974, a fitting and memorable finale to Les Ames's reign as county manager. They were John Player League champions in two successive seasons in 1972 and 1973 and winning finalists in the Benson and Hedges competition in 1973.

The foundations for these achievements had been diligently and patiently laid by Ames, Cowdrey and Page. The emergence of Underwood and Knott, the vibrant champions of Kent's revival, was an enormous stroke of luck, in the words of Colin Cowdrey. 'Neither Les, Colin, nor I, could take credit for these talents. The good Lord dropped them into Kent.' Alan Dixon, Brian Luckhurst, Norman Graham, Mike Denness, Graham Johnson and Bob Woolmer were other key players who reached maturity as Kent slowly put together the pieces in their jigsaw. An invigorating blend was given two vital ingredients with the recruitment of Pakistani stylist, Asif Iqbal and West Indian, John Shepherd. Asif had first come to the notice of Kent as a member of the Pakistan Eaglets team which beat the county by an innings at Dartford in 1963. In the later eventful years Les Ames responded enthusiastically to the urgency of the dashing Asif. 'You bat like I did, only more gracefully,' he told him. Shepherd was a 16-year-old when he was discovered by Ames on a Cavaliers' tour of Barbados. He was essentially a product of the Kent nursery, groomed and nurtured by Colin Page and his staff. 'If you took Shep out of our team, you would have cut out its heart,' recalled Page. Derek Underwood also acknowledged the value of Shepherd, one of the most respected of all-rounders, in Kent's piping time of triumph. Even more significantly, he believed that Les Ames recognised, before most others, the importance of the all-rounder in the modern game.

In 1970, Kent's centenary year, the omens for the first championship since 1913 were less then propitious. At the beginning of July, to the dismay of their expectant supporters, Kent were bottom of the table. In their first seven championship matches they recorded only one victory. Adding to the unease was the chastening experience of defeat by Sussex, against the odds, in the third round of the Gillette Cup at Canterbury. The subsequent team meeting at Maidstone could not have been recommended to the tender-hearted. Les Ames was in magisterial mood. The variations of his invective can rarely have been excelled. Colin Page was present at the meeting. 'We had played terribly badly in preceding weeks. That day Les blew his top. He got very worked up. He made it very clear what he thought about the situation.' Norman Graham, the lofty north-easterner, gravely replied to the rallying call. 'Ay, manager, you're right. Let's get cracking.'

Colin Cowdrey remembered Ames's blistering broadside. By general consent it was agreed that the remedy—the only way out of the impasse—was to go hell-for-leather for bonus points. 'I shall always think that the spirit generated at that meeting provided the basis for winning the championship,' he said. Kent went on to beat Hampshire and Sussex. They stepped up the tempo in the hectic pursuit of bonus points. In four out of seven victories the acceleration brought over 20 points in each game, and the batting chase culminated in a record 23 points in the last home game against Leicestershire at Folkestone. Within a month Kent had emerged from their turmoil to become serious contenders for the championship. Asif's batting, blazingly defiant and rippling with outrageous adventure, reaped a largesse of bonus points. As Kent's amazing season moved to a thrilling conclusion, Asif forecast that the championship would be decided in their favour at The Oval. Cowdrey, after a dismal personal start to the season, led a full-strength team on a magnificent last lap. He remembered batting with Asif against

Championship tonic: Ames, as the esteemed secretary-manager, toasts Kent's first title since 1913 in the county's centenary year in 1970. Other celebrants are (left to right): David Clark, Colin Cowdrey and the Prime Minister, Edward Heath, who was also a winner in the General Election (L. Ames)

Middlesex at Canterbury. 'What a tragedy the season isn't a week longer. We would win the title the way we are playing now,' he told his colleague. Asif was astonished by his remark. 'No, skipper, you've got it wrong,' he replied. 'We've got enough time. If it was any longer we would get stale.' Asif's prophecy was handsomely fulfilled, and the champagne glasses were lifted at The Oval to toast Kent's first championship for 57 years.

The shadows of the Packer affair cast a blight on Kent and England cricket in 1978. In his reflections on the integrity of Les Ames, Derek Underwood recalled his former manager's fierce defence of his players during the controversy: 'The Kent players involved were told that their contracts would not be renewed at the end of the season. This meant that Les's boys, Knotty, Asif and myself were, to all intents and purposes, going to be sacked.'

Ames was by this time in retirement; but it did not prevent him from standing up at the club's annual general meeting to express 'his repugnance' at the treatment meted out to the players. Underwood remembered the astonishing sight of Ames, the revered elder, being subjected to the jeers of the Kent members. 'Les was very brave. He was being loyal to the players who had done so well for Kent over the years. He knew that we cared and saw very little justification for our sackings.'

Underwood said that Les, as a former player, recognised the overriding claim of security at the heart of the contentious issue. 'Kent were not offering us contracts and this man from Australia was. Les was 100 per cent behind us in a worrying and traumatic time.'

Ames always had a proper respect for authority, except in circumstances which, he considered, placed officialdom in a bad light. An example was Les's involvement with the celebrated Hoppers Club, formed in a fit of pique by the Kent players in 1939. That year the Kent management had brought out a tie, only available, as it transpired, to paid-up members. Les, without knowledge of the qualification, decided he would buy one for his father, who was a Kent member. The manager of the Canterbury shop, where he went to make the purchase, told him that he had received strict instructions that players were not allowed to wear the tie. Les did not want the tie for himself; but he was angry at the disclosure. He went to the county office to protest to the secretary about the discourtesy. Two weeks later the ruling was reversed; it was announced that the players could wear the tie. Before that happened Les consulted with his team-mates. Howard Levett, who was to become a co-founder of the Hoppers Club, shared Ames's indignation. 'We'll have our own tie,' he said. The pattern of the players' tie bears the logos of a beer barrel and hops on a navy background. The tie has to be worn on Mondays—with the forfeit, if caught not wearing it, of buying a drink for the challenger, or challengers. It can be an expensive business if a forgetful member meets an accuser in a playful mood. Les once caught out his close friend, Jack Godden. He enlisted the support of other challengers. Godden, laughing at his friend's effrontery, had to pay up.

The Hoppers Club, which reached its 50th anniversary in 1989, is now a thriving organisation. Its biennial dinner is a convivial event on the cricket calendar. With Ames as the Hop Controller (or president), the club now boasts a membership of around 600 members. The honorary ranks include such personalities as Alec Bedser, Peter May and Denis Compton, among the former cricketers, and writers and broadcasters, Jim Swanton, Peter West and Christopher Martin-Jenkins.

Les Ames travelled along a distinctive highway in the post-war years. His marvellous second innings included a seven-year term as a Test selector, beginning in 1950. He was the first professional cricketer to be accorded this honour. Wilfred Rhodes and Jack Hobbs preceded him but only as co-opted members in the 1920s. Ames served under five chairmen, Bob Wyatt, Norman Yardley, Freddie Brown, Harry Altham and Gubby Allen. At Test and county level Ames was challenging and forthright in his assessments. England players, with seemingly impeccable credentials, were not exempt from his criticism. Any flaws would come under severe scrutiny. Colin Cowdrey and Doug Insole remembered Les as a man who took a well-balanced view of events and people. He was a quick-fire executioner of cricketing myths. Cowdrey believed that Ames, as a selector, would generally extend his advice in a firm but respectful manner. If he disagreed with a choice, he would make it abundantly clear to the other panellists, not excluding the most venerable of luminaries in the Lord's hierarchy. The pattern of the discourse might involve his outright rejection of a selected player. Then he would go along with the majority decision and say: 'I respect your view; I hope I'm wrong. Good luck!'

Gubby Allen, Bob Wyatt and Norman Yardley all considered that Ames was a very sound judge of a cricketer. Allen, who nominated Les as a selector, paid high tribute to his friend and colleague in regarding him as one of the best of his collaborators. Allen's six years as chairman preceded and followed Ames's resignation after taking over the Kent managership. 'We were fortunate in the resources available to us during this time. Selectors are great and captains are good in the years when you have the talents,' said Allen. 'They cannot succeed, through no fault of their own, when the right calibre players don't exist.'

The view has been expressed by Sir Leonard Hutton, England's path-finder captain in the 1950s, and Wilfred Wooller, another fellow selector, that Ames was never patronising in his attitude to players. He did not criticise unfairly or publicly. Hutton, with memories of Ames's kindness when he was injured on his first overseas tour to South Africa in 1938–9, championed his administrative qualities. 'I was delighted that Les was a selector during my time as England captain. He did not dwell in the past, or probe too deeply into the technical abilities of current players.' Norman Yardley considered that Ames's strengths as a selector were in keeping with his style as a player. 'He looked to attack and always advocated candidates with a positive approach to cricket.'

Ames's shrewdness as a selector, in the friendliest of Lord's assemblies, prompted Gubby Allen to offer him the post of chairman. Les had to decline the invitation because of his Kent commitments. Ames regarded his period as a Test selector as a signal honour. It was especially pleasing because it enabled him to maintain his association with international cricket. Aiding him in his tasks were the umpires of the day, former cricket rivals and colleagues—John Langridge, Fred Price, Frank Lee, Sam Pothecary, Sid Buller and Charlie Elliott. Standing as they did, day by day in county cricket, the old umpires were invaluable guides to form and potential.

As a former professional cricketer, Ames was also eavesdropping on a dramatic change in the status of the professional. The elevation of Hutton to the England captaincy in 1952 was an unanimous choice. It was, though, an indication of a new climate. Ames believed that Hutton's appointment was an acceptance of the long-established Australian policy of picking the best team, with the captain included as of right. Until the 1950s England, and most first-class counties for that matter, had persisted in their adherence to the amateur tradition. There were examples of players being given the leadership when they were not worthy of a place in teams. Despite his admiration for Percy Chapman as a man, Ames doubted whether his Kent colleague was ever quite good enough to captain England. Chapman's success in leading one of the finest sides to visit Australia in 1928-9 brought him tremendous acclaim. 'He was fortunate in the talents at his command on that tour. It made him as a captain,' said Ames. 'Percy was a great fielder; he had a delightful personality—and he was an amateur—which clinched the issue until his later decline.'

From his time as a selector Ames nominated Hutton, Compton, Edrich and Washbrook, whose careers bridged the war, as the outstanding batsmen. Peter May, among the post-war breed, earned his accolade as the greatest English batsman. May first unfurled his exceptional talents as a 21-year-old against South Africa at Leeds in 1951. 'His equanimity from first to last, his subordination of self for side, even after completing a century, and his sound technique stamped him as a player well above the ordinary,' commented *Wisden*. The calculated fury of May's driving, his onside dominance, vied with that of another proven master batsman, Leonard Hutton, at Headingley. 'Peter was, perhaps, a better player than Hammond against fast bowling,' recalled Ames. 'Australian bowlers like Lindwall and Miller might have worried Wally even in his prime. In his great years he did not have to face such hostile bowling. On the other hand, May's talents might not have prospered as they did, had he been faced with the spin of O'Reilly and Grimmett.'

England countered the menace of Lindwall and Miller with the ferocity of Trueman and the injury-prone Tyson (regarded by Ames as the quickest bowler in the world for three years). Statham was the immaculate foil at the other end, his unyielding accuracy contributing to the shattered morale of opponents. Peter Loader, spotted by Ames at The Oval, was another outstanding prospect whose Test opportunities were limited in days when fast bowlers hunted in pairs rather than quartets.

Ames ranked his Kent wicket-keeping successor, Godfrey Evans, as a 'keeper of unparalleled excellence in the post-war era. Jim Laker, in his later, brilliant years, he considered as probably the finest off-spinner in his experience. Along with the late Bill Bowes, he judged that the Yorkshireman, Bob Appleyard, deserved the rating of one of the finest bowlers in the history of the game. Bowes linked Appleyard with O'Reilly and S. F. Barnes as an unsurpassed trio. 'I would have picked Appleyard in any England side,' said Ames. 'He was a magnificent bowler, amazingly versatile with his quick off-breaks and awayswingers, and he bowled a slower one which was difficult to detect.'

One of the most controversial issues of the 1950s involved the rivalry between Tony Lock and Johnny Wardle for the place as England's slow left-arm bowler. Wardle was incensed at the preference given to Lock, despite the Surrey bowler's dubious and widely considered illegal action. Ames, as a selector, conceded a measure of regret at the opportunities denied to Wardle. He did not shrink from shouldering blame in the choice of Lock through the 1950s. Explaining the dilemma, he said:

> There was a big question mark against Lock. But we had to rely upon the umpires, who were the real adjudicators, and they only called Lock once in England. In any event, it was a big decision for the chairman of the selectors. If we had come out with a statement that Lock was to be omitted because he threw, there was a danger of being sued for jeopardising his livelihood.

Given the acceptance of Lock, however vexing the circumstances, Ames believed that he was more dangerous as an orthodox slow left-arm bowler, especially in England. Lock also had the advantage of being a superb fieldsman close to the wicket. Wardle's great asset, only fully realised towards the end of his career with Yorkshire and England, was his remarkable control in his unorthodox style. 'When he bowled in this manner he was unfailingly accurate. He always seemed to drop the ball on the spot,' recalled Ames. 'As an exponent of the chinaman and assorted googlies, he was undoubtedly in the great class.'

The series against Australia in England in 1956 was dominated by Laker's record-breaking achievement of 19 wickets in the fourth Test at Old Trafford. It included 10 wickets in the second innings, the first time this had been recorded in a Test match. Laker also took 10 wickets for 88 runs for Surrey against the Australians at The Oval. The extent of his dominance can be gauged from the fact that in seven matches he took 63 wickets against the tourists.

Australia won the second Test at Lord's by 185 runs and made a rousing start in the next match at Leeds. England lost three wickets, those of

Richardson, Cowdrey and Oakman dismissed by Archer, for 17 runs in the first hour. They were rescued by the 41-year-old Cyril Washbrook, an England selector and a heavily criticised choice for the match. Washbrook, in his first Test appearance for five years, survived two chances to score 98. He added 187 for the fourth wicket with Peter May in what was to prove a match-winning partnership. Laker and Lock shared 18 wickets, as England won by an innings and 42 runs.

Wilf Wooller, a member of the Test selection committee in 1956, remembered the foreboding of the selectors, including Ames, after the tumble of England wickets. 'Les took his selection duties very seriously. By the time we got to Headingley England were in deep trouble. Les was threatening to go home (perhaps only half in jest), but May and Washbrook saved the day and we went on to win the Ashes.' Ames also recalled the tremors of anxiety at Leeds. 'Washbrook played beautifully. He couldn't have gone in at a worse time. The Aussies had their tails up.'

At Manchester the selectors made another inspired choice in recalling the Reverend David Sheppard. Sheppard, after going into the ministry, had almost completely severed his connection with first-class cricket. He had played only four innings for Sussex before the Old Trafford Test. One of the curiosities of the match was that the first five England batsmen were all amateurs. (The last time this had happened against Australia was in 1899, when Fry, MacLaren, Ranjitsinhji, Townsend and Jackson had gained selection.) An opening stand of 174 between Cowdrey and Richardson paved the way for a resplendent century by Sheppard. It was an innings of unquenched mastery; a precise sermon in batting, which gave no hint of lack of match practice. Before the end of the first day there were ominous signs of a crumbling wicket. Accusations were made that the pitch had been specially prepared for England's spin bowlers and these were denied by the Lancashire authorities. Ian Johnson, the Australian captain, maintained a commendable dignity amid the bitterness. After the match he said: 'When the controversy and the side issues are forgotten, Laker's wonderful bowling will remain.' Ames recalled: 'The Australians were not good players against off-spin. They did rather give up the ghost. The top of the wicket went after the first day. Jim, with his marvellous control, turned the ball at right angles.' Laker, in a flash of vintage humour, slyly took his spinning partner, Tony Lock to task. 'Lockie spoilt my day by taking one wicket and depriving me of all 20.'

One of the mysteries of the match was the failure of Lock to exploit the conditions. It was rumoured that such was his self-disgust that he did not speak to Laker for several weeks following the Test at Old Trafford. 'Lock turned the ball too much at Manchester,' said Ames. 'In his frustration he bowled too short. Godfrey Evans was at times having to take the ball shoulder high behind the wicket.' Bill O'Reilly, the great Australian leg-spinner, in another context, endorsed Ames's verdict. 'Big spin on the ball is not worth a candle. The telling factor is accuracy. All a bowler needs to do is just move the ball. If a batsman finds he is not getting you in the middle of the bat he starts to worry.'

O'Reilly and Ames were old hands in the allurements of spin, the one as a deadly practitioner, and the other either as a keeper of its secrets behind the wicket, or as a batsman who danced to glory or doom in his attempts to conquer it.

13
RIOTS IN PAKISTAN

Les emerged from a sorry experience with great honour.
I do not like to think what would have been the outcome
with a less able manager.

E. M. WELLINGS

L es Ames's unflappability and powers of diplomacy as a tour manager established him as a cricket statesman of the highest stature on three MCC tours in the 1960s. Colin Cowdrey, the England captain on two of the tours—to the West Indies and Pakistan—admired his Kent senior's sternly honest dealings with overseas authorities.

Ames possessed a priceless, instinctive gift of communication which averted a major crisis on the riot-strewn tour of Pakistan in 1969. 'One of the things that helped me in the troubles was the fact that I had been through the mill myself as a Test player,' he said. His international reputation as a cricketer and the friends he had made over a long career did assist him in steering his ship through the roughest of waters. 'He could be unnervingly direct,' said Colin Cowdrey. 'But he was never arrogant or rude. He could make his hosts laugh and respect him. He was superb and as independent with them as he was with us as a team. They trusted him absolutely in a way I cannot measure.'

The MCC tour of Ceylon and Pakistan, which replaced the cancelled visit to South Africa, was an ill-fated venture. After the serenity of a successful four-match tour of Ceylon, Ames and his team were pitched into a country in a state of turmoil and student unrest. The contrast between the two tours was alarming. Michael Melford, writing in *The Cricketer*, said 'an evil genie seemed to brood over everything that happened. This was no time for a cricket tour. Yet it was not for the MCC manager and captain to call it off. There was no apparent hostility towards the MCC or Britain in general but one of the most likely events to have changed this was a cancellation of the tour.'

Towards the end of the stay in Ceylon, the reports of riots in Pakistan grew and the East Pakistan section of the tour was initially called off. Unsuccessful attempts were made to delay the departure from Colombo. Two days before the team flew on to Karachi on Sunday, 2 February, Ames received a cable from the Pakistan Board of Control suggesting substitute fixtures in Bahawalpur and Lyallpur. He replied that he would prefer the

Ames, the MCC tour manager, whose gifts of diplomacy earned him high praise on the riot-strewn tour of Pakistan in 1969 (Sport and General)

team to stay in Karachi for a few days, to give him time to appraise the fluctuating events. On the Monday Ames and Cowdrey spent almost the entire day in consultation with the Deputy High Commissioner, the Commissioner of Karachi and over the telephone with Fida Hassan, the President of the Board and, at this time of political tension, adviser to President Ayub Khan. It seemed likely that the tour would be abandoned; but eventually it was agreed to play the match at Bahawalpur.

E. M. Wellings, a London cricket correspondent on the tour, recalled the first two rescheduled games at Bahawalpur and Lyallpur.

> They were peaceful but the living conditions were bad, but not as deplorable as those at Sahiwal, where fortunately play was abandoned on the second day through torrential rain, and the side could travel to Lahore, which was far from peaceful. There were riots in the town and trouble on the ground during the first Test.

The Lahore Test, frequently interrupted by the rebellious students, was drawn. 'Concentration was almost impossible,' wrote Melford, 'and Cowdrey's 100 after England had lost three wickets for 113, was quite a feat in the circumstances.' The police at Lahore could not contain the disruptions. It was left to Aftab Gul, a student leader and the Pakistani opening batsman to quieten the crowd. After he had been dismissed by Underwood, he went over to one of the noisiest of the stands and managed to achieve a measure of peace. 'Here was a young man who, if he lifted his hand, could stop or start a riot,' commented Derek Underwood. Aftab Gul was then, ironically, a law student at Punjab University. He was the first player to appear in first-class cricket while on bail for alleged political activities. He enjoyed a vast following as a student leader and it was said that the Pakistan officials did not dare to stage the Lahore Test without him.

Politics loomed again when pressure was exerted on the MCC to go to Dacca in East Pakistan, even though the state of emergency there had not been lifted. There was no actual proposition from the Pakistan Board; but Ames and Cowdrey deemed it unwise and hazardous to embark on another Test on the following Friday, as was one suggestion, at a venue 1,000 miles away and with only a day separating the two Tests. This cricketing reason was accepted by the High Commissioner. However, Ames was then asked to issue a statement explaining that the MCC would, after all, be going to Dacca. There had been much resentment in East Pakistan at the previously abandoned fixture, much of it from the East–West rivalry and directed at the government officials in West Pakistan rather than the MCC. In a speech next day Ames maintained that he had not been officially approached by the Board to visit Dacca, a statement which was denied by Fida Hassan. Later in the week during which the Lahore Test was being played, Ames was asked to switch the last Test from Karachi to Dacca. Ames's response was to fly to Rawalpindi for a belated interview with Hassan. The MCC considered it important from a cricket point of view to play in Karachi, along with Lahore, one of the major cricket centres in Pakistan. The proposed switch was yet more evidence of the intrusion of politics.

Melford wrote:

> The MCC were at last able to address themselves to the what should have been the overriding issue of the tour, the winning of the Test series. On numerous occasions previously when it had seemed that the tour might be about to end, or when a wrangle was taking place about where the Tests should be played, it had been very hard to concentrate on the main business. It was a preparation for a Test series which in modern times must be without precedent.

Wellings related that the second Test in Dacca was played on an unworthy pitch, in a town in a rebellious mood. Even so, Ames had been assured by the High Commissioner that Dacca was peaceful and that the army and the police were in full control. Wellings wrote:

> The team could blame only the High Commissioner that they were exposed to the perils. The Deputy High Commissioner was astonished by our arrival. He had told his senior well in advance that Dacca and

the whole of East Pakistan was in a state of dangerous confusion and that he was making plans to evacuate those Britons who were in the south around Chittagong.

The situation, according to Wellings, was that the MCC team were 'virtually prisoners' of a students' committee which had taken over in Dacca. The army's nearest forces were 15 miles away, and the police were off the streets, which were largely deserted.

Ames recalled: 'We had had some demonstrations in Lahore and then we were due to go to Dacca, which was supposed to be the worst place of all. Quite a number of people had been killed in the political furore. It was touch and go whether we went there.'

The match was run by the student leaders. Ames had a number of meetings with them before allowing the game to go ahead. 'They seemed a jolly, nice set of chaps, all young between 18 and 19. I may have been naive. But I was assured that if I agreed to their taking control, there would be no trouble.' It was a situation calling for restraint and care. Ames was nervous about the outcome. For the first and only time as a tour manager he contacted Lord's to point out his dilemma. 'We understand all your troubles out there, Les,' was the reply. 'We shall back you in whatever you decide to do.' Ames did not find the message from headquarters especially comforting; but he remembered his surge of bravado afterwards. 'Bloody Englishmen have never run away from anything,' he said to one of the tourists. 'And I'm not going to capitulate. Come on, let's go.' Ames's decision was not a popular one: there was intense pressure from the cricketers' wives back home, who were understandably worried about reports of fatalities in the region and the safety of their husbands.

Derek Underwood remembered a reception at the High Commissioner's home on the eve of the Dacca Test. 'We were told that troops were at hand if danger threatened. In the event, there was no trouble and this was one Test which proceeded, against expectations, without any disturbance at all.' John Snow and David Brown shared seven wickets in bowling out Pakistan for 246. England lost seven wickets for 130 on a deteriorating wicket before Basil D'Oliveira, assisted by Snow, Underwood and Pocock, brought welcome resistance. D'Oliveira struck an unbeaten century, holding on valiantly for three and three-quarter hours, and the match was drawn.

During the earlier riots in Lahore Ames narrowly escaped a serious injury as he left the stand at one interval. 'It could have been pretty nasty,' he recalled. 'I was coming down an outside staircase when the leg of a chair came flying just beside me. If it had hit me I would certainly have been badly hurt. The blow would also have knocked me off balance and resulted in a heavy fall down the steps.'

Ames soldiered on, carrying an awesome burden, until the ugliest riot of all—on the third day of the Karachi Test in March—brought the tour to an end. The MCC tourists, along with the rest of the townspeople, were subject to a nightly curfew and not allowed out of their hotel. Underwood remembered a bizarre and extraordinary climax to the tour. 'It was quite ridiculous. The best part of it was that we batted for three days until the final riot finished it.' England totalled 502 for 7. Colin Milburn, whose jaunty humour had done much to keep his team-mates cheerful, reached a magnificent century. Then came the first pitch invasion which held up play for 50 minutes.

'It was already clear that the match was unlikely to be finished,' reported *The Cricketer.* Another half-hour was lost on the second day. Alan Knott, who finished on 96, and Brown were engaged in the most exhilarating stand of the series when the game was abandoned on the third day. 'It had seemed that the spark for the final explosion might be kindled by Knott's 100,' ran another report. 'But before that well-deserved distinction could be achieved a mob arrived from outside the ground, swarming over the railings. Hundreds of youths, some with red banners, advanced on the pitch as the players fled. They seized the stumps, tried to dig up the pitch, and wrecked the VIP stand.' The object of the invasion was allegedly to stop cricket being played during a strike in support of teachers. Brian Johnston, who was commentating on Pakistan television, remembered abandoning his attempts to describe the scenes of vandalism. 'I made my way hurriedly to the back of the England dressing-room. We were locked in there for quite some time with all the uproar going on outside.' Les Ames also recalled the violent and frightening occasion. 'They came over in their hordes. The president of the Pakistan Cricket Board came into our dressing-room and said: "The tour is finished." I didn't disagree with him.'

The MCC team and the accompanying cricket correspondents were eventually smuggled out of the ground. A small fleet of overcrowded cars whisked a relieved assembly back to their hotel. By a miracle of resource Ames was able to arrange a flight home later in the evening. 'As usual he was calm and efficient and we all owed him a debt of thanks for handling the situation so well,' added Johnston.

In retrospect Ames believed that the Pakistan cricket authority did not appreciate the extent of the students' dissension. 'I don't basically think there was any animosity or that the riots were directed against the team. A cricket match, with 20,000 people in attendance, was a focal point at which the students could air their grievances and stir up trouble.'

The strength and resolve displayed by Les Ames on a formidable and exacting managerial assignment earned him tributes in many quarters. In Pakistan he was praised for his unflagging efforts to continue the tour. Derek Underwood, one of his Kent cricket graduates, marvelled at his composure in circumstances of extreme provocation. 'I cannot think from a manager's point of view that there has ever been a tougher tour.'

E. M. Wellings also reflected on Ames's calmness and skill in the crisis. 'Les emerged from a sorry experience with great honour. I do not like to think what would have been the outcome with a less able manager. He had a mammoth task contending with British diplomats, Pakistan officials and unofficial bodies such as the students' committee in Dacca.'

As a result of Ames's leadership, the England team left for home with a clear conscience. In a rare departure from modesty, Les recalled his delight at the letter he received from the MCC committee which congratulated him on his conduct of the tour. 'I was very proud of keeping the show on the road,' he said.

14
MASTER OF ARTS

The memories of his career are precious because he belongs to an era of quality, which I fear has gone forever.

LEO O'BRIEN, *the former Australian Test cricketer.*

A stately procession wormed its way slowly down the aisle of Canterbury Cathedral. Les Ames was on the winner's path once again among the congregation of robed celebrants. In a moving and colourful ceremony he was invested with the honorary degree of Master of Arts by Kent University.

'Games are a metaphor for life,' said the public orator, Professor Colin Seymour-Ure, on this day of distinction in November 1988. In his citation he reflected on the fact that English was rich in the imagery of cricket. Students were 'stumped' by examination questions as were examiners by the answers. Moralists urged people to play with a 'straight bat' unless they wanted to be trapped on a 'sticky wicket'. The rallying cries had become sporting cliches of everyday usage. Fulfilment in Les Ames's own sporting quest had come as a result of 'his marvellous attitude to life and his enduring professionalism'.

Ames had written many years ago of the importance of the will to succeed: 'If you think you can, then you can.' 'Such character bred enjoyment not only for himself but for the thousands who relished his game—moving the score sweetly and swiftly along, never slogging but with all the shots in the book; or clipping a bail to stump yet another victim with a typical lack of ostentation.'

The ceremony of honour was yet another signal of respect for a revered sportsman. It followed his term as Kent president—he was the first former professional to occupy the post in 1975—and the award of the CBE for his services to cricket two years earlier. Other celebrations followed on his 80th birthday when this milestone was acknowledged by two dinners in Kent and a reception, hosted by Earl Attlee at the House of Lords, which was attended by a distinguished assembly of cricket friends.

At the degree presentation in the time-hallowed setting of Canterbury Cathedral, Les was quietly thrilled by the remembrance of his exploits. He remembered how his feet, unaccustomed to the snailpace walk, trembled as he moved forward to receive his award. Although he did not say so, there

SIR DONALD BRADMAN, A.C.

30—10—85.

Mr. F. C. Bernardes,
32 Albemarle Road,
BECKENHAM.

Dear Mr. Bernardes,

I understand that on 30th November next you will be chairing a celebration dinner to honour Les Ames, the President of the Kent County Cricket Supporters Club, and that he will be celebrating his 80th birthday on December 3rd.

Might I take the liberty of saying that I would like to be identified with these occasions by sending this brief letter of greetings and good wishes.

As you are well aware Les and I were friendly adversaries in the International Cricket World more than fifty years ago. Although I chased far too many runs off his very broad bat and suffered from his safe and slick hands behind the stumps we have remained staunch friends over that long period.

Please convey to him my best wishes for a very happy birthday and I trust the dinner will fittingly celebrate the occasion.

With warmest regards,

Yours sincerely,

A letter of congratulation from Sir Donald Bradman on Ames's 80th birthday

*Canterbury distinction: Invested with the honorary degree of Master of Arts by
Kent University in November 1988 (University of Kent)*

was surely also at least a quiver of apprehension at this salute to a modest
man.

His nimble feet, which sallied merrily down the wicket in his playing days,
now carry him briskly on his morning walks over nine miles to his boyhood
village of Elham. At the King's Arms he catches up on the local gossip over a
pint of beer before, as a concession to his years, he boards the bus back
home to Canterbury. All of his contemporaries admire and envy the vigour
of his old age. He is to be found on the hottest of summer days, tending his
garden for long hours. It is a joke among friends, which he secretly relishes,
that his immaculate lawn is not his own achievement but that of the county
club groundsman at Canterbury. His physical stamina is quite amazing.
Gubby Allen, a close and devoted companion, considered him to be one of
the sprightliest octogenarians he had ever known.

Les has always been temperate in his habits although it was well-known
that he enjoyed a gin and tonic or two and a night out with the boys in his
playing days. In their horseplay at the end of an arduous season, as Derek
Underwood recalled, Kent's young men might overstep the bounds of propriety and break a few glasses in away dressing-rooms. A bill for damages
would arrive on the Kent manager's desk. 'How can I tell these boys off?,' Les
would ponder as he remembered his own frolics as a player. Ames did not
encourage irresponsibility; but he was never a puritan. He would join in the
revels at the close of play with the most extrovert of colleagues during his
time as player and manager. 'Les did look after himself,' said former Kent

149

colleague, Howard Levett. 'But I've known him take a snooze in the dressing-room and then go out and make a hundred, which was anything but sleepy.'

Tom Pearce and Tony Pawson both remembered Les's dry wit, never in any way malicious, and how he delighted in other people's humour on cricket's social round. 'You couldn't have had a better friend,' said Pearce, 'He is so reliable.' Les never forgot the friends of his youth. Doug Insole, at the time a young Essex player, provided one instance of Ames's recall. Insole had an uncle, John Galbraith, who had played soccer with Ames at Clapton Orient. Galbraith had asked him to pass on his best wishes to his former football colleague. During an interval in a match against Kent, Insole duly relayed his uncle's message. He was immensely struck by Ames's reaction. 'John Galbraith,' replied Les. 'I've often wondered what happened to him. He was one of the nicest people I have known in sport. Please tell him that and remember me to him.' Insole thought that this was a spontaneously delightful reaction from someone who had become a major international figure to a man with whom he was only briefly acquainted, and who had never had pretensions to anything other than average club standard.

At Les's side, and helping to keep him on his toes, almost literally so, is his vivacious wife, Bunty, a former dancer from Cheshire. It is an engaging partnership. It is illuminating to eavesdrop on their affectionate banter; the cross-talk is often quite hilarious; and they are fierce rivals as jam-makers, which marks the point of Les's rare excursions into her kitchen domain. Bunty's hospitality is legendary as befits a North-country lady. Jack Godden, one of Ames's long-standing friends, is among those captivated by her kindness. 'If you walked into their home in the middle of the night and asked for a meal, she would get up and make you one.' Anger surfaces if you rebuff, however innocently, her generous nature. On one occasion Les was invited to a cricket function with Kent committee member, John Pocock. Bunty was content to be left to her own devices, but not when she heard that Pocock's wife, Joan was also without company. 'Why didn't you bring Joan to spend the evening with me?' inquired Bunty. 'When John protested that he wouldn't presume upon her hospitality without an invitation, Bunty was very cross,' remembered Les.

'Bunty is so proud of Les,' said Colin Page. 'She is steady and sensible and a person who earns your gratitude.' The description offered by Page and other friends of the pair is that she can truly be regarded as the first lady of Kent cricket. As Les, in his years as manager, sought to encourage and nurture the county's young men, Bunty looked after the distaff side. She exercised a soothing influence, ironing out problems and complaints, in her care of the players' wives and girl friends.

As he nears his mid-eighties, Les plays straight down the middle and wields an adept club as a golfer. He is, by all accounts, a mean opponent in his regular rounds on the Royal Cinque Ports Club course at Deal. He plays off a handicap of 15. His score for a round is likely to be lower than his own

Where it all began: Ames revisits his boyhood home at Chichester House, Elham, in 1986 (L. Ames)

age. As he whimsically confirms, this is a task which gets easier with each passing year. Sir Leonard Hutton, among other cricketing friends, shares Ames's passion for golf. They enjoyed many rounds together during the 1938-9 tour of South Africa. On one occasion, playing on a championship course in Durban, Hutton remembered that Les strung together four birdies in an overwhelming start to the round. 'I was four down after four holes. Watching him race ahead, I thought he had taken up the wrong game.'

Wilf Wooller remembered the custom of a golfing foursome on the Sunday of Tests during their days as selectors. They were always keenly contested and could spill over into tantrums at times. Gubby Allen part-nered Walter Robins, a notorious prankster, in one match against Ames and Wooller on a Midlands course during a Test match at Trent Bridge, in the 1950s. Golf is a game which can lead to odd situations and feelings of injustice. This was a round which severely tested Les's good nature. Allen recalled: 'Robbie hit his first ball on the short hole; it was an awful shot and, as usual when this happened, he marched ahead to discover the lie of the ball.' Les also played an indifferent shot. Out on the fairway Robins found his opponent's ball and tossed it, unbeknown to the following trio, into a gorse bush. The position of the ball in the bush was highly suspicious; it did give the appearance of having been placed there.

Robins adamantly denied that he was the culprit. Les was not convinced and did not relent in his accusations as they moved on to the next tee. This

151

was a long hole, with only a solitary tree standing sentinel between them and the distant green. It seemed an unlikely hazard. Les said: 'Well, I can't hit the ball into the gorse this time.' Robins replied: 'No, but I should look out. You might hit the tree.' Les's tee shot did inevitably strike the tree, the ball flying off to the left and out of sight. It was a signal for an outburst of hysterics among his companions. Allen said: 'We just couldn't stop laughing, which was very unfair on poor old Les.' As so often happens on days of mis-adventure, Ames's plight was compounded by the sequel in the clubhouse. The wager on the match was ten shillings but Les could not pay. He had left his money in his coat in the locker room, and it had been stolen. The jesting Robins insisted on payment. 'I don't care whether your money has been pinched. I want my ten bob.'

A truce was eventually declared in this episode. Les was able to shrug off his displeasure. Robins had dared where others would have quailed; his infuriating banter fuelled by Ames's heated remonstrations. When the golf-ing battle was rejoined Les had doubtless worked out an avenging ploy with which to recoup his losses. Gamesmanship, in the rivalry of cricket, would have incurred a withering and less easily assuaged condemnation. On this field, Ames, as a player and onlooker, deplored cheating in any form. 'He played the game in the right spirit,' said Howard Levett. 'I have known him come back to the dressing-room after being given out lbw when he had clearly played the ball.' Ames was stoically quiet on these occasions. Luck would swing his way on another day and Les, wise in such matters, knew that he must not challenge the umpire's authority.

Colin Cowdrey has reflected on Ames's stern apprenticeship in first-class cricket. This formative period did, he believed, contribute to Les's 'no nonsense' approach in his dealings with Kent's young cricketers. As a conscientious man, Ames could never condone falling standards. He could instinctively judge and separate the slackers from the triers. 'If we hadn't played particularly well, Les could be quite scornful. "What a load of rubbish! I hope you do better tomorrow," would be his reflex response.' Even on more successful days Ames would still be circumspect in his reaction to achievements. Only gradually would he lower his guard to deal out the cards of praise. 'He was unerringly direct and would never alter,' said Cowdrey. 'Once you knew him—and this took time—you came to realise that this was his great strength.'

A sense of fairness relieved the austerity of an iron-clad sportsman. Doug Insole recalled one of his early matches for Essex against Kent at Clacton. He was much in awe of Ames's standing as a cricketer. He had also been warned by his county seniors that his Kent opponent was a hard man on the field. Insole was fielding in the slips when Les came in to bat. 'He nicked a ball low to my right and I dived to my right to take the catch very close to the ground. Les did not look at the umpire; he just turned to me and asked: "Did you catch it?" I told him that I had, and off he went without demur.' It was a telling gesture from a gentleman of cricket. Insole has never forgotten his lesson in sportsmanship.

The unyielding honesty which governed all the actions of Les Ames has earned him a legion of friends in Kent and far beyond its borders. If life had a second edition, he would only marginally need to correct his proofs. 'The memories he holds are precious,' said one of his Australian rivals, Leo O'Brien, 'because he belongs to an era of quality, which I fear has gone forever.'

A STATISTICAL SURVEY OF LES AMES'S FIRST-CLASS CRICKET CAREER

Compiled by Peter Wynne-Thomas and Howard Milton

The records and statistics contained in this section conform to the first-class lists of matches as set out in the *Guides to First-class Cricket* compiled by the Association of Cricket Statisticians. The assistance of Philip Bailey in checking the details in this compilation is gratefully acknowledged.

TEST CAREER: INNINGS BY INNINGS

1929 *v* SOUTH AFRICA			Caught/Stumped
5th Test (The Oval)	c Mitchell b McMillan	0	2
1929-30 *v* WEST INDIES			
1st Test (Bridgetown)	b Constantine	16	0
	not out	44	1
2nd Test (Port of Spain)	c Achong b Constantine	42	1
	c sub b Small	105	2/1
3rd Test (Georgetown)	c Hunte b Francis	31	2/2
	c Francis b Constantine	3	0/1
4th Test (Kingston)	b Griffith	149	1/0
	c Nunes b Scott	27	0/1
1931 *v* NEW ZEALAND			
1st Test (Lord's)	c James b Weir	137	1/1
	not out	17	0
2nd Test (The Oval)	c James b Vivian	41	3
3rd Test (Old Trafford)	did not bat	—	—
1932 *v* INDIA			
1st Test (Lord's)	b Nissar	65	0
	b Amar Singh	6	0
1932-3 *v* AUSTRALIA			
1st Test (Sydney)	c McCabe b O'Reilly	0	3
	did not bat	—	1
2nd Test (Melbourne)	b Wall	4	0
	c Fingleton b O'Reilly	2	2
3rd Test (Adelaide)	b Ironmonger	3	1
	b O'Reilly	69	0
4th Test (Brisbane)	c Darling b Ironmonger	17	1/2
	not out	14	0
5th Test (Sydney)	run out	4	0

			Caught/Stumped
1932-3 _v_ NEW ZEALAND			
1st Test (Christchurch)	b Vivian	103	0
2nd Test (Auckland)	b Badcock	26	0+
1933 _v_ WEST INDIES			
1st Test (Lord's)	not out	83	0
2nd Test (Old Trafford)	c Headley b Martindale	47	1
	did not bat	—	1/1
3rd Test (The Oval)	c Headley b Martindale	37	2/2
	did not bat	—	4
1934 _v_ AUSTRALIA			
1st Test (Trent Bridge)	c Wall b O'Reilly	7	2
	b O'Reilly	12	2
2nd Test (Lord's)	c Oldfield b McCabe	120	1
	did not bat	—	1
3rd Test (Old Trafford)	c Ponsford b Grimmett	72	1
4th Test (Headingley)	c Oldfield b Grimmett	9	1
	c Brown b Grimmett	8	—
5th Test (The Oval)	retired hurt	33	2
1934-5 _v_ WEST INDIES			
1st Test (Bridgetown)	lbw b R. S. Grant	8	0/2
2nd Test (Port of Spain)	c R. S. Grant b Martindale	2	0+
	c Achong b Hylton	6	1+
3rd Test (Georgetown)	c Christiani b Hylton	0	1
	not out	5	0/1
4th Test (Kingston)	c Constantine b Mudie	126	0
	c R. S. Grant b Constantine	17	—
1935 _v_ SOUTH AFRICA			
1st Test (Trent Bridge)	c Viljoen b Vincent	17	1
2nd Test (Lord's)	b Balaskas	5	0+
	lbw b Langton	8	1+
3rd Test (Headingley)	b Vincent	0	0
	b Bell	13	0/1
5th Test (The Oval)	not out	148	3
	did not bat	—	0/2
1936-7 _v_ AUSTRALIA			
1st Test (Brisbane)	c Chipperfield b Ward	24	2
	b Sievers	9	0
2nd Test (Sydney)	c sub b Ward	29	0
	did not bat	—	1
3rd Test (Melbourne)	b Sievers	3	1/2
	b Fleetwood-Smith	19	1

155

			Caught/Stumped
4th Test (Adelaide)	b McCormick	52	2
	lbw b Fleetwood-Smith	0	3
5th Test (Melbourne)	b Nash	19	3
	c McCabe b McCormick	11	—
1937 *v* NEW ZEALAND			
1st Test (Lord's)	b Vivian	5	1
	c sub b Roberts	20	1
2nd Test (Old Trafford)	not out	16	0/2
	lbw b Dunning	39	1
3rd Test (The Oval)	not out	6	1
	did not bat	—	1
1938 *v* AUSTRALIA			
1st Test (Trent Bridge)	b Fleetwood-Smith	46	2
2nd Test (Lord's)	c McCormick b Fleetwood-Smith	83	0
	c McCabe b O'Reilly	6	0
1938-9 *v* SOUTH AFRICA			
1st Test (Johannesburg)	c Wade b Gordon	42	0/1
	not out	3	0
2nd Test (Cape Town)	b Gordon	115	0/1
	did not bat	—	1
3rd Test (Durban)	not out	27	1
	did not bat	—	3
4th Test (Johannesburg)	b Langton	34	1
	b Gordon	17	—
5th Test (Durban)	c Dalton b Langton	84	2
	not out	17	0

SERIES BY SERIES SUMMARY

	M	I	NO	Runs	HS	Avge	100	50	c/s
1929 *v* SOUTH AFRICA	1	1	0	0	0	0.00	0	0	2/0
1929-30 *v* WEST INDIES	4	8	1	417	149	59.57	2	0	7/5
1931 *v* NEW ZEALAND	3	3	1	195	137	97.50	1	0	4/1
1932 *v* INDIA	1	2	0	71	65	35.50	0	1	0
1932-3 *v* AUSTRALIA	5	8	1	113	69	16.14	0	1	8/2
1932-3 *v* NEW ZEALAND	2	2	0	129	103	64.50	1	0	0
1933 *v* WEST INDIES	3	3	1	167	83†	83.50	0	1	8/3
1934 *v* AUSTRALIA	5	7	1	261	120	43.50	1	1	10
1934-5 *v* WEST INDIES	4	7	1	164	126	27.33	1	0	2/3
1935 *v* SOUTH AFRICA	4	6	1	191	148†	38.20	1	0	5/3
1936-7 *v* AUSTRALIA	5	9	0	166	52	18.44	0	1	13/2

	M	I	NO	Runs	HS	Avge	100	50	c/s
1937 *v* NEW ZEALAND	3	5	2	86	39	28.66	0	0	5/2
1938 *v* AUSTRALIA	2	3	0	135	83	45.00	0	1	2
1938-9 *v* SOUTH AFRICA	5	8	3	339	115	67.80	1	1	8/2
TOTAL	47	72	12	2,434	149	40.56	8	7	74/23

Corrections to scorecards published in Wisden:
1933 2nd Test E. Achong should be c Ames b Langridge, not st Ames b Langridge
1934–5 3rd Test C. M. Jones should be lbw b Hollies, not c Ames b Hollies
†*Did not keep wicket in this innings.*

BATTING: ALL FIRST-CLASS MATCHES

	M	I	NO	Runs	HS	Avge	100	50
1926	2	3	0	65	35	21.00	0	0
1927	30	41	5	1,211	111	33.63	1	9
1928	37	60	6	1,919	200	35.53	4	7
1928-9 (Australia)	8	8	3	295	100*	59.00	1	1
1929	34	53	3	1,795	145	35.90	5	9
1929-30 (West Indies)	11	19	2	818	149	48.11	4	0
1930	33	54	5	1,434	121	29.26	1	8
1931	35	50	6	1,711	172	38.87	4	6
1932	35	50	7	2,482	180	57.72	9	13
1932-3 (Australia/New Zealand)	18	24	1	736	107	32.00	2	5
1933	36	57	5	3,058	295	58.80	9	13
1934	27	43	6	2,113	202*	57.10	5	12
1934-5 (West Indies)	11	18	5	566	126	43.53	1	3
1935	31	54	5	1,730	148*	35.30	6	5
1936	9	16	0	717	145	44.81	3	2
1936-7 (Australia)	14	23	0	811	109	35.26	1	6
1937	30	52	4	2,347	201*	48.89	7	10
1938	17	27	1	1,116	170	42.92	2	5
1938-9 (South Africa)	13	16	3	683	115	52.53	2	2
1939	25	46	6	1,846	201	46.15	5	9
1945	1	2	0	64	57	32.00	0	1
1946	24	40	3	1,336	114*	36.10	2	8
1947	22	42	7	2,272	212*	64.91	7	14
1948	26	45	2	1,943	212	45.18	7	9

	M	I	NO	Runs	HS	Avge	100	50
1949	25	47	2	2,125	160	47.22	7	9
1950	22	39	4	1,422	131	40.62	5	7
1950–1 (India)	16	21	3	626	116*	34.77	2	3
1951	1	1	1	7	7*	—	0	0
Total	593	951	95	37,248	295	43.51	102	176

BATTING: FIRST-CLASS MATCHES FOR KENT

	M	I	NO	Runs	HS	Avge	100	50
1926	2	3	0	65	35	21.66	0	0
1927	28	39	5	1,193	111	35.08	1	9
1928	33	53	5	1,736	200	36.16	4	6
1929	29	46	2	1,777	145	40.38	5	9
1930	28	46	4	1,214	84	28.90	0	8
1931	28	41	4	1,344	172	36.32	3	5
1932	28	40	6	2,100	180	61.76	7	11
1933	28	48	4	2,428	295	55.18	8	9
1934	18	31	4	1,559	202*	57.74	3	9
1935	26	46	3	1,427	139	33.18	4	5
1936	7	12	0	531	145	44.25	2	2
1937	22	39	2	1,997	201*	53.97	6	10
1938	12	20	1	892	170	46.94	2	3
1939	25	46	6	1,846	201	46.15	5	9
1946	23	38	3	1,264	114	36.11	2	7
1947	20	39	7	2,156	212*	67.37	7	12
1948	26	45	2	1,943	212	45.18	7	9
1949	25	47	2	2,125	160	47.22	7	9
1950	21	37	3	1,347	131	39.61	5	7
1951	1	1	1	7	7*	—	0	0
Total	430	717	64	28,951	295	44.33	78	139

HUNDREDS IN FIRST-CLASS MATCHES

1	111	Kent v Hampshire (Southampton)	1927
2	129	Kent v Somerset (Taunton)	1928
3	109	Kent v Warwickshire (Tunbridge Wells)	1928
4	200	Kent v Surrey (Blackheath)	1928
5	113	Kent v Warwickshire (Edgbaston)	1928
6	100*	MCC v Tasmania (Hobart)	1928–9

7	101	Kent *v* Essex (Folkestone)	1929
8	106	Kent *v* Surrey (Blackheath)	1929
9	109	Kent *v* Surrey (The Oval)	1929
10	118	Kent *v* Sussex (Hastings)	1929
11	145	Kent *v* South Africans (Canterbury)	1929
12	105	England *v* West Indies (Port of Spain)	1929–30
13	107	MCC *v* British Guiana (Bridgetown)	1929–30
14	142*	MCC *v* Jamaica (Kingston)	1929–30
15	149	England *v* West Indies (Kingston)	1929–30
16	121	An England XI *v* Australians (Folkestone)	1930
17	172	Kent *v* MCC (Lord's)	1931
18	137	England *v* New Zealand (Lord's)	1931
19	112	Kent *v* Sussex (Tunbridge Wells)	1931
20	115	Kent *v* New Zealanders (Canterbury)	1931
21	130*	Kent *v* Middlesex (Tunbridge Wells)	1932
22	149	Kent *v* Northamptonshire (Tunbridge Wells)	1932
23	120	Kent *v* Surrey (Blackheath)	1932
(nos 21, 22 and 23 were in consecutive innings for Kent)			
24	130	Kent *v* Glamorgan (Canterbury)	1932
25	133	Kent *v* Sussex (Hastings)	1932
26	180	Kent *v* Hampshire (Dover)	1932
27	101	Kent *v* Worcestershire (Dover)	1932
28	105*	An England XI *v* Indians (Folkestone)	1932
29	105	MCC Australian XI *v* The Rest (Folkestone)	1932
30	107	MCC *v* Tasmania (Launceston)	1932–3
31	103	England *v* New Zealand (Christchurch)	1932–3
32	143*	Kent *v* Derbyshire (Derby)	1933
33	115	Kent *v* MCC (Lord's)	1933
34	210	Kent *v* Warwickshire (Tonbridge)	1933
35	295	Kent *v* Gloucestershire (Folkestone)	1933
36	137	Kent *v* Surrey (Blackheath)	1933
37	132	Kent *v* Northamptonshire (Dover)	1933
38	145*	Kent *v* Northamptonshire (Dover)	1933
39	125	Kent *v* Middlesex (Lord's)	1933
40	201	Players *v* Gentlemen (Folkestone)	1933
41	109	Kent *v* Hampshire (Portsmouth)	1934
42	202*	Kent *v* Essex (Brentwood)	1934
43	146*	England *v* The Rest (Lord's)	1934
44	115	Kent *v* Warwickshire (Edgbaston)	1934
45	120	England *v* Australia (Lord's)	1934
46	126	England *v* West Indies (Kingston)	1934–5

47	128	Kent *v* Nottinghamshire (Trent Bridge)	1935
48	138	Kent *v* Warwickshire (Edgbaston)	1935
49	139	Kent *v* Gloucestershire (Bristol)	1935
50	118	Kent *v* Worcestershire (Worcester)	1935
51	148*	England *v* South Africa (The Oval)	1935
52	111*	MCC *v* H. D. G. Leveson-Gower's XI (Scarborough)	1935
53	120	Kent *v* Yorkshire (Dover)	1936
54	145	Kent *v* Indians (Canterbury)	1936
55	107	An England XI *v* Indians (Folkestone)	1936
56	109	MCC *v* Tasmania (Launceston)	1936–7
57	201*	Kent *v* Worcestershire (Gillingham)	1937
58	182	Kent *v* Leicestershire (Leicester)	1937
59	125	Kent *v* Worcestershire (Worcester)	1937
60	119	Kent *v* Surrey (Blackheath)	1937
61	127	Kent *v* Surrey (Blackheath)	1937

(nos 59, 60 and 61 were in consecutive innings for Kent)

62	108	Kent *v* Derbyshire (Folkestone)	1937
63	149	Over 30s *v* Under 30s (Folkestone)	1937
64	170	Kent *v* Essex (Gravesend)	1938
65	139	Kent *v* Australians (Canterbury)	1938
66	109	MCC *v* Transvaal (Johannesburg)	1938–9
67	115	England *v* South Africa (Cape Town)	1938–9
68	177	Kent *v* Glamorgan (Tonbridge)	1939
69	136*	Kent *v* Surrey (The Oval)	1939
70	159*	Kent *v* Derbyshire (Gravesend)	1939
71	201	Kent *v* Worcestershire (Worcester)	1939
72	108	Kent *v* Lancashire (Old Trafford)	1939
73	106	Kent *v* Warwickshire (Gravesend)	1946
74	114*	Kent *v* Middlesex (Lord's)	1946
75	104	Kent *v* Derbyshire (Canterbury)	1947
76	179	Kent *v* Hampshire (Southampton)	1947
77	212*	Kent *v* Nottinghamshire (Gravesend)	1947
78	109	Kent *v* Northamptonshire (Gravesend)	1947
79	152	Kent *v* Essex (Maidstone)	1947
80	145*	Kent *v* Nottinghamshire (Trent Bridge)	1947
81	127	Kent *v* Leicestershire (Dover)	1947
82	104	Kent *v* Hampshire (Southampton)	1948
83	113	Kent *v* Northamptonshire (Tunbridge Wells)	1948
84	123	Kent *v* Somerset (Maidstone)	1948
85	120	Kent *v* Sussex (Hastings)	1948
86	212	Kent *v* Gloucestershire (Dover)	1948

87	112	Kent _v_ Gloucestershire (Gloucester)	1948
88	104	Kent _v_ Middlesex (Dover)	1948
89	100	Kent _v_ Combined Services (Gillingham)	1949
90	131	Kent _v_ Surrey (The Oval)	1949
91	160	Kent _v_ Warwickshire (Maidstone)	1949
92	125	Kent _v_ Sussex (Hove)	1949
93	146	Kent _v_ Somerset (Weston-super-Mare)	1949
94	152*	Kent _v_ New Zealanders (Canterbury)	1949
95	119	Kent _v_ Lancashire (Folkestone)	1949
96	112	Kent _v_ Gloucestershire (Bristol)	1950
97	119	Kent _v_ Gloucestershire (Bristol)	1950
98	114*	Kent _v_ Nottinghamshire (Trent Bridge)	1950
99	130	Kent _v_ Essex (Maidstone)	1950
100	131	Kent _v_ Middlesex (Canterbury)	1950
101	110	Commonwealth _v_ Mysore (Bangalore)	1950–1
102	116*	Commonwealth _v_ Prime Minister's XI (Bombay)	1950–1

MAJOR WICKET PARTNERSHIPS

2nd	273	with L. J. Todd	Kent _v_ Essex (Maidstone)	1947
3rd	259	with L. J. Todd	Kent _v_ Gloucestershire (Folkestone)	1933
4th	278	with E. H. Hendren	MCC _v_ British Guiana (Georgetown)	1929–30
5th	277	with F. E. Woolley	Kent _v_ New Zealanders (Canterbury)	1931
5th	242	with W. R. Hammond	England _v_ New Zealand (Christchurch)	1932–3
7th	194	with T. A. Pearce	Kent _v_ Middlesex (Tunbridge Wells)	1932
8th	246	with G. O. B. Allen†	England _v_ New Zealand (Lord's)	1931

†_Highest partnership for wicket against all countries._

SEASON BY SEASON RECORD IN THE FIELD

SEASON	FOR KENT			ALL FIRST-CLASS		
	As wicket-keeper	Other	Total dis.	As wicket-keeper	Other	Total dis.
	ct	st.	ct	ct	st.	ct
1926			4	4			4	4
1927	21	18	6	45	23	18	6	47
1928	65	49		114	69	52	1	122
1928–9					8	10		18
1929	71	45		116	79	49		128
1929–30					16	9		25
1930	44	41		85	49	47		96

SEASON	FOR KENT				ALL FIRST-CLASS			
	As wicket-keeper		Other	Total dis.	As wicket-keeper		Other	Total dis.
	ct	st.	ct		ct	st.	ct	
1931	29	35		64	38	39		77
1932	35	56		91	40	64		104
1932–3					11	8	5	24
1933	16	23	7	46	29	31	9	69
1934	18	21	1	40	32	24	1	57
1934–5					9	3	2	14
1935	24	28	5	57	31	31	5	67
1936	9	4		13	11	5		16
1936–7					23	4	2	29
1937	39	9	1	49	58	15	1	74
1938	11	1	2	14	15	1	2	18
1938–9					14	7		21
1939			15	15			15	15
1945							1	1
1946			26	26			28	28
1947			8	8			9	9
1948			21	21			21	21
1949			21	21			21	21
1950			12	12			12	12
1950–1							3	3
1951			1	1			1	1
Totals	382	330	130	842	555	417	149	1121

Ames holds the record for the most dismissals by a wicket-keeper in an English first-class season, namely 128 in 1929. In addition he is the only wicket-keeper to capture more than 100 in a season three times. He also holds the record for most stumpings in a season, 64 in 1932.

WICKET-KEEPING RECORDS

SIX DISMISSALS IN AN INNINGS			
4ct	2st	Kent *v* Sussex (Maidstone)	1929
5ct	1st	Kent *v* Sussex (Folkestone)	1930
SEVEN OR MORE DISMISSALS IN A MATCH			
8ct	1st	Kent *v* Oxford University (The Parks)	1928
3ct	4st	Kent *v* Leicestershire (Tonbridge)	1928
6ct	2st	Kent *v* Hampshire (Folkestone)	1929
3ct	5st	Kent *v* Derbyshire (Chesterfield)	1929
5ct	4st	Kent *v* Sussex (Maidstone)	1929

4ct	4st	Kent *v* Gloucestershire (Bristol)	1929
3ct	4st	Kent *v* Leicestershire (Tunbridge Wells)	1929
1ct	7st	Kent *v* Warwickshire (Tonbridge)	1930
5ct	2st	Kent *v* Sussex (Folkestone)	1930
3ct	4st	The Rest *v* Lancashire (The Oval)	1930
6ct	2st	England *v* West Indies (The Oval)	1933
3ct	4st	Kent *v* Essex (Brentwood)	1934
2ct	5st	Kent *v* Middlesex (Maidstone)	1935
6ct	2st	Players *v* Gentlemen (Lord's)	1937
7ct		Kent *v* Lancashire (Maidstone)	1937

WICKET-KEEPING RECORD FOR KENT

DISMISSALS OFF EACH BOWLER SEASON BY SEASON 1927-32

	1927		1928		1929		1930		1931		1932		Total	
	c	s	c	s	c	s	c	s	c	s	c	s	c	s
Beslee	2	0	6	0	12	0	1	0					21	0
Freeman	4	12	12	37	19	36	17	37	8	29	4	37	64	188
A. C. Wright	8	0	18	0	14	0	10	0					50	0
Capes	4	4	0	3									4	7
A. J. Evans	1	0											1	0
Woolley	1	0	3	3	10	4	1	2					15	9
Ashdown	1	2	12	1	11	0	4	0	6	0	9	1	43	4
Howlett			10	0									10	
Hardinge			0	2	2	4	8	2	4	1	5	8	19	17
Marriott			4	3	2	1			5	5	8	5	19	14
Todd					1	0					1	0	2	0
Peach							3	0					3	0
Watt									6	0	7	4	13	4
C. Fairservice											1	1	1	1
Totals	21	18	65	49	71	45	44	41	29	35	35	56	265	244

DISMISSALS OFF EACH BOWLER SEASON BY SEASON 1933-8

	1933		1934		1935		1936		1937		1938		Total	
	c	s	c	s	c	s	c	s	c	s	c	s	c	s
Freeman	7	18	2	15	4	17	0	1					13	51
Valentine	1	0	1	0									2	0
Woolley			0	1			0	1	1	2	1	0	2	4
Ashdown	1	3	4	1	1	0	1	0	0	1			7	5
Marriott	1	2	0	2	4	4							5	8
Todd	1	0	2	0	6	0	4	0	8	0	3	0	24	0
Watt	5	0	4	0	1	1			12	1	1	0	23	2

	1933		1934		1935		1936		1937		1938		Total	
	c	s	c	s	c	s	c	s	c	s	c	s	c	s
D. V. P. Wright			4	0	5	1	2	1	9	5	3	0	23	7
Lewis			1	2	2	5					3	1	6	8
C. G. Cole					1	0	1	1	4	0			6	1
Davies							1	0	1	0			2	0
Taylor									1	0			1	0
Harding									2	0			2	0
Whitehouse									1	0			1	0
Totals	16	23	18	21	24	28	9	4	39	9	11	1	117	86

The remarkable statistic revealed from the above figures is the success of Ames in partnership with A. P. 'Tich' Freeman. For Kent the pair dismissed 77 batsmen caught and 239 stumped; in other first-class matches they accounted for 5 caught and 22 stumped, thus being responsible together for the removal of 343 batsmen. No comparable figures have been issued for other successful pairs, but it is most unlikely that any equalled the success of Ames and Freeman.

LEADING KENT WICKET-KEEPERS
(Kent matches only)

	Career	Mtchs	Ct†	St.	Total
F. H. Huish	1895–1914	469	901	352	1253
A. P. E. Knott	1964–1985	349	828	87	915
L. E. G. Ames	1926–1951	430	512	330	842
J. C. Hubble	1904–1929	343	411	217	628
T. G. Evans	1939–1967	258	451	103	554

†*Some catches taken while not keeping wicket.*

BOWLING

	Runs	Wickets	Average	Best
Kent	697	22	31.68	3/23
Other matches	104	2	52.00	1/16
Total	801	24	33.37	3/23

Best Bowling: 3/23 Kent v Surrey (The Oval) 1946.

SOME NOTABLE KENT WICKET-KEEPER/BOWLER PARTNERSHIPS
(First-class matches only)

		Kent			Tests		
	Period	Mtchs	Ct	St.	Mtchs	Ct	St.
c/st Huish b Blythe	1899–1914	368	147	178	—	—	—
c/st Ames b Freeman	1926–1936	242	89 (77)	239	1	—	—
c/st Knott b Underwood	1964–1985	338	108	54	72	22	5

		Others			Total			
	Period	Mtchs	Ct	St.	Mtchs	Ct	St.	Total
c/st Huish b Blythe	1899–1914	3	—	1	371	147	179	326
c/st Ames b Freeman	1926–1936	26	7 (5)	22	269	96 (82)	261	357 (343)
c/st Knott b Underwood	1964–1985	33	4	5	443	134	64	198

NB Ames made a number of catches off Freeman when not keeping wicket. The figures in brackets represent those made as a wicket-keeper. Note also Ames's first catch off Freeman as a wicket-keeper did not occur until 1927.

COUNTRY-BY-COUNTRY SUMMARY

	M	I	NO	Runs	HS	Avge	100	50	Ct	St
ENGLAND										
Kent *v*										
Derbyshire	25	43	6	1458	159*	39.40	4	6	31	30
Essex	30	49	6	1823	202*	42.39	5	7	27	34
Glamorgan	16	27	2	1125	177	45.00	2	8	15	13
Gloucestershire	28	51	2	2309	295	47.12	6	12	30	33
Hampshire	28	44	6	1950	180	51.31	5	12	47	14
Lancashire	23	38	–	1176	119	30.94	2	8	25	13
Leicestershire	24	39	3	1308	182	36.33	2	8	27	24
Middlesex	29	50	3	1737	131	36.95	5	8	32	22
Northamptonshire	21	34	4	1412	149	47.06	5	5	27	24
Nottinghamshire	28	52	7	2263	212*	50.28	4	13	24	16
Somerset	22	36	6	1295	146	43.16	3	6	33	18
Surrey	29	52	3	2425	200	49.48	9	8	33	12
Sussex	26	42	3	1608	133	41.23	5	9	31	20
Warwickshire	20	32	4	1759	210	62.82	7	6	24	21
Worcestershire	26	37	5	1906	201*	59.56	5	9	33	17
Yorkshire	24	41	2	954	120	24.46	1	2	27	5
MCC	9	17	–	941	172	55.35	2	6	14	6
Cambridge University	1	1	–	85	85	85.00	–	1	1	1
Oxford University	4	5	1	120	80*	30.00	–	1	13	4
Australians	3	5	–	194	139	38.80	1	–	4	–
Indians	3	4	–	261	145	65.25	1	1	3	2
New Zealanders	4	7	1	450	152*	75.00	2	2	2	–
West Indians	3	5	–	112	86	22.40	–	1	2	–
Combined Services	1	1	–	100	100	100.00	1	–	1	–
KENT TOTAL	430	717	64	28951	295	44.33	78	139	512	330
Test Matches	22	30	6	1106	148*	46.08	3	4	36	9
Other Matches	50	75	8	2656	201	39.64	8	13	63	37
ENGLAND TOTAL	502	822	78	32713	295	43.96	89	156	611	376
AUSTRALIA										
Test Matches	10	17	1	279	69	17.43	–	2	21	4
Other Matches	25	32	3	1302	109	44.89	3	9	26	17
AUSTRALIA TOTAL	35	49	4	1581	109	35.13	3	11	47	21

	M	I	NO	Runs	HS	Avge	100	50	Ct	St
NEW ZEALAND										
Test Matches	2	2	—	129	103	64.50	1	—	—	—
Other Matches	3	4	—	132	97	33.00	—	1	2	1
NEW ZEALAND TOTAL	5	6	—	261	103	43.50	1	1	2	1
SOUTH AFRICA										
Test Matches	5	8	3	330	115	67.80	1	1	8	2
Other Matches	8	8	—	344	109	43.00	1	1	6	5
SOUTH AFRICA TOTAL	13	16	3	683	115	52.53	2	2	14	7
WEST INDIES										
Test Matches	8	15	2	581	149	44.69	3	—	9	8
Other Matches	14	22	5	803	142*	47.23	2	3	18	4
WEST INDIES TOTAL	22	37	7	1384	149	46.13	5	3	27	12
INDIA	14	18	2	595	116*	37.18	2	3	2	—
CEYLON	2	3	1	31	16	15.50	—	—	1	—
TOTAL	593	951	95	37248	295	43.51	102	176	704	417

GROUND-BY-GROUND SUMMARY

	M	I	NO	Runs	HS	Avge	100	50	Ct	St
ENGLAND										
Bath	3	6	1	176	74	35.20	—	1	7	1
Birmingham (Edgbaston)	8	15	3	825	115	68.75	3	3	11	2
Birmingham (Mitchell & Butler's Ground)	1	1	—	18	18	18.00	—	—	1	1
Blackheath	15	26	1	1222	200	48.88	6	1	19	6
Bournemouth	1	1	—	4	4	4.00	—	—	2	—
Bradford	4	6	—	54	26	9.00	—	—	—	3
Brentwood	1	1	1	202	202*	—	1	—	3	4
Bristol	11	21	2	1000	139	52.63	3	8	14	17
Cambridge	1	1	—	85	85	85.00	—	1	1	1
Canterbury	50	77	3	3272	152*	44.21	8	18	58	41
Cardiff (Arms Park)	4	5	—	97	41	19.40	—	—	5	5
Chatham	2	3	—	92	59	30.66	—	1	4	—
Chelmsford	3	4	2	45	33*	22.50	—	—	1	—

	M	I	NO	Runs	HS	Avge	100	50	Ct	St
Cheltenham (Victoria Park)	1	2	–	52	52	26.00	–	1	1	–
Chesterfield	5	8	1	154	41*	22.00	–	–	10	6
Clacton	1	2	–	24	14	12.00	–	–	–	–
Colchester (Castle Park)	1	1	–	70	70	70.00	–	1	2	–
Colchester (Garrison Ground)	1	2	–	67	67	33.50	–	1	–	1
Coventry (Butts)	1	1	–	6	6	6.00	–	–	1	1
Derby	4	7	1	240	143*	40.00	1	–	1	1
Dover	28	47	5	2035	212	48.45	8	6	28	18
Dudley	3	4	–	156	62	39.00	–	1	2	–
Folkestone	45	76	4	3126	295	43.41	10	12	57	43
Gillingham	11	20	4	789	201*	49.31	2	3	13	–
Gloucester (Wagon Works)	2	3	–	188	112	62.66	1	1	2	2
Gravesend	21	37	8	1880	212*	64.82	5	9	27	17
Harrogate	1	2	–	110	58	55.00	–	2	–	–
Hastings	15	24	2	994	133	45.18	4	5	16	8
Horsham	1	2	–	19	19	9.50	–	–	–	–
Hull	1	–	–	–	–	–	–	–	–	–
Ilford	2	4	1	84	61*	28.00	–	1	5	–
Ilkeston	3	5	–	93	27	18.60	–	–	3	6
Kingston-upon-Thames	1	2	1	75	42	75.00	–	–	–	–
Leeds	6	11	–	186	41	16.90	–	–	5	1
Leicester (Aylestone Road)	6	8	2	561	182	93.50	1	4	6	11
Leicester (Grace Road)	1	2	–	18	11	9.00	–	–	–	–
Leyton	4	6	–	178	69	29.66	–	1	4	9
Lord's	39	60	4	2433	172	43.44	7	14	61	21
Loughborough (Park Road)	2	3	–	85	62	28.33	–	1	1	–
Maidstone	29	48	1	1746	160	37.14	4	8	38	27
Manchester	17	24	1	691	108	30.04	1	4	13	8
Melton Mowbray	1	2	–	7	7	3.50	–	–	1	–
Neath	1	2	1	43	31*	43.00	–	–	–	–
Newport (Monmouth)	1	2	–	130	69	65.00	–	2	–	–
Northampton	10	17	1	391	71	24.43	–	2	12	8
Nottingham	18	33	3	1374	145*	45.80	3	7	19	5
Oakham	2	3	–	96	86	32.00	–	1	1	–
Oval	25	40	7	1639	148*	49.66	4	9	40	22
Oxford	4	5	1	120	80*	40.00	–	1	13	4
Peterborough (Town Ground)	1	2	–	100	52	50.00	–	1	1	4
Portsmouth	3	6	2	278	109	69.50	1	1	7	1

	M	I	NO	Runs	HS	Avge	100	50	Ct	St
Scarborough	2	4	1	128	111*	42.66	1	–	3	–
Sheffield (Bramall Lane)	1	2	–	48	44	24.00	–	–	2	–
Southampton	10	20	4	858	179	53.62	3	4	13	4
Southend	2	4	–	48	35	12.00	–	–	–	2
Stourbridge	3	4	1	41	27*	13.66	–	–	8	3
Swansea	3	5	–	151	71	30.20	–	2	2	3
Taunton	7	11	3	385	129	48.12	1	2	9	6
Tonbridge	21	31	2	1311	210	45.20	2	9	25	27
Tunbridge Wells	24	40	3	1495	149	40.40	5	4	23	23
Weston-super-Mare	1	2	–	218	146	109.00	1	1	–	–
Worcester	6	9	1	700	201	87.50	3	2	10	3

AUSTRALIA

	M	I	NO	Runs	HS	Avge	100	50	Ct	St
Adelaide	6	10	1	324	69	36.00	–	4	10	1
Brisbane (Exhibition Ground)	1	1	–	10	10	10.00	–	–	–	4
Brisbane (Woolloongabba)	4	7	1	245	80	40.83	–	2	5	3
Hobart	2	2	1	152	100*	152.00	1	1	3	1
Launceston	3	3	–	250	109	83.33	2	–	1	7
Melbourne	6	8	–	137	64	17.12	–	1	11	3
Perth	3	4	–	78	36	19.50	–	–	2	–
Sydney	10	14	1	385	90	29.61	–	3	15	2

NEW ZEALAND

	M	I	NO	Runs	HS	Avge	100	50	Ct	St
Auckland	1	1	–	26	26	26.00	–	–	–	–
Christchurch	2	3	–	135	103	45.00	1	–	–	–
Wellington	2	2	–	100	97	50.00	–	1	2	1

SOUTH AFRICA

	M	I	NO	Runs	HS	Avge	100	50	Ct	St
Bulawayo	1	1	–	47	47	47.00	–	–	–	–
Cape Town	2	2	–	160	115	80.00	1	–	2	1
Durban (Kingsmead)	3	4	2	172	84	86.00	–	1	8	–
East London	1	1	–	3	3	3.00	–	–	–	–
Johannesburg (Old Wanderers)	4	6	1	211	109	42.20	1	–	2	1
Kimberley	1	1	–	28	28	28.00	–	–	–	4
Pietermaritzburg	1	1	–	62	62	62.00	–	1	2	1

WEST INDIES

	M	I	NO	Runs	HS	Avge	100	50	Ct	St
Bridgetown	6	8	2	192	44*	32.00	–	–	7	3

	M	I	NO	Runs	HS	Avge	100	50	Ct	St
Georgetown	5	7	1	184	107	30.06	1	—	7	6
Kingston	5	10	2	647	149	80.87	3	1	6	1
Port of Spain	6	12	2	361	105	36.10	1	2	7	2
INDIA										
Bangalore	1	1	—	110	110	110.00	1	—	—	—
Bombay (Brabourne Stadium)	4	5	2	148	116*	49.33	1	—	1	—
Calcutta	3	4	—	82	60	20.50	—	1	—	—
Dehra Dun	1	2	—	15	10	7.50	—	—	—	—
Hyderabad	1	1	—	45	45	45.00	—	—	—	—
Indore	1	1	—	15	15	15.00	—	—	1	—
Kanpur	1	2	—	19	17	9.50	—	—	—	—
Madras (Chepauk)	1	1	—	69	69	69.00	—	1	—	—
Poona	1	1	—	92	92	92.00	—	1	—	—
CEYLON										
Colombo (Oval)	2	3	1	31	16	15.50	—	—	1	—

BIBLIOGRAPHY

L. E. G. Ames: *Close of Play* (Stanley Paul, 1953).

R. L. Arrowsmith: *A History of Kent* (Arthur Barker, 1971).

Revd. J. Howard Brown: *A History of Harvey Grammar School, Folkestone* (1962).

Neville Cardus: *Australian Summer* (Rupert Hart-Davis, 1949).

Colin Cowdrey: *M.C.C.—The Autobiography of a Cricketer* (Hodder and Stoughton, 1976).

B. Curtis (editor): *One Hundred Years of Kent Cricket 1870-1970* (J. A. Jennings Ltd., Canterbury, 1970).

P. G. H. Fender: *The Turn of the Wheel—M.C.C. Team, Australia, 1928-29* (Faber and Faber, 1929).

——: *Kissing the Rod—The Story of the Tests of 1934* (Chapman and Hall, 1934).

Jack Fingleton: *Cricket Crisis* (Pavilion Books, 1985).

Bill Frindall (editor): *The Wisden Book of Cricket Records* (Queen Anne Press, 1981).

George L. Greaves: *Over the Summers Again* (Harrogate C.C., 1976).

Bruce Harris: *The 1937 Australian Tour* (Hutchinson and Co., 1937).

Rt. Hon. Lord Harris (editor): *History of Kent County Cricket* (Eyre and Spottiswoode, 1907).

Brian Hart: *The Elham Valley Line 1887-1947* (Wild Swan Publications, 1984).

Alan Hill: *Hedley Verity: A Portrait of a Cricketer* (Kingswood Press, 1986).

Gerald Howat: *Walter Hammond* (George Allen and Unwin, 1984).

D. R. Jardine: *Ashes and Dust* (Hutchinson and Co., 1935).

Brian Johnston: *It's Been a Piece of Cake* (Methuen, 1989).

John Kay (editor): *Cricket Heroes* (Phoenix Books, 1959).

Harold Larwood: *The Larwood Story* (W. H. Allen, 1965).

David Lemmon: *'Tich' Freeman and the Decline of the Leg-Break Bowler* (George Allen and Unwin, 1982).

Christopher Martin-Jenkins: *The Complete Who's Who of Test Cricketers* (Orbis Publishing, 1980).

Ronald Mason: *Ashes in the Mouth* (Hambledon Press, 1982).

Dudley Moore: *The History of Kent C.C.C.* (Christopher Helm, 1988).

Patrick Murphy: *The Centurions* (J. M. Dent and Sons Ltd., 1983).

Gerald Pawle: *R. E. S. Wyatt, The Fighting Cricketer* (George Allen and Unwin, 1985).

Tony Pawson: *Runs and Catches* (Faber and Faber, 1980).

BIBLIOGRAPHY

Ian Peebles: *Woolley, the Pride of Kent* (Stanley Paul, 1969).
Mary Smith: *History of Elham.*
Herbert Sutcliffe: *For England and Yorkshire* (Edward Arnold and Co., 1935).
E. W. Swanton: *Gubby Allen, Man of Cricket* (Hutchinson, 1985).
Hedley Verity: *Bowling 'Em Out* (Hutchinson, 1937).
H. W. Warner: *Story of Canterbury Cricket Week* (Canterbury, 1960).
R. E. S. Wyatt: *Three Straight Sticks* (Stanley Paul, 1951).

Contemporary reports in *The Times*, the *Daily Telegraph*, the *London Evening News* and *Star*, the *Kentish Gazette*, *The Cricketer*, and various editions of *Wisden Cricketers' Almanack* and *Kent County Cricket Club Yearbook* have provided the nucleus of printed sources in the book.

INDEX

by L. F. Hancock